NATURE AS SUBJECT

Studies in Social, Political, and Legal Philosophy
General Editor: James P. Sterba, University of Notre Dame

This series analyzes and evaluates critically the major political, social, and legal ideals, institutions, and practices of our time. The analysis may be historical or problem-centered; the evaluation may focus on theoretical underpinnings or practical implications. Among the recent titles in the series are:

NATURE AS SUBJECT

Human Obligation and Natural Community

Eric Katz

ROWMAN & LITTLEFIELD PUBLISHERS, INC.
Lanham • Boulder • New York • London

ROWMAN & LITTLEFIELD PUBLISHERS, INC.

Published in the United States of America
by Rowman & Littlefield Publishers, Inc.
4720 Boston Way, Lanham, Maryland 20706

3 Henrietta Street
London WC2E 8LU, England

Copyright © 1997 by Rowman & Littlefield Publishers, Inc.

British Cataloging in Publication Information Available

Library of Congress Cataloging-in-Publication Data
Katz, Eric, 1952–
    Nature as subject : human obligation and the natural community /
Eric Katz.
        p.   cm.—(Studies in social, political and legal philosophy)
    Includes bibliographical references and index.
    Romanized record.
    ISBN 0-8476-8303-6 (hard : alk. paper).—ISBN 0-8476-8304-4
(pbk. : alk. paper)
    1. Environmental ethics.   2. Human ecology—Philosophy.
I. Title.   II. Series.
GE42.K37   1997
179′.1—dc20   96-26920
                                                              CIP

ISBN 0–8476–8303–6 (cloth : alk. paper)
ISBN 0–8476–8304–4 (pbk. : alk. paper)

Printed in the United States of America

♾ ™ The paper used in this publication meets the minimum requirements of
American National Standard for Information Sciences—Permanence of Paper
for Printed Library Materials, ANSI Z39.48–1984.

For
Emma, Ani, Jonah
and Susan

Contents

III. Justice, Genocide, and the Environment

IV. History and Tradition

Foreword

Mark Sagoff

The white-tailed deer on Fire Island, although no longer truly wild, carry the tick that causes Lyme disease. They forage in flower gardens and beat the hopeful planter to the vegetable patch. We watch for these deer when we ride our bikes at night, fearing an accident. What value, then, do these creatures possess? Surely, it is not an instrumental one. The prices of vacation homes on Fire Island do not rise because more deer infest the area. Yet these deer, as this wonderful collection of essays explains, belong to the place more rightfully than vacationers do. They were certainly there first. As the vestiges of a truly wild natural community, they remind us that our technological imperative to control and dominate nature does not and—if this book is correct—should not always succeed.

Eric Katz celebrates the grass that grows in the cracks of the pavement, the raptors that nest upon a skyscraper, the spray thrown up from the tide. These things will not appeal to those who see everything as a means to something else and who regard intrinsic value—the idea that something is worthy of love and attention for what it is in itself—as a subversive notion, a threat to their way of thought. For these people, value is a function of our welfare or well-being as measured by the amount we are willing to pay for what we enjoy or consume. They will not understand a book that recognizes the intrinsic magnificence of the natural world and that argues that our duty to protect it goes beyond the categories of instrumental rationality or utility.

In these persuasive essays, Eric Katz parts company with many environmentalists who insist that prudence and morality teach the same lesson—that by protecting nature, for example, we serve our long-run economic interests as well as meet our ethical obligations. By example and by argument, Katz shows convincingly that to dominate, control, and as technology progresses, replace nature is the central prescription of instrumental rationality or prudence, which yields to the natural world only as one would yield to an enemy, until one develops the technology needed to accomplish its total defeat. The reasons to protect nature are essentially the reasons to love, respect, and appreciate it. These reasons concern the qualities of the natural world as they are perceived in our best cultural and spiritual traditions. They are not to be understood in instrumental terms.

One of the many great strengths of this book lies in its willingness to debunk arguments that seek to reconcile an environmental ethic with the logic of utility—arguments that favor anthropocentric and instrumental reasons for environmental preservation. Many of these arguments—for example, the idea that a greater diversity of species contributes to the stability of ecosystems—have been thoroughly criticized in the scientific literature. Katz argues, for example, that commonplace instrumental arguments for the protection of rain forests in Amazonia and elsewhere are seriously flawed. While he agrees with other environmental ethicists that natural environments should be preserved, he rightly acknowledges that "arguments based on human interest fail to provide an adequate justification for the preservation of ecosystems in the Third World."

Many readers who are used to accepting uncritically instrumental arguments for protecting nature will find much in these essays provocative. But Katz is fundamentally right. A consistent environmental ethic cannot be utilitarian. The most magnificent aspects of nature—those environments which we regard as sacred—are often economically less valuable, indeed, less useful and less beneficial to humankind, than the urban sprawl and commercial blight that is everywhere replacing them. This collection of essays presents the sound principle, to which all environmentalists may inevitably come, that our moral obligation is to nature, not to our own wants or interests, and that all the most valuable things may be useless.

Acknowledgments

Since these essays represent my most important work in philosophy since graduate school, I must acknowledge my debt to almost everyone with whom I have discussed these ideas since at least 1975. Of particular importance are my graduate school teachers, Alasdair MacIntyre, Michael Martin, David Solomon, Robert Cohen, Marx Wartofsky, Paul Sagal, and Jay Hullet.

In the field of environmental philosophy, I owe enormous thanks to Eugene Hargrove, Holmes Rolston, Mark Sagoff, Bryan Norton, and J. Baird Callicott. A major influence on my personal and professional life has been Andrew Brennan. I have benefited from many discussions and correspondence with Ned Hettinger, Thom Heyd, Avner de-Shalit, Sara Ebenreck, Karen Warren, Will Aiken, Jim Cheney, Tom Birch, Richard Sylvan, Richard Watson, George Sessions, Tom Regan, Peter Miller, Don Marietta, Donald Scherer, Jack Weir, Michael Black, Anthony Weston, Eric Higgs, Bill Jordan, and my colleague at New Jersey Institute of Technology, David Rothenberg.

In the field of philosophy of technology, I am deeply indebted to Carl Mitcham and Paul Durbin.

I thank all my colleagues at NJIT for humoring me and, in particular, John Opie and Norbert Elliot for intellectual stimulation and editorial clarification. The members of the Science, Technology, and Society program—John O'Connor, Maarten de Kadt, Burt Kimmelman, and Nancy Jackson—have always been kind enough to listen to my ideas. Special thanks to Winnifred Cummings for making my office run smoothly.

Finally, three personal debts of thanks: to Rabbi Steven Shaw of the Jewish Theological Seminary; to my good friends, Andrew Light and Gary Varner; and to my family.

I thank the following publishers and individuals for permission to reprint these essays:

Eugene Hargrove and *Environmental Ethics* for "Utilitarianism and Preservation," 1 (1979): 357–64; "Organism, Community, and the 'Substitution Problem,' " 7 (1985): 241–56; "Searching for Intrinsic Value: Pragmatism and Despair in Environmental Ethics," 9 (1987): 231–41; "The Call of the Wild: The Struggle Against Domination and the Technological Fix of Nature," 14 (1992): 265–73; and "Moving Beyond Anthropocentrism: Environmental Ethics, Development, and the Amazon," co-author, Lauren Oechsli, 15 (1993): 49–59.

Harlan Miller and the Society for the Study of Ethics and Animals for "Is There a Place for Animals in the Moral Consideration of Nature? *Ethics and Animals* 4 (1983): 74–87.

The Department of Philosophy of Bowling Green State University and Bowling Green State University Press for "Buffalo-Killing and the Valuation of Species," from *Values and Moral Standing* (Bowling Green Studies in Applied Philosophy Vol. 8), ed. L. W. Sumner (Bowling Green, Ohio: Bowling Green State University Press, 1986), 114–23.

"Defending the Use of Animals by Business: Animal Liberation and Environmental Ethics" appeared in *Business, Ethics and the Environment: The Public Policy Debate* ed. W. Michael Hoffman, Robert Frederick, and Edward S. Petry, Jr. (New York: Quorum Books, 1990), 223–32, and is reprinted with permission of Greenwood Publishing Group, Inc., Westport, Connecticut. Copyright © 1990 by the Center for Business Ethics at Bentley College.

JAI Press for "The Big Lie: Human Restoration of Nature," *Research in Philosophy and Technology* 12 (1992): 231–41.

The University of Wisconsin Press for excerpts from "Restoration and Redesign: The Ethical Significance of Human Intervention in Nature," *Restoration and Management Notes* 9, 2 (Winter 1991): 90–96. Reprinted by permission of the University of Wisconsin Press.

The White Horse Press and *Environmental Values* for "Artefacts and Functions: A Note on the Value of Nature," *Environmental Values* 2 (1993): 223–32.

Social Theory and Practice for "Imperialism and Environmentalism," *Social Theory and Practice* 21, 2 (Summer 1995): 271–85.

"Biodiversity and Ecological Justice" appeared in *Biodiversity and Landscapes: A Paradox of Humanity*, ed. Ke Chung Kim and Robert Weaver (Cambridge: Cambridge University Press, 1994), 61–74. Copyright © Cambridge University Press 1994. Reprinted with the permission of Cambridge University Press.

Rowman & Littlefield and Andrew Light and Jonathan M. Smith, the editors of *Space, Place, and Environmental Ethics: Philosophy and Geography I* for "Nature's Presence: Reflections on Healing and Domination," (Lanham, Md., 1996).

Associated University Presses and Bucknell University Press for "Judaism and the Ecological Crisis" from *Worldviews and Ecology*, ed. Mary Evelyn Tucker and John A. Grim (Lewisburg, Penn.: Bucknell University Press, 1994), 55–70.

"The Traditional Ethics of Natural Resources Management" is reprinted with permission from *A New Century for Natural Resources Management*, ed. Richard L. Knight and Sarah F. Bates (Washington, D.C. and Covelo, Calif.: Island Press, 1995), 101–16. Copyright © Island Press 1995.

Introduction

Is there a moral reason for the preservation of the natural environment? Can that moral reason be articulated in terms that transcend the direct consideration of human interests? These are the basic questions that motivate my work in philosophy. They are the foundation and the inspiration of the essays collected in this volume. This book is about environmental ethics, the field of environmental philosophy. Through these essays I raise, and attempt to answer, fundamental philosophical questions about the human relationship to nature and the moral justification of human activity within the natural world.

There are obvious prudential reasons for preserving a healthy and well-functioning natural environment. Human survival and the human desire for a comfortable and beautiful world are clear and powerful motivations for maintaining natural habitats and ecosystems. But prudence is not the same as moral justification. The interesting question for environmental philosophy is whether a moral justification can be given for traditional environmentalist policies such as pollution prevention, the conservation of natural resources, the protection of endangered species, and wilderness preservation. It is the primary task of environmental philosophy—of environmental ethics—to develop ethical principles appropriate for the practice of environmentalism. In this way, environmental policy will be based on a secure foundation of philosophical and ethical reasoning, not the unstable and variable dictates of prudential self-interest.

One approach within this conception of environmental philosophy would be to seek these "environmentally appropriate" ethical principles in the direct application of traditional ethical theories—such as utilitarianism, Kantianism, rights theory, or contractarianism—to the newly emerging problems of the environmental crisis. From this perspective, environmental philosophy would be a version of a basic applied ethics. Its subject matter—the justification of environmental policies—would be new, but the philosophical principles and ethical ideals used to analyze and solve these new problems would be the familiar positions and ideas of Western philosophy. A rather different approach to environmental philosophy would eschew the traditional versions of ethical theory and offer a radical reinterpretation or critique of the dominant philosophical ideas of the modern age. From this critical perspective, traditional ethical systems must be modified, expanded, or transcended in order to deal with the fundamental philosophical issues raised by the existence of the contemporary environmental crisis. The crucial change would be an expansion of ethical thought beyond the limits of the human community to include the direct moral consideration of the natural world.

In these essays I have chosen this second path. My basic critical idea is that human-centered (or "anthropocentric") ethical systems fail to account for a moral justification for the central policies of environmentalism. From this negative account of anthropocentrism I derive my fundamental position in environmental ethics: *the direct moral consideration and respect for the evolutionary processes of nature*. I believe that it is a basic ethical principle that we must respect Nature as an ongoing subject of a history, a life-process, a developmental system. The natural world—natural entities and natural ecological systems—deserves our moral consideration as part of the interdependent community of life on Earth. Hence the title of this collection. I consider Nature as analogous to a human subject, entitled to moral respect and subject to traditional ethical categories. I do not anthropomorphize Nature; I do not ascribe human feelings and intentions to the operations of natural processes. I do not consider natural processes to be sentient or alive. I merely place Nature within the realm of ethical activity. The basis of a moral justification of environmental policy is that we have ethical obligations to the natural world, just as we have ethical obligations to our fellow human beings. In these essays I explain and analyze this nonanthropocentric perspective in environmental philosophy.

A Brief Intellectual History

Perhaps the best way to introduce my position is to give a brief account of the development of my ideas, a personal intellectual history that runs parallel to the development of environmental ethics as a distinct subdiscipline in the field of philosophy. Although the contemporary postwar environmental movement is generally dated from the publication of Rachel Carson's *Silent Spring* in 1962,[1] academic philosophers did not begin to approach the subject until the early 1970s. The first book-length treatment of environmental issues from the perspective of mainstream philosophy was John Passmore's *Man's Responsibility for Nature: Ecological Problems and Western Traditions*, published in the United States in 1974.[2] The principal journal in the field, *Environmental Ethics*, did not begin publication until 1979, but it immediately served as a catalyst for an exponential growth in the professional literature of environmental philosophy.

I entered graduate school in the philosophy department at Boston University in September 1974, and began formal work on my dissertation (*The Moral Justification for Environmentalism*) in 1978. I was awarded my degree in the spring of 1983. Thus my graduate career, my research in environmental philosophy, and the writing of my dissertation took place within the first decade of the development of the field of environmental philosophy. Many of my ideas were influenced by the discussions taking place within the new discipline at that time, and I like to think that my ideas—which began to be published in 1979—also served to influence the direction of the field.

My interest in environmental ethics arose indirectly, as an outgrowth of a comprehensive project within the Boston University Department of Philosophy concerning another new field of applied philosophy, medical ethics. Under the direction of its chairman, Alasdair MacIntyre (who was later to be one of my two dissertation advisers), the philosophy department had begun a wide-ranging program of developing curricula, holding interdisciplinary seminars, and teaching premedical and nursing students about medical ethics. The central issues in medical ethics concerned the nature of the moral obligations that existed between patients and medical personnel. Philosophical problems arose because many kinds of patients did not fit the traditional models of the rational and autonomous subject of ethical theory. Patients who were comatose, senile, insane, or severely retarded—not to mention the problematic fetuses of the abortion controversy—could not enter into the traditional vision of ethical consideration and obligation. These atypical or marginal cases of humanity did not seem to possess the requisite status as "persons"—how then could moral theory and moral obligations apply to them?

My interest in the philosophical analysis of issues in medical ethics was not at all directed to the development of the proper procedures of medical care; rather my interest was in the challenge to traditional categories of ethical consideration represented by these cases of atypical human beings. Why, exactly, were some humans entitled to full moral status while others were not? What was the justifiable criterion or criteria that made a human being worthy of moral consideration? These were questions that went to the heart of any justifiable theory of ethics.

Thinking about this issue led me to consider the moral status of the nonhuman animal kingdom, and fortunately I found a sympathetic ear in Professor Michael Martin, who agreed to direct me in a course of reading. Peter Singer's *Animal Liberation* had recently been published, as well as the first article by Tom Regan in his development of the theory of animal rights, "The Moral Basis of Vegetarianism."[3] Singer based his argument on a basic utilitarianism—since animals could feel pleasure and pain, they had an interest in avoiding pain and maximizing pleasure, and human moral agents had no reason not to take these interests into account in their moral deliberations. Regan argued that animals were the subjects of a conscious life, and thus had a right not to be killed. Although I was not convinced by the arguments of Singer and Regan, I began to imagine the possibility of analogous arguments for the moral consideration of natural entities—could we say that natural entities such as plants, rivers, and endangered species had interests worthy of moral consideration, rights that might protect them from development and destruction by human activity? Could such an argument serve as a moral justification for policies of environmentalism?

This was the origin of my interest in environmental ethics, an interest that has dominated my philosophical life for over twenty years. In the summer of 1977, I began research as a prelude to developing a dissertation proposal. I remember a frightening sense of total freedom, frightening because there were no traditional signposts, no accepted texts, and no clear direction from which to begin. I was on my own, unaware of any other professional philosophers who were interested in the idea of my planned research. MacIntyre had written a critique of utilitarian reasoning in the electric power industry, and Martin was fascinated by the arguments over animal rights, but neither had any knowledge of the field we now call environmental ethics. I was forced to chart my own path.

At first I naively believed that the arguments for the justification of environmental policy would be rather straightforward. I would only need to show that the protection of the natural environment was part of the general human obligation not to harm other human individuals and the human community. The degradation of the natural environment—pollution, the elimination of species, and the waste of natural resources—was only a contemporary means of inflicting harm on other people. Policies of environmental protection clearly helped humanity. There was no reason to develop any radical new ethical theory, no reason to stretch the analogy from the arguments of animal liberation (which I thought were weak enough as is) to the rest of the natural world. In fact, my chief concern while writing the dissertation proposal was the fascinating subject of obligations to future generations: was the protection of the natural environment an obligation we owed to posterity? How could we owe obligations to people who did not yet exist? As there existed at that time a large literature on this subject, involving the proper method for ascertaining obligations and utility calculations in the distant future,[4] I comfortably settled into an analysis of the issues, confident and happy that I had narrowed down a vast uncharted subject into a clear, practical, and relevant dissertation topic.

Then I read an essay by Martin H. Krieger, "What's Wrong with Plastic Trees?" in *Science*[5]—and I understood how Kant must have felt when he first appreciated the argument of David Hume. As Kant writes in the *Prolegomena*, Hume's ideas interrupted his "dogmatic slumber" and started him on the new path of critical philosophy. Just as Hume dismantled the entire rational basis of knowledge, offering up a challenge to Kant to reestablish a secure epistemological foundation, Krieger dismantled the entire strategy of basing environmental policies on the benefits for the human community. Krieger destroyed any anthropocentric foundation for environmental preservation—thus challenging all who follow to develop a justification for environmentalism that is nonanthropocentric, that is not based on the satisfaction of human interests.

Krieger's argument plays a central role in several of the essays collected in this volume, and to avoid repetition, I will not outline or discuss his position here in any detail. It is sufficient to see that Krieger undermines any anthropocentric argument for environmentalism—i.e., any argument based on the satisfactions, interests, and goods of the human community regarding the natural world—by showing that humans do not require the preservation of nature to achieve social and individual satisfaction. The human valuation of nature changes over time, and so does our ability to technologically reproduce those aspects of the natural world in which we are interested. If our central concern is the satisfaction of human beings, then we may be better off by developing or even artificially duplicating the beneficial processes of nature, rather than preserving areas of the natural environment. "There is no lack of merit in natural environments," writes Krieger, "but this merit is not canonical."[6] Moreover, humans can be educated to appreciate different kinds of environments—so why not use this educational process to teach appreciation of artificial environments that are plentiful and available at low cost? Krieger claims that "Artificial prairies and wildernesses have been created, and there is no reason to believe that these artificial environments need be unsatisfactory for those who experience them."[7] Since even environmentalists claim that human good is the goal of social policy, we should focus on the maximization of human good and the development of social justice. Preserving trees, argues Krieger, cannot be the ultimate goal of a human-based social policy.

My first published essay, "Utilitarianism and Preservation," set forth the challenge represented by Krieger's analysis of the basis of environmental policy. Anyone who understood Krieger's argument as I did would see that it severely damaged the claims of the entire mainstream political movement of environmentalism—for since the publication of Carson's *Silent Spring*, the crucial focus of the environmental movement was to show a disbelieving or uneducated public that the destruction of the natural environment produces harmful effects for human life, and that the preservation of nature would produce benefits for humanity. This useful political claim was no longer, to my mind, philosophically defensible. Humanity's interest in the preservation of the natural world was merely contingent, easily replaced by new technology, artificial environments, and reeducation. I concluded that a justification of environmentalism must be based on moral arguments that transcended the interests and goods of the human community.

But where was one to find an ethic not based on human goods and interests? I had as a model the arguments of Singer and Regan for the moral consideration of nonhuman animals, but I thought that these arguments would prove inadequate for a moral justification of environmentalism. Singer's version of "animal liberation" was based on a hedonistic utilitarianism, but much of the natural environment did not experience pleasure and pain. Regan's version of "animal rights" was based on respecting the interests of entities that experienced a conscious life, but here again most natural entities did not have this kind of experience. Current ethical theory regarding the proper application of rights (or moral consideration) was based on the idea that only entities that had clearly defined interests could be said to deserve moral recognition.[8] Did the natural world and the nonhuman entities that comprised it have interests—interests in life, development, growth? I was not sure that the interests of natural entities by themselves could be the basis of a sustainable ethical theory concerning the nonhuman natural word, for the concept of "interest" as applied to nonhumans and nonrational entities was itself problematic.[9]

I discovered the best direction for the development of a nonanthropocentric environmental ethic after reading the work of Aldo Leopold, and his contemporary interpreters Holmes Rolston and J. Baird Callicott.[10] Leopold's essay "The Land Ethic," published in his posthumous collection of nature and biographical essays, *A Sand County Almanac*, has become the core text of environmental philosophy. Leopold argued for a community-based ethic, in which one would owe moral obligations and respect to one's fellow community members, but his innovation was to include "soils, waters, plants, and animals, or collectively: the land" in the membership of the moral community. He distilled the essence of environmental ethics into one memorable commandment: "A thing is right when it tends to preserve the integrity, stability, and beauty of the biotic community. It is wrong when it tends otherwise." Here was a clear expression of an ethic that included humanity in its moral evaluations but also transcended human concerns by engaging the health and stability of the entire natural world as a moral issue.

Leopold's contemporary commentators, Rolston and Callicott, stressed that the importance of Leopold was his development of a "holistic" ethic, an ethic that was primarily focused on the *systems* of the natural world, rather than on the individuals that comprised the systems. A holistic environmental ethic, following Leopold, would have as its basic concern the welfare of ecosystems, habitats, wilderness areas, and natural communities—not the pleasure, happiness, goods, or interests of individual animals and plants. As Callicott writes, "The moral worth of individuals (including, n.b., human individuals) is relative, to be assessed in accordance with the particular relation of each to the collective entity which Leopold called 'land.' " And this is because "the good of the biotic *community* is the ultimate measure of the moral value, the rightness or wrongness, of actions."[11] No individual has any kind of intrinsic or absolute value, for all moral value is measured according to the good for natural systems. An ethic concerned with the justification of the preservation of the natural environment must be focused on *environments*—natural communities, habitats, and ecosystems. Within these environmental systems, individuals often are killed or harmed, but the overall community continues to function at an appropriate level.

Ecological or environmental holism marked a clear departure from traditional methods and structures of modern ethical theory. Traditional modern ethics, at least in the West, is based on the fundamental value of individual human beings. Not all human beings are always recognized as full participants in the moral realm—and thus we have slavery and other forms of human discrimination and oppression—but the basic framework of modern ethics has remained focused on this preeminent value. The holistic environmental ethic that seemed to justify environmentalism was radically different. It was a *nonanthropocentric* theory of ethical value, in that it recognized the existence of value in entities other than human beings and human institutions. Moreover, it was a *holistic* theory, not based on the value of individuals but rather on the value of collective entities, communities, or systems. Although it challenged the basic structure of modern ethics, the new environmental ethic was supported by ancient traditions in Greek ethics that focused on the importance of communal relationships (as in the work of Aristotle and Plato) and by developments in the ecological and biological sciences that stressed organic interdependence and mutuality. Environmental ethics appeared to be both new and old—fresh and exciting yet comfortable and secure.

My work began to focus on the analysis and clarification of the main ideas and problems in a holistic environmental ethic. Despite the publication and discussion of a major work from the perspective of a nonanthropocentric individualism—Paul Taylor's *Respect for Nature*[12]—I considered all forms of individualism to be a dead end. An ethic that would be adequate for the justification of environmental preservation would have to be holistic, would have to focus directly on the preservation of environments and ecosystems, not merely on natural individuals. But the details of this holistic environmental ethic still needed to be worked out.

It is clear from this personal history of the origin of contemporary environmental ethics that for me the development of an environmental ethic must follow one of several clearly defined routes, marked by basic choices in the primary focus of the ethic. The first choice is between an anthropocentric ethic and a nonanthropocentric one: is environmental policy to be morally justified by a consideration of human benefit or the good of the nonhuman natural world? I chose nonanthropocentrism. The second choice is between individualism and holism: is the moral value of the natural environment to be found in the value of natural individuals or in the natural systems comprised by these individuals? I chose holism. But was there a third choice, between various forms of nonanthropocentric holism? It was to this question that my major philosophical work was first directed.

Communal Holism and the Autonomy of Nature

If we direct our moral concern to the systems of the natural world, precisely to what are we directing our gaze? Leopold himself had an ambiguous sense of the holistic entity that was to be the main focus of his ethical evaluation. As I discuss in the essay "Organism, Community, and the 'Substitution Problem,' " one can conceive of nature as one large organic whole, analogous to a biological *organism*, or one can conceive of nature as a model of a *community* of interacting but interdependent individuals. The former view is similar to the popular "Gaia Hypothesis" advocated originally by James E. Lovelock, but Leopold played with a version of this idea as early as the 1920s, influenced by the organismic philosophy of P. D. Ouspensky.[13] The latter view, that of community, plays the major role in the exposition of Leopold's "land ethic"—which was written much later, just before his death in 1948. Is there a significant difference between these views of the natural holistic system?

I believe that there are clear differences. The conception of the natural system as one vast organism is an extreme form of holism in which individual entities have no worth outside of their function for the welfare of the system. The conception of the natural system as a community is a modified form of holism in which the individual members of the community contribute to the welfare of the overall system, but also maintain independent value as autonomous individuals. An organism has parts; a community is composed of members. The degree of autonomy of the individual entities serves to distinguish one model from another. And this autonomy also leads to differing decisions in the realm of environmental policy. The community model of modified holism will support policies of action that tend to preserve both ecological systems and the individual entities within these systems; the organism model will tend to sacrifice individual well-being for the good of the entire system. The community model is thus immune to the charge made by Tom Regan and others that environmental holism is a form of "environmental fascism,"[14] for this modified holism protects the value (and rights) of the individual members of the natural community.

Of course I am here presenting only a brief summary of arguments that are developed more fully in the essays in this volume. The early essays explore the basis and justification for a modified form of holism based on the community model of natural systems. But a central concern throughout all of my work is the notion of *autonomy*—an idea that first gains its importance in my thought through the analysis of the model of community-based holism. Autonomy is the free development of individuals and natural processes—its opposite is domination. This focus on autonomy and domination becomes more emphatic throughout the development of my philosophical views, but its seeds are present from the very beginning. Several themes recur repeatedly in these essays, as I work out the details of a theoretical position in environmental ethics:

(1) The moral consideration of both individuals and systems, as I have already noted in the explanation of modified holism. In recent years, a view similar to my modified holism has developed into a position called "pluralism" that has been debated to a large extent in the literature.[15]

(2) Concern for temporality and history as crucial factors in the determination of moral value. In my view, we cannot understand the identity, integrity, value, or meaning of any natural entity or system unless we understand its history, its genesis. The source of an entity or system is a primary determinant of value and meaning.

(3) Concern for the identity and integrity of ecological systems and the natural entities that comprise the systems. There is a connection between ontology and ethics: what an entity is, free of the imposition of human desires and interests, determines its moral value and the moral obligations owed to it.

(4) Criticism of the imposition of human ideals and human projects on the free development of nature and natural processes. When humans shape and manipulate the natural world to meet their own interests, to satisfy their desires, it is a form of anthropocentric domination, the oppression and denial of the autonomy of nature.

(5) The idea that Nature is an autonomous moral subject, analogous to the traditional human subject of modern ethical theory. As a temporally situated multidimensional system of both interdependent individuals and interacting subsystems, Nature is the subject of an ongoing history, similar to human individuals and

human institutions and systems. As such a subject, it is the legitimate focus of direct moral concern and obligation.

The final conclusion to these themes is thus, as I noted above, that humanity has moral obligations to the natural world, similar to the obligations that exist from one human being to another, to preserve its integrity, identity, and free development. As moral agents, our primary moral goals are to preserve autonomy and to resist all forms of domination, both within the human community and within the natural world. In much of my philosophical work, I have attempted to apply this theoretical position to practical problems of environmental policy, with a dual purpose in mind: to effect changes in environmental policy itself and to test the coherence of my philosophical standpoint.

Plan of the Book

The essays in this collection are grouped into four sections. In the first section, "The Moral Consideration of Nature," I explore the possibility and justification of an ethic that considers nature and natural entities to be the direct objects of moral concern and obligation. I criticize two traditional ethical theories, utilitarianism and a basic form of classical American pragmatism, as being too anthropocentric to justify environmental policies. I also examine the arguments for the moral consideration of nonhuman animals and compare these "animal liberation" positions to a workable environmental ethic. I explain the limitations of individualistic theories of ethical obligation as the basis of an environmental ethic and investigate the differences between two versions of holistic theories—nature as one complex organism and nature as a community. I defend a nonanthropocentric community-based holism, modeled after the work of Aldo Leopold, in which ethical obligations regarding the environment are owed directly to the natural community in which human society is embedded.

In the second section, "Restoration and Domination," I explore the philosophical meaning of human intervention in the natural word. If Nature is a moral subject, a member of our ethical community, then actions which serve to modify or destroy natural processes are problematic. I focus specifically on the processes of ecological restoration, the development of sustainable forestry, and the repair of damaged environments. My argument is based on the difference between human-created artifacts (which are designed for a human purpose) and natural entities (which evolve without a specifically human-based design). The attempts by humanity to manage natural environments are a form of domination, a human imperialism over natural entities. The purpose of this domination is to mold nature into a human-friendly artificial world, one that at best resembles the natural world.

The four essays in the third section, "Justice, Genocide, and the Environment," apply the theoretical position developed in the first two sections to the problems of development in the Third World, global biodiversity, and the comparison between the destruction of the natural world and policies of genocide. I argue that a nonanthropocentric ethic—because it does not consider human benefits the primary goal of environmental policy—will result in different decisions than traditional human interest arguments. I also argue that a nonanthropocentric ethic will require broader conceptions of justice and reparations between the industrialized world and developing nations. In two essays consideration is given to the values underlying the environmental crisis and the destruction caused by the Holocaust of European Jewry.

The final section, "History and Tradition," contains two essays that explore older arguments and positions in environmental ethics and policy. One essay examines the traditions of Jewish law regarding the environment, with particular emphasis on the principles in Judaism that are compatible with a nonanthropocentric environmental ethic. Since Judaism is a theocentric religion, principles are justified by God's commands, not necessarily by human interests. The second essay examines the origins of resource management ethics in the philosophy of John Locke, specifically his view that nature is only useful as private property. I discuss this anthropocentric tradition of human use-value as adopted by the first head of the U.S. Forest Service, Gifford Pinchot, in a famous clash between Pinchot and John Muir over the development of Hetch Hetchy in Yosemite National Park.

Although the essays in this volume were written over a seventeen-year period, and were originally published (or presented as talks) as individual works, the collection as a whole sets forth a unified and coherent position in environmental philosophy—the direct moral consideration of the processes of Nature. If we are to develop a moral response to the environmental crisis that surrounds us, we must treat the natural world as an autonomous subject, worthy of moral respect.

Notes

1. Rachel Carson, *Silent Spring* (Boston: Houghton Mifflin, 1962). Other important popular environmentalist books were Paul Ehrlich, *The Population*

Bomb (New York Ballantine, 1968); Lewis Herber (Murray Bookchin) *Our Synthetic Environment* (New York: Knopf, 1962); and Barry Commoner, *The Closing Circle: Nature, Man, and Technology* (New York: Knopf, 1971).

2. John Passmore, *Man's Responsibility for Nature: Ecological Problems and Western Traditions* (New York: Scribner's, 1974).

3. Peter Singer, *Animal Liberation* (New York: Random House, 1975). Tom Regan, "The Moral Basis of Vegetarianism," *Canadian Journal of Philosophy* 5 (1975): 181–214.

4. This literature included, but was not limited to, the following: Jan Narveson, "Utilitarianism and New Generations," *Mind* 76 (1967): 62–72; Jan Narveson, "Moral Problems of Population," *Monist* 57 (1973): 62–86; J. Brenton Stearns, "Ecology and the Indefinite Unborn," *Monist* 56 (1972): 612–25; R. I. Sikora, "Utilitarianism: The Classical Principle and the Average Principle," *Canadian Journal of Philosophy* 5 (1975): 409–19; M. P. Golding, "Obligations to Future Generations," *Monist* 56 (1972): 85–99; Hardy Jones, "Genetic Endowment and Obligation to Future Generation," *Social Theory and Practice* 4 (1976): 29–47; and Edwin Delattre, "Rights, Responsibilities, and Future Persons," *Ethics* 82 (1972): 254–58. Eventually, I discussed obligations to future generations in the second chapter of my dissertation.

5. Martin H. Krieger, "What's Wrong with Plastic Trees?" *Science* 179 (1973): 446–55.

6. Ibid., p. 451.

7. Ibid., p. 453.

8. See Joel Feinberg, "The Nature and Value of Rights," *Journal of Value Inquiry* 4 (1970): 243–57, and "The Rights of Animals and Unborn Generations," in *Philosophy and Environmental Crisis*, ed. William T. Blackstone (Athens: University of Georgia Press, 1974), pp. 43–68.

9. One of the best criticisms of the notion of "interests" is R. G. Frey, "Rights, Interests, Desires and Beliefs," *American Philosophical Quarterly* 16 (1979): 233–39. The problematic nature of the notion of interests is best exemplified by a debate concerning moral obligations to works of art. See Alan Tormey, "Aesthetic Rights," *Journal of Aesthetics and Art Criticism* 32 (1973): 163–70 and David Goldblatt, "Do Works of Art Have Rights?" *Journal of Aesthetics and Art Criticism* 35 (1976): 69–77.

10. Aldo Leopold, *A Sand County Almanac* (New York: Oxford University Press, 1949). Rolston's early work was collected in Holmes Rolston, III, *Philosophy Gone Wild: Essays in Environmental Ethics* (Buffalo: Prometheus, 1986) and rewritten as one book, *Environmental Ethics: Duties to and Values in the Natural World* (Philadelphia: Temple University Press, 1988). Callicott's essays have been collected in J. Baird Callicott, *In Defense of the Land Ethic: Essays in Environmental Philosophy* (Albany: SUNY Press, 1989).

11. J. Baird Callicott, "Animal Liberation: A Triangular Affair," *Environmental Ethics* 2 (1980): 327, 320.

12. Paul W. Taylor, *Respect for Nature: A Theory of Environmental Ethics* (Princeton: Princeton University Press, 1986).

13. See J. E. Lovelock, *Gaia: A New Look at Life on Earth* (Oxford: Oxford University Press, 1979). For Leopold's early fascination with Ouspensky see his posthumous essay, "Some Fundamentals of Conservation in the Southwest," *Environmental Ethics* 1 (1979): 131–41.

14. Tom Regan, *The Case for Animal Rights* (Berkeley: University of California Press, 1983), pp. 361–62.

15. For more on pluralism see Christopher Stone, *Earth and Other Ethics: The Case for Moral Pluralism* (New York: Harper & Row, 1987), Peter Wenz, *Environmental Justice* (Albany: SUNY Press, 1988), J. Baird Callicott, "Animal Liberation and Environmental Ethics: Back Together Again," *Between the Species* 4 (1988): 163-69, Callicott, "The Case Against Moral Pluralism," *Environmental Ethics* 12 (1990): 99–124, Wenz, "Minimal, Moderate, and Extreme Moral Pluralism," *Environmental Ethics* 15 (1993): 61–74, and Gary Varner, "No Holism Without Pluralism," *Environmental Ethics* 13 (1991): 175–79.

Notes on the Texts

These essays were written between 1979 and 1996, and are here reproduced virtually unchanged from the form of their original publication. I have made minor alterations in a few texts to avoid detailed repetition, but this is not always possible, as discussed below. I have made a few minor stylistic changes and in several essays have modified the footnote format to conform with the rest of this volume.

Reprinting a collection of essays such as this creates one major disadvantage for the reader, and one major advantage. The disadvantage is that the reader who begins with chapter 1 and reads the collection straight through will undoubtedly find passages and arguments that are repeated. This repetition is unavoidable, since I often build my arguments in later essays based on work in previous essays. The major advantage is for those who wish to read particular essays without reading the entire collection. Those readers will find that each essay is a self-contained argument, not dependent on any other chapter in the book. If I had deleted sections in some later essays because they were echoes of arguments set forth earlier, the reader of the later essays would miss crucial points necessary for a full understanding of my position.

In the interest of academic and scholarly integrity, I have thus decided to reprint these essays without significant changes—even in those places where I am now less than completely satisfied with my argument or its expression. Readers interested in researching my work in environmental philosophy can use this volume instead of returning to the original sources.

Each of the essays is introduced by a brief description of the circumstances surrounding its creation. Where necessary, the relevant issues and arguments of other environmental philosophers are summarized to provide the appropriate context for the essay.

Part I

The Moral Consideration of Nature

.

1

Utilitarianism and Preservation

"Utilitarianism and Preservation" was my first published essay. It was written in the spring of 1979 as a response to an article by John N. Martin that had appeared in the first issue of Environmental Ethics. *In discussing the idea of "the irreplaceable" in the context of environmental decision making, Martin had advocated a utilitarian basis for the preservation of rare and unique natural entities. I use Martin's faith in utilitarian thinking as a starting point to discuss Martin Krieger's challenge to human-centered environmentalism. The central idea in my position is that human benefits, desires, and interests are only contingently related to the preservation of the natural environment. If the goal of environmental policy— of any social policy—is the maximization of human satisfaction, then we may achieve higher levels of satisfaction by developing, using, or destroying the natural world. Humans may be happier in an artificial world, Krieger's world of plastic trees. Krieger's argument dooms any anthropocentric attempt to base environmental policy on human interests. My essay is essentially negative and critical—I had not yet worked out a positive conception of what a nonanthropocentric environmental ethic might look like. Nevertheless, within this basic criticism of anthropocentrism there are many hints of my later essays: a concern for the genetic properties of a natural entity; consideration of the identity and the integrity of an entity, system, or place; and an emphasis on history and uniqueness as the basis for environmental value.*

I

At the end of his analysis of arguments for the preservation of the irreplaceable,[1] John N. Martin discovers that he is puzzled by the peculiar two-sided use of utilitarian reasoning in debates over the environment. His conclusion is that "the vast majority of preservationist cases can be explained by a version of utilitarianism," and by the term *explained* he seems to mean "justified." However, he continues, "Given that the major foes of preservation are utilitarians, this consequence is surprising. It looks as if the foes may be defeated by turning their own theory against them and using it more carefully." Martin is thus proposing that with more careful philosophical groundwork, a complete utilitarian justification of the environmentalist-preservationist position can be formulated, routing once and for all the anti-environmentalist forces of development.

I argue that Martin's view is wrong, that utilitarianism in its most basic forms cannot explain or justify the preservationist position in the preservation vs. development debate—although it often appears to do so. In fact, the widespread use of utilitarian arguments to justify policy decisions about the protection of the environment is detrimental to preservation. The essential elements of utilitarianism only provide a justification for the satisfaction of human need, for this satisfaction is the standard by which utilitarianism measures goodness or moral worth. But human needs and the needs of the natural environment are not necessarily similar or in harmony; thus, any ethical theory—such as utilitarianism—which tries to explain the preservation of the natural environment by means of the satisfaction of human wants, need, and desires will be only contingently true: it will depend on the factual circumstances, the actual desires of the human community at any given time. This empirical limitation does not bode well for the security of the preservationist argument.

II

What then is the preservationist position? Essentially, we can define it as an argument for the protection and preservation of some object or state-of-affairs in an unaltered condition. Martin himself is concerned with irreplaceable entities, but environmentalists do not always restrict themselves to that class of objects.[2] Generally, they use the argument to justify the preservation of plants, wildlife, rock formations, the land, ecological systems, wilderness areas, etc.

Martin believes that the major problem in the application of utilitarian ethical theory to this preservationist position lies in the justification of the importance of genetic properties. Any worthwhile argument for preservation would have to explain why a perfect reproduction of a work of art or an artificially produced Yosemite Valley is not as valuable as the original. The reason—of course—is that the historical genetic properties of the object—the process by which it was created—cannot be separated from the nongenetic properties in a determination of the worth of the object. Martin, however, claims that utilitarianism is unable to evaluate the genetic properties of an object because of its "blindness to the past."[3] When evaluating the consequences of an action in order to determine its moral worth, the utilitarian has his "eyes [directed] towards the future."[4] The sole concern of the utilitarian is whether a world in which a certain entity is preserved will be a better world than one in which the entity will not be preserved. According to Martin, the utilitarian is not interested in the historical properties that the entity may possess, and thus how the entity came into being is a fact which is irrelevant to the moral calculation. The utilitarian is forward-looking: the measurement of future utility is the criterion of goodness or moral value.

Martin admits to being troubled by this apparent inability of utilitarian moral theory to evaluate entities on the basis of genetic properties. As he notes, it creates numerous instances in which preservationist intuitions are in conflict with utilitarian calculations. "The utilitarian counts astro-turf as the equal to grass; he allows roads and motels within the boundaries of national parks; he dams rivers and lumbers forests. In all cases he is unswayed by genetic considerations."[5] In order to alleviate this problem with utilitarianism, Martin proposes a method by which genetic considerations are *indirectly* introduced into the utilitarian calculation of benefit and harm. Since it is an obvious truth that people "have special attitudes towards objects based on genetic considerations," the utilitarian ought to consider these attitudes when calculating the utility of an act of preservation. Thus Martin concludes that preservation may be a better policy of action, not because of any intrinsic worth of the object being preserved, but because preservation—given present attitudes—produces a more satisfied population.[6]

This indirect calculation of genetic properties of objects—by means of an evaluation of the population's attitudes—yields a number of problems. Martin notes three areas of possible controversy. The first is the "contingency of [a] preservationist obligation" which is based on human attitudes. Because the utilitarian bases his policy of preservation on the satisfaction of certain human attitudes, the policy will be justified only as long as these attitudes remain in effect. As Martin

comments: "If people did not now and in the future care about Yosemite Valley, arguments for its preservation based on genetic properties
would not seem to carry any force."[7] Arguments for environmental
preservation, then, depend for their validity on the contingent existence of certain human attitudes.

This reliance on contingent human attitudes creates a second problem: the "possibility of deception." If the utilitarian argument for preservation rests on the satisfaction of human attitudes and feelings, then
actual objects considered important need not be preserved as long as
people believe that they are. The belief that a certain object is "natural"
or "real" will satisfy human needs and increase social utility. As long
as the population continues to be deceived, there will be no decrease
in the levels of satisfaction. What is preserved, then, is the *belief* that
objects with important genetic properties continue to exist—the actual
objects need not be preserved. Tourists to Paris, for example, do not
have to know that the original *Mona Lisa* was slashed by a knife-wield-
ing intruder. Martin does not approve of this conclusion: "What we
see here is that serving people's feelings is sometimes not enough."[8]
As traditional arguments against utilitarianism have stressed, there
exist some values—such as truth and justice—which are important regardless of consequences. The *prima facie* value of truth would thus
seem to override a utilitarian calculation about the benefits of deception in actual cases of preservation. Martin thus calls for a further elab-
oration of utilitarian theory.

Finally, Martin notes the actual "unpopularity of preservation." People seem to get more satisfaction from using motor boats on lakes,
damming rivers for hydroelectric power, and building access roads
into national parks than they would by preserving these natural resources in a pristine state. Thus it seems that "the utility derived from
serving the attitudes of those favoring preservation is an insignificant
part of total utility."[9] Given the actual state of contemporary society,
utilitarian arguments concerning preservation appear to clash with the
intuitive judgments of environmentalists.

III

This analysis of certain problems in an indirect utilitarian argument
for the preservation of objects with important genetic or historical
properties is the key point of Martin's essay. It is therefore surprising
to discover that despite these problems, his conclusion is that a more

careful use of utilitarian arguments can buttress the environmental cause. I believe that the contrary conclusion is much more obvious: these problems reveal the complete failure of utilitarian arguments to explain the subtlety and crucial importance of the environmentalist position on preservation.

Martin employs a standard version of utilitarianism in his analysis. In his argument a given world is better than an alternative if and only if it possesses more social utility, and utility "is identified with the satisfaction of citizen preferences."[10] The significant fact about such an ethical theory is that the criterion of moral value is the satisfaction of human preferences—the satisfaction of human needs, wants, and desires. Any natural resource, object, or ecological area will only be preserved, therefore, if its preservation satisfies some obvious human need. Moreover, because of the utilitarian calculus, the satisfaction derived from the act of preservation will have to outweigh any or all satisfactions produced by the development or nonpreservation of the resource, object, or area.

Basing moral value or goodness on the satisfaction of human needs and desires can only harm the environmentalist goal of preserving natural entities. A result of this theory is that the preservation of nature as a policy of action has only secondary and contingent value. The only primary value is the production of greater amounts of social utility: the satisfaction of human preferences and needs. The promulgation of environmentalist or preservationist policy will thus depend upon the contingent existence of relevant preservationist needs of the human community. To use one of Martin's examples: the chincona tree will be preserved only as long as the human community needs the quinine which is produced from it.[11] But this act of preservation is only a contingent moral obligation: if no human need is satisfied by the tree's preservation, if, for example, an artificial source of quinine is discovered, there will be no moral reason to preserve the species. Thus the best result which an environmentalist can achieve by the use of a utilitarian argument is an unstable, contingent justification of preservation. Preservation will be the acceptable moral position only when human beings want it as a social policy.

The problems associated with contingency which Martin raised in his discussion of the *indirect* utilitarian argument forcibly demonstrate the precarious nature of a utilitarian justification of environmental preservation. I have noted these problems in the previous section and need not repeat them here. What Martin fails to see, however, is that even his "safe," nongenetic cases of preservation—those involving conservation, cost-benefit analyses, externalities, and ecology[12]—are not sufficiently explained or justified by a *direct* utilitarian approach. A good counterexample is the preservation of endangered species which are of little or no importance to humanity or the world ecological system. The preservation of the snail darter, a freshwater fish whose protected status has halted the completion of the Tellico dam,[13] cannot be explained rationally by the concept of utility. No cost-benefit analysis could favor the preservation of the fish: the loss in dollars spent and energy unused is staggering. Nor can the preservation of the snail darter be justified in terms of ecology: except for the interest of scholars in the field, the fish has no known beneficial effects on the human community or environment. If utilitarian arguments are presented to fortify the environmentalist-preservationist position, absurd claims have to be made. The environmentalist is forced to argue that the existence of a fish (or a plant, or a wilderness area) which is not utilized by the human community has more social utility than the obvious economic gains resulting from the nonpreservation of the fish (or plant or wilderness area) and the development of the affected region. It seems clear that this kind of utilitarian argument for preservation will rarely justify the environmentalist position.

This point has been amply demonstrated by Martin H. Krieger in an article entitled "What's Wrong with Plastic Trees?"[14] described by Mark Sagoff as "a *reductio ad absurdum* of contemporary 'utilitarian' arguments for preserving the environment."[15] Krieger states that "Artificial prairies and wildernesses have been created, and there is no reason to believe that these artificial environments need be unsatisfactory for those who experience them."[16] In fact, since "the way in which we experience nature is conditioned by our society,"[17] public choice and desire can be manipulated so that "people learn to use and want . . . environments that are likely to be available at low cost."[18] Here then is the ultimate utilitarian position: environments artificially created to produce the most human satisfaction, and human minds conditioned to enjoy the artificial environments. Surely no greater amount of social utility could be imagined! Unfortunately, the effect of this theory on environmental policy would be disastrous. Any or all natural objects and environments could be destroyed to further the interests, to increase the satisfaction, of the human community.

An artificial but satisfying utilitarian world clearly demonstrates the flaw in Martin's analysis and the danger that analysis holds for the policy of preservation. Utilitarianism, as Martin conceives it, only measures the moral worth or goodness of an action by the satisfaction of human preferences and needs which is produced. These human needs are connected only contingently with the preservation of any given natural object, resource, or ecological system. Humanity could enjoy an artificial, plasticized world which produces more social utility than a world filled with natural objects and resources. As our space program has demonstrated, humans can even *survive* in an artificial environment. The simple fact of the matter is that the interests of humanity are not necessarily connected with the preservation of the natural environment. Any ethical theory which places its emphasis on the satisfaction of human needs can support a policy of preservation only on a contingent basis. Obligations to preserve natural objects and resources are overridden whenever a greater amount of human satisfaction can be attained by nonpreservation.

There is no danger then, as Martin believes, for the foes of environmental preservation who use utilitarian arguments. On their side is the essential premise of utilitarian theory that the satisfaction of human desires and needs is the sole criterion of goodness or moral worth. The real danger lies in the use of utilitarian arguments by preservationists. Basing arguments for environmental preservation on the premises of utilitarian moral theory will only reveal the precarious relationship which exists between the satisfaction of human needs and the preservation of natural objects. Once it is accepted that the satisfaction of human needs is the primary measure of value, the continued existence of the natural world is reduced to a mere contingency.

IV

In conclusion, I would like to note two different approaches which the preservationist might take to avoid Martin's "more careful" formulation of utilitarian arguments. These observations are not meant as finished theories of environmental obligation, but as suggestions for further work.

(1) Utilitarianism might be salvaged for use in the environmentalism debate if it is stripped of its bias towards the satisfaction of *human* needs and preferences. Bentham, it should be remembered, considered the pains and pleasures of the animal kingdom to be of importance in a utilitarian calculation.[19] According to this kind of position, the needs and desires of the wildlife in a given area would have to be considered prior to any development or destruction for the purpose of human betterment.

Unfortunately, the problems with this kind of broad utilitarianism appear insurmountable. How does the satisfaction of animal needs compare in utility with the satisfaction of human needs? Can we bring plant life into the calculation? What about nonliving entities, such as rock formations (e.g., the Grand Canyon) or entire ecological areas? Does a marsh have an interest in not being drained and turned into a golf course, a need or desire to continue a natural existence? It is clear that difficult—if not impossible—problems arise when we begin to consider utility for nonhuman and nonsentient entities.

(2) A second alternative, highly tentative, is a movement away from a "want-oriented perspective" in ethical theory.[20] Rather than evaluating the moral worth of an action by the consequences which satisfy needs and desires in the human (or even nonhuman) world, we can look at the intrinsic qualities of the action, and determine what kind of values this action manifests. The question which the debate over environmental preservation raises is *not* "Does preservation of this particular natural object lead to a better world?" but rather "Do we want a world in which the preservation of natural objects is considered an important value?" The question is not whether the preservation of a certain entity increases the amount of satisfaction and pleasure in the world, but rather, whether these pleasures, satisfactions, and needs ought to be pursued. The question, in short, is about what kind of moral universe ought to be created.[21] Only when the preservation of natural objects is seen to be an intrinsically good policy of action, rather than a means to some kind of satisfaction, will a policy of environmental protection be explained and justified. The development of an ethical theory which can accomplish this task will be a difficult undertaking, but it is the only choice open to preservationists who wish to avoid the easy, self-defeating trap of utilitarianism.

Notes

1. John N. Martin, "The Concept of the Irreplaceable," *Environmental Ethics* 1 (1979): 46.

2. In a somewhat trivial sense, of course, all objects are irreplaceable: any object replacing a unique individual object is a different individual. Martin seems concerned with objects which are irreplaceable in a nontrivial sense: species of life, strange and beautiful natural formations and ecosystems (Yosemite Valley, the Everglades, etc.), and works of art. Environmentalists generally place less emphasis on the absolute uniqueness of the entity they wish to protect. A marsh is protected from development into a golf course, not because

it is the last marsh in the world, nor because it is a uniquely beautiful marsh. Exactly why it is protected is, of course, a question which only a more detailed system of environmental ethics can answer.

3. Martin, "The Irreplaceable," p. 42

4. Ibid., p. 43.

5. Ibid.

6. Ibid., p. 44.

7. Ibid.

8. Ibid., p. 45.

9. Ibid., p. 46.

10. Ibid., p. 39.

11. Ibid.

12. Ibid., p. 40.

13. For an account of the snail darter and other endangered species which have halted industrial development, see Philip Shabecoff, "New Battles over Endangered Species," *New York Times Magazine,* June 4, 1978, pp. 38–44.

14. Martin H. Krieger, "What's Wrong with Plastic Trees?" *Science* 179 (1973): 446–55.

15. Mark Sagoff, "On Preserving the Natural Environment," *Yale Law Journal* 84 (1974): 205.

16. Krieger, "Plastic Trees," p. 453.

17. Ibid.

18. Ibid., p. 451.

19. In an oft-quoted passage, Jeremy Bentham discusses the importance of animal suffering as a criterion of moral respect. See *An Introduction to the Principles of Morals and Legislation* (1789), chap. 17, par. 4, note.

20. Laurence H. Tribe, "Ways Not to Think About Plastic Trees," in *When Values Conflict,* ed. Laurence H. Tribe, Corinne S. Schelling, and John Voss (Cambridge, Mass.: Ballinger, 1976), p. 62. Also published in *Yale Law Journal* 83 (1974): 1315–48. Tribe, an opponent of "instrumental" or utilitarian reasoning in environmental decision making, has tried to develop a new ethic to justify environmental concerns. See also his "Technology Assessment and the Fourth Discontinuity: The Limits of Instrumental Rationality," *Southern California Law Review* 46 (1973): 617–60.

21. It should be noted that Mark Sagoff, although a critic of the view suggested here, appears to agree that something is wrong with simply satisfying human desires: "As long as policies are intended to maximize the general satisfaction, they will be no better, morally or spiritually, than the interests they serve." The problem then becomes one of replacing hedonistic human desires with desires more in harmony with the preservation of the natural environment. See Sagoff, "Natural Environment," p. 225.

2

Is There a Place for Animals in the Moral Consideration of Nature?

In the spring of 1983 the Society for the Study of Ethics and Animals (SSEA) organized a session for the December 1983 American Philosophical Association meeting. The theme of the session was the relationship between environmental ethics and the ethical treatment of animals, a topic that was both puzzling and controversial at that time. Since it was a nonanthropocentric ethic, animal liberation appeared to have a close affinity with mainstream environmental ethics. In its early years, the journal Environmental Ethics *had published essays on the moral consideration of animals (e.g., Tom Regan, "Animal Rights, Human Wrongs," 2 (1980): 99–120), even when the essays made no explicit connection between the moral treatment of animals and environmental issues. But two important articles raised serious questions about the compatibility of these branches of applied "nonhuman" ethics. J. Baird Callicott, in "Animal Liberation: A Triangular Affair,"* Environmental Ethics *2 (1980): 311–38, had argued that a truly ecological ethic must be holistic, on the model of Aldo Leopold's land ethic. Animal liberationists, because of their concern for every individual animal, including domesticated animals, were arguing from an entirely different foundation. But Lilly-Marlene Russow, in "Why Do Species Matter?"* Environmental Ethics *3 (1981): 101–12, argued that ecological holism had severe difficulty in accounting for many environmentalist intuitions and policies about the preservation of rare and unique species. In "Is There a Place for Animals in the Moral Consideration of Nature?" I make a first attempt at analyzing the relationship between an environmental ethic and an ethic that considers the moral treatment of animals. I argue for a modified holism that places its major emphasis on the protection*

13

of environmental systems while at the same time respecting the moral value of individuals. This essay was published in the journal of the SSEA, Ethics and Animals, in September 1983, prior to the actual meeting, and I presented an outline of the paper before the society in December. Evelyn Pluhar also presented a paper ("Two Conceptions of an Environmental Ethic and Their Implications," Ethics and Animals 4 (1983): 110–27) that argued for a compromise position; however, her emphasis was on the moral consideration of individual animals.

I

The compatibility of an "animal liberation" ethic and an environmental ethic depends primarily on how one interprets the meaning and moral structure of a theory of environmental ethics. In part this is because the meaning and moral structure of an animal liberation ethic is fairly straightforward: it focuses on the absence of morally relevant differences between humans and animals, and on the moral significance of animal pain and suffering.[1] But the form of an environmental ethic is not so clear. Does an environmental ethic advocate moral concern for natural individuals, for species, for ecosystems, or perhaps for nature as a whole? An answer to this question is required before one can judge the relationship between animal liberation and environmental ethics, but an answer, unfortunately, is not easily discernible. In what follows I will argue, first, that several versions of an environmental ethic yield problematic environmental and moral conclusions; second, that an environmental ethic must be interpreted as a complex balancing of different kinds of moral concern—i.e., moral concern for individuals, for species, and for natural ecosystems—and third, that this balancing will produce moral results that are troubling to the advocate of an animal liberation ethic.

An analysis of the form of an environmental ethic can proceed most easily if the potential objects for moral concern are divided into three major groups: individuals, species, and ecosystemic communities. Thus one interpretation of an environmental ethic will hold that moral obligations, duties, or rules are applicable to all natural individuals—animals, plants, bodies of water, soil, rocks, minerals, etc. Another interpretation of an environmental ethic will consider natural species as the proper object of moral concern. A final interpretation of an environmental ethic will hold that moral concepts are applicable to ecosystems or natural communities as a whole. Restricting the discussion to these possibilities will greatly facilitate the analysis, and the cost in terms of conceptual clarity will not be significant. The form of an environmental ethic that considers obligations to nature as a whole, for example, can easily be assimilated into the ecosystemic interpretation, once one considers the earth's biosphere as one large and complex ecosystemic community.

In analyzing the meaning and form of an environmental ethic, two central points need to be considered. First, is the formal structure of the ethic coherent, reasonable, and in general agreement with normal ethical practice? Of course an environmental ethic is different from traditional ethical theories that consider only human actions, concerns, and institutions the primary objects of moral value—but nonetheless, an environmental ethic cannot be so radically different from traditional ethical theories that it defies credibility. It must be a plausible revision in the meaning and justification of moral concepts. Second, the interpretation of an environmental ethic must be in accord with the general policies of environmentalism, i.e., of environmental protection. Although it might seem strange to cite this as a significant consideration in the analysis of an environmental ethic—isn't it obvious that an environmental ethic is in accord with a policy of environmentalism?—the fact is that certain interpretations of the meaning of an environmental ethic actually undermine environmentalist principles. These interpretations of an environmental ethic will thus be rejected on the practical ground that they fail to achieve the goal of environmental protection.

II

Perhaps the most obvious interpretation of an environmental ethic is the moral consideration of the ecosystem, or the natural community as a whole. Aldo Leopold's oft-quoted definition of the moral rightness of human environmental action is generally used as a thematic signpost for this position: "A thing is right when it tends to preserve the integrity, stability, and beauty of the biotic community. It is wrong when it tends otherwise."[2] In the more recent literature, J. Baird Callicott and Don Marietta, Jr., have each argued for this model of an environmental ethic. Callicott describes Leopold's vision in this way: "the good of the biotic *community* is the ultimate measure of the moral value, the rightness or wrongness, of actions." Or in other words: "the effect upon ecological systems is the decisive factor in the determina-

tion of the ethical quality of actions."[3] Similarly, Marietta writes that
"morally acceptable treatment of the environment is that which does
not upset the integrity of the ecosystem as it is seen in a diversity of
life forms existing in a dynamic and complex but stable interdependency."[4] Thus, in this version of an environmental ethic, the natural
ecosystem or community is the primary object of moral concern. The
morality of human deliberative action will be judged by various criteria of ecosystemic goodness—the stability, integrity, health, and diversity of the natural biotic community. Actions which affect an ecosystem as a whole—e.g., the damming of a river, the clearing of forest
land, the draining of a marsh—will be morally judged by their relation
to ecological concepts concerning the entire natural community under
consideration. Even actions directed towards individual natural entities will be judged by ecosystemic criteria: shooting a deer or chopping
down a single tree will be morally evaluated by the effect the action
has on the natural community.

A number of comments can be made about this interpretation of an
environmental ethic. First, it is clear that this model of moral concern
in an environmental ethic is incompatible, as such, with an ethic of
animal liberation. An ethic which evaluates action in terms of communal health and stability cannot be seriously interested in the welfare
of individual entities—such as animals—unless these individuals are
particularly important to communal functions. As Bryan Norton has
recently argued, "the relationship between the individual interests of
organisms, individual plants, and nonliving objects, on the one hand,
and the healthy functioning and integrity of the ecosystem, on the
other hand, is a contingent one."[5] The overall healthy functioning of
the natural community may require the death, destruction, or suffering
of individual natural entities, animals included. From the perspective
of the natural community, the sacrifice of individual entities may be
the morally correct course of action. Callicott thus argues that a major
thesis of an animal liberation ethic—the moral significance of the suffering of animals—is irrelevant in the moral evaluations of an ecosystemic environmental ethic. "Pain and pleasure seem to have nothing
at all to do with good and evil if our appraisal is taken from the vantage point of ecological biology. . . . If nature as a whole is good, then
pain and death are also good."[6] Or rather, if the well-being of the natural community or ecosystem is the primary good of moral judgment,
then pain and death that contribute to this overall good cannot be
judged as moral evils, as an animal liberation ethic would require. Because an animal liberation ethic is concerned with the welfare of indi-

vidual animals, while a community-based environmental ethic may require the sacrifice of individual animals, the two ethical systems cannot be compatible.

The second point to notice about the interpretation of an environmental ethic that focuses on the natural community is that it may also require the suffering or death of human individuals. The attempt to determine the moral worth of animals in a system of environmental ethics includes the determination of the moral worth of human beings. Callicott, again, notes that in an environmental ethic "the moral worth of individuals (including, n.b., human individuals) is relative, to be assessed in accordance with the particular relation of each to the collective entity," i.e., the natural community.[7] Thus, humans are not to be given their traditionally special moral status based on rationality, moral autonomy, or whatever. Instead, human individuals, just as all other natural entities, will be morally evaluated by their contribution to the welfare, the healthy functioning, of the natural community. This revision of the traditional lofty moral status of human individuals is a source of serious criticism of an environmental ethic. Why, it might be argued, should humans accept a system of moral rules that may require harmful consequences to human individuals or human projects and institutions? One need only consider the existence of species—such as the smallpox virus or disease-bearing mosquitoes—which threaten human individuals. Must the species still be protected at the cost of human life? It does no good to respond to this criticism by arguing that in the long run restricting human activity or sacrificing human individuals for the protection of the natural community will benefit human society. Although this is a popular argument of many environmentalists, it is only a contingent possibility. Indeed, a different point seems more probable: since the primary goal of moral action is the good of the natural community, and since human technology and population growth create many of the threats to environmental health, an environmental ethic may demand the elimination of much of the human race and human civilization. This consideration casts serious doubts on the plausibility of the environmental ethic based on the welfare of the natural community as a whole.

The only possible method of defending an environmental ethic from this criticism is to insist that human life and institutions are part of the natural community whose good is the primary end of all action. Human flourishing is important because it is an essential component of the natural community. An environmental ethic that *excluded* humans from the natural community would clearly threaten the continuation of all human projects and activities—whatever humans did would have an adverse effect on the moral unit, the natural community. An environmental ethic that excluded humans from the natural community, for example, would prohibit humans from filling in a small marsh area in order to expand a pre-existing housing development on its border. But an environmental ethic that considers human well-being as *part* of the natural community (not, of course, the supreme part), as part of the moral end of action, *might* permit the expansion of the housing development after a comparison of the benefits and harms to the human population and the natural environment (the marsh).

At best, however, including humans in the natural community is only a partial deflection of the criticism of an environmental ethic based on its anti-human tendencies. An environmental ethic with an appropriate perspective on the place of humanity in the natural system will save a few human projects and activities, but it will still require major changes in human activity, major human sacrifices for the sake of the overall community. Unfortunately, specifying these changes and sacrifices by means of concrete examples is a difficult—and perhaps impossible—task. The making of environmental decisions is not a job for the armchair philosopher: a proper environmental decision requires a multitude of scientific and sociological data as a factual basis. Nevertheless, even if humans are included in the natural community so that their interests are taken into account in the determination of communal well-being, it should be clear that dumping toxic pollutants into a lake—a lake that is not used in any other way by humans— would be a moral evil, an injury to the natural environment. Whether humans would be permitted to dam a river for electrical power is a more problematic case, since the harm to the natural environment as a whole is less severe; in this kind of case specific facts would be needed to make the moral determination. The crucial point to remember is that this form of an environmental ethic claims that humans are no different than any other species; the measure of their worth and the worth of their activities is decided by the overall well-being of the natural community. If I plan to dig a well on my property in the country I will have to consider the effect of my drawing water not only on my human neighbors and their water supplies, but also on the surrounding countryside and its nonhuman inhabitants. An environmental ethic thus requires a major revision in traditional human moral practice. In an environmental ethic moral decisions transcend inter-human relationships to consider the natural community as a whole. Moral decisions cannot be made by simply considering consequences to human life. But this revision in moral practice is not easily granted; humans must relinquish their special place in the moral universe. Thus an environmental ethic may not be acceptable to humans because it implausibly revises traditional moral practice.

A final comment concerning this interpretation of an environmental ethic undermines its validity even more. The fact is that an environmental ethic that considers the overall well-being of the community as the primary goal of all action cannot explain the moral rightness of all the policies desired by the contemporary environmentalist movement. This version of an environmental ethic is unable to explain the protection of rare and endangered species, species so threatened that they play little or no part in the ecology of their natural communities. In this regard, Lilly-Marlene Russow cites as an example the David deer, a species now preserved only in zoos, a species whose original habitat or natural ecosystem is unknown to humanity.[8] Similarly, the snail darter or the bald eagle are examples of species which have little or no ecological function in their natural habitats. In a sense, then, these species are not members of the natural community, not functioning parts of the ecological system. Their preservation, therefore, cannot be guaranteed by simply securing the moral goal of communal or ecosystemic well-being. An environmental ethic designed to treat communal welfare as the primary good cannot explain the preservation of species so rare that they no longer serve an ecological function. But since the preservation of rare species is an important goal of environmentalists, this interpretation of an environmental ethic must be rejected.

The problem of the role of endangered species in ecological communities leads to a second possible interpretation of an environmental ethic: perhaps an environmental ethic is an ethical system that considers species as the primary object of moral concern. An advocate of this version of an environmental ethic could argue then that rare and endangered species ought to be preserved because natural species are the primary recipients of moral obligation. Destroying a species would be morally wrong, because it is equivalent to the traditional prohibition against killing an individual human being. In addition, a species-based environmental ethic could also explain obligations to ecological communities as a whole, since these communities contain species of living things or they are the habitats necessary for the survival of species. This interpretation of an environmental ethic might therefore be more attuned to the needs of the environmentalist, i.e., to the protection of rare and endangered species and the preservation of natural ecological communities and habitats.

The first point to notice about this "species" interpretation of an environmental ethic is that, like the community model, it is basically incompatible with an animal liberation ethic. Although it restricts moral concern to a much smaller group of entities than the natural community, it still focuses on a *collection* of entities rather than on individuals. Since the primary moral goal is the well-being and survival of species, the pain or death of individual members of the species is of secondary importance. It may be necessary, for example, to manage or "harvest" an animal species that is overpopulating an area and threatening its own food supply. The death (even if painless) of individual animals in order to insure the continuance of the entire species would be a moral evil in a system of animal liberation ethics.

In addition, there are conceptual problems with this interpretation of an environmental ethic. In a practical sense, the moral consideration of species does not provide direct reasons for the protection of the nonliving environmental background, the natural objects that form the material structure of ecosystems. Environmentalists, for example, seek the preservation of beautiful natural rock formations, free-flowing rivers, and undeveloped wetlands. They seek this preservation, not simply because of the life forms which live in and around these natural areas, but because of some direct interest in the nonliving objects themselves. But this concern for nonliving natural objects cannot be explained by a moral consideration of species.

A more serious problem is the justification of an environmental ethic that focuses on species as the primary object of moral consideration. Why should species count so much? Why should species be so important? Joel Feinberg, for one, discounts species entirely as the proper objects of direct moral concern: "A whole collection, as such, cannot have beliefs, expectations, wants, or desires . . . individual elephants can have interests, but the species elephant cannot."[9] For Feinberg, at least, an entity without interests cannot have moral rights or be an object of moral consideration. Now although I am not suggesting agreement with Feinberg's views, he does emphasize the *oddity* of considering a whole species a morally relevant entity. Indeed, this interpretation of an environmental ethic has rather an ad hoc aura to it: since environmentalists desire the protection of rare and endangered species, they create an ethic that considers species in themselves as morally valuable. But on what can this moral value be based? Either a species is important because it fulfills an ecological function in the natural community, in which case the community model of an environmental ethic will explain its preservation; or a species is important because the individual members of the species are valuable, in which case an individualistic model of an environmental ethic will explain the act of preservation.[10] In itself, a species-based environmental ethic seems to be an uneasy, groundless compromise between the broad view that the natural community is the environmentally appropriate moral object and the narrow view that natural individuals are themselves the bearers of moral worth.[11]

Thus one arrives at the third interpretation of an environmental ethic: an environmental ethic is a system of ethical rules and obligations pertaining to individual natural entities directly. Natural entities have moral value in themselves, and so they must be protected by environmentally correct policies of action. Human deliberative action will be morally evaluated by its relationship to the individual natural entities in the environment. Draining a marsh or damming a river will be judged by the effects produced on the individual entities in these natural areas. The ecosystem or natural community as a whole will be protected because the individuals who make up the community will be protected in themselves. At first glance, this interpretation has much to recommend it. It has a structure similar to traditional moral theories that consider human individuals the primary objects of moral concern. Since natural individuals are being considered, there is no need to introduce peculiar ontological questions about the interests or desires of collections or communities. Moreover, Leopold suggests an analogy with various historical extensions of moral consideration and rights to groups of human individuals: blacks, women, children, etc.[12] And Christopher Stone has argued that the legal concept of guardianship can be used to provide this moral conception with a substantive content: i.e., the consideration of individual natural entities as the beneficiaries (in themselves) of human action.[13] In sum, the third interpretation of an environmental ethic considers natural entities in themselves, as individuals, the proper objects of moral concern to whom moral rules and obligations apply. As morally valuable entities they deserve protection and preservation.

Several comments can also be made about this version of an environmental ethic. First, it is clear that this environmental ethic is the most similar to an ethic dealing with the moral status of animals. An animal liberation ethic considers the moral worth of animals in themselves as individuals; this individualistic environmental ethic considers the moral worth of all natural entities. An animal liberation ethic considers as morally relevant certain properties of the animals themselves—e.g., sentience—rather than merely the relationship the animals have to morally "superior" autonomous humans. Animals have intrinsic or inherent value based on some aspect of their existence and not simply an instrumental value for humans. Similarly, an individualistic environmental ethic considers natural entities as inherently valuable because of some objective property they possess in themselves; they are not valuable simply because of their instrumental value to human society and human interests.[14] Thus an environmental ethic conceived on the model of individual rights or moral consideration for natural objects is most similar to an animal liberation ethic; the two ethical theories have identical formal structures.

But there are problems with this version of an environmental ethic. As with the species-based interpretation of an environmental ethic, the problem of justification proves to be insolvable. If one grants that an environmental ethic must find some objective property of natural entities as the source of intrinsic moral value, then one is hard pressed to discover a coherent and plausible candidate. Clearly, the criterion most often chosen by advocates of an animal liberation ethic, sentience or the ability to feel pleasure and pain, is largely irrelevant to an ethic that considers the moral significance of plants and other natural entities that do not feel pain and pleasure. Kenneth Goodpaster has thus argued for the moral considerability of all living entities, and he makes a powerful case in that he does not argue for the moral equivalence of all such living beings.[15] Nevertheless, a reverence for all life criterion cannot justify an environmental ethic. Even assuming that a non-arbitrary or unbiased scale of moral worth could be developed to show when it was morally acceptable to kill other forms of life (Goodpaster, e.g., postpones this extremely difficult task), the ethical consideration of all living entities does not extend the moral boundaries far enough. An environmental ethic that is true to the principles of environmentalism must be able to explain the moral consideration of nonliving natural entities as well as living ones. An environmental ethic that considers the moral worth of all natural entities is considering rocks, bodies of water, and the shifting sands of a beach to be morally considerable. This moral consideration cannot be based on the moral criterion of life, since these natural entities are not alive. On what, then, can the moral consideration be based?

It is at this juncture that one begins to question the entire plan of finding a morally relevant property of all natural objects as the basis of an environmental ethic. As even Goodpaster discovers, in a revision of his earlier views, the extension of moral consideration beyond humans reaches a "breaking point" where talk of morally relevant interests and properties seems highly implausible.[16] The breaking point, of course, is the moral consideration of inanimate natural objects. Can rocks or streams be morally considerable? Unless one postulates an ethical doctrine of the sacredness of all nature, there does not seem to be any method of justifying the moral worth of individual nonliving natural entities. But a doctrine of the sacredness of all nature is highly problematic. Does it mean, for example, that disease organisms or disease-carrying insects cannot be exterminated? What about domesticated animals and plants? Do these require an additional moral principle? Basically, the idea that an individual natural nonliving entity has inherent moral worth is too implausible to be seriously considered. Although one may wish to develop a theory that will protect all animals and plants, a moral criterion based on all of natural existence is so broad that it excludes virtually nothing.

The problem with inanimate natural entities forces a return to a community or ecosystemic approach to an environmental ethic. Only if nonliving natural entities are considered as ecologically significant parts of a natural community can they be plausibly judged as morally worthwhile. They do not possess intrinsic or inherent value as such, but as functioning parts of a morally valued natural community. The analysis has thus returned to its starting point, and with disappointing results: all of the interpretations of an environmental ethic considered so far prove to be problematic.

III

Despite the problems encountered in all three of the interpretations of an environmental ethic, it may be feasible to attempt some kind of compromise or combination of the various alternatives. Perhaps a blending of the differing interpretations will yield an environmental ethic that combines the strong points of each version and avoids the implausibilities and areas of contention and criticism. Therefore, I would like to suggest the following version of an environmental ethic, as an outline of a comprehensive and plausible system of ethics to insure the protection of the natural environment.

A meaningful and practical environmental ethic must be composed of two principles or two kinds of moral consideration. The primary form of moral consideration is the moral regard for the ecosystem or the natural community, as discussed above as the first interpretation of an environmental ethic. This must be the *primary* principle of an environmental ethic because environmental protection means more than just the protection of natural individuals and natural species—it means the protection of complete ecological systems. Environmentalists and wilderness preservationists (for example) are interested in protecting *environments*, i.e., ecological systems and natural communities. The preservation of individual natural entities or natural species in isolation from their natural habitats and communities is at best a last ditch effort to prevent extinction; it cannot be the primary goal of a policy of environmentalism. Thus the preeminent goal of action in a theory of environmental ethics is the well-being, health, or stability of the ecological community. Moral rules, obligations, and duties, or the moral evaluation of consequences of action, will be developed and determined by a concept of the *ecological good*, i.e., the good for the ecological community as a whole.

Nonetheless, this primary goal of ecosystemic well-being must be augmented by a secondary goal of the protection of natural individuals. This secondary goal will serve to limit the excessive use of the primary principle in cases where it should not apply. What I have in mind are cases such as the rare endangered species that is no longer a functioning part of the natural ecosystem, or even disease organisms such as the smallpox virus that are on the verge of being totally eradicated. If ecosystemic well-being were the *only* principle of moral action, then it would seem permissible to eliminate the disease organisms or to let the endangered species become extinct. But if an environmental ethic has a secondary moral principle which is activated, so to speak, after questions of ecosystemic well-being are decided, then rare and endangered species can be protected despite their irrelevance to ecosystemic health and stability. Thus in cases where the health or welfare of the natural community is not at issue, human action affecting the environment should be judged by its relationship to natural individuals and species. As long as they do not adversely affect the well-being of the natural ecological community, all individuals and species ought to be preserved and protected. This is the second and subsidiary principle of a practical environmental ethic.

At the risk of repeating myself, let me be a bit more specific about the ordering of these two principles. The primary principle must be the moral consideration of natural communities as a whole, for this is the only method of protecting environmental systems and the inanimate and nonsentient components of these systems. If, on the contrary, the moral consideration of natural individuals were primary, then a coherent and plausible explanation for the protection of inanimate natural objects would have to be given to insure the basic tenets of environmental policy. But it is not at all clear what theory of value could show how inanimate natural entities—stones and streams—are inherently valuable. It seems that only as parts of an ecologically healthy well-functioning community (that is itself valuable) do these inanimate and nonsentient entities become valuable. Moreover, if the consideration of natural individuals were primary, it is not obvious how or why one would protect ecological systems or communities. As long as the individual animals, e.g., were healthy, there would be no need to protect their natural habitats. One could create artificial habitats—parks and preserves—that would maintain the well-being of the individual animals but would not, of course, be consistent with environmentalist principles of preservation. Thus, I have suggested that the moral consideration of ecosystemic communities is the moral principle most compatible with environmental policies; augmenting this principle with a secondary concern for natural individuals—e.g., endangered species of animals—will yield a complete environmental ethic that is plausible and in agreement with environmentalist intuitions.

Although this ordering of two kinds of moral consideration for the environment—i.e., consideration for the natural ecosystemic community and consideration for natural individuals and species—yields a fairly precise practical system of moral action and evaluation, it is not without its hard cases. Perhaps the most intriguing is the case in which the existence of a particular species (or individual) actually threatens the natural community as a whole. Despite environmentalist beliefs about the preservation of species, the use of the two principles in this type of case requires the elimination of the threatening species. Since the primary principle of an environmental ethic, the primary goal of all action relating to the environment, is the health, stability, and well-being of the entire natural community, the community must be protected from the threat. Of course it is likely that in an actual instance the well-being of the ecosystem could be preserved by transferring the species to a different ecosystem where it would not be harmful, or by controlling the size of the species population; nevertheless, if ecosystemic health or stability requires the elimination of the species, the species must be eliminated. If an environmental ethic permitted the destruction of natural environments, natural ecosystems, and communities, it would be meaningless or incoherent.

In sum, then, an environmental ethic should be interpreted as a complex balancing of two forms of moral consideration regarding natural entities and systems. Moral consideration should first be directed toward the natural community or ecosystem as a whole, so that the overall good for the ecosystem is the primary goal of action. But this communal good should be supplemented by a consideration of natural individuals and species, so that in cases where ecosystemic well-being is not an issue, the protection of endangered species or natural individuals can be morally justified. This supplementary or secondary moral consideration of individuals will yield a much richer environmental ethic than the mere consideration of ecosystemic good, and it will help avoid the objections to the first community-based environmental ethic discussed above. Augmented by a secondary consideration of natural individuals, this theory will be able to explain the protection of rare endangered species that are no longer functioning members of a natural community. It will also help to soften the revolutionary character of an environmental ethic that considers the ecosystemic good superior to the good of human individuals; because of the secondary principle natural individuals (including humans) will not be excluded from direct moral consideration. Thus, the balancing of these two kinds of moral consideration yields the most plausible and practical environmental ethic, an environmental ethic that is essentially in accord with environmentalist intuitions about the protection of the natural environment, and that is reasonable enough to be accepted by human moral agents.

IV

Finally, then, a comment on the relationship between this environmental ethic and an animal liberation ethic. It should be clear that if the primary ethical goal or principle of an environmental ethic is the well-being of the ecosystemic natural community *as a whole*, then the well-being of individual animals in the community will sometimes be sacrificed for the communal good.[17] The problem is that ecosystems function, develop, and survive by means of the life and death struggle of competing natural forces, competing living beings. Humans cannot act to prevent the suffering and death of all animal life and remain true to an *environmental* ethic. Indeed, there may be times when human action to improve the health of the ecosystemic community will require the death, destruction, or suffering of individual animals or animal species. Humans may have to eliminate disease organisms, insects, or even higher animals—rabbits, deer, or wolves, e.g.,—which have overpopulated their natural communities and threaten ecosystemic stability. But an animal liberation ethic holds that the death and suffering of animals is a moral evil, because it violates the moral worth of individual animals. When this death and suffering is a result of human action, even for the sake of ecosystemic well-being, it is a direct violation of the principles of an animal liberation ethic. Thus, as I noted above, an animal liberation ethic and an environmental ethic based on the good of the ecosystemic natural community will tend to be incompatible.

The advocate of an environmental ethic has, I believe, only one method for removing this incompatibility: a revision of the basic structure of an environmental ethic. An environmental ethic can be made compatible with an animal liberation ethic if it is conceived as an ethic primarily concerned with the satisfaction of sentient beings—the higher animals and humans. Natural entities and ecological communities would be preserved, not because of any intrinsic value, but simply because they provide satisfaction or pleasure to sentient beings. But this model of an environmental ethic will not operate as a preserver of environmentalist policies; it makes an environmental ethic compatible with an animal liberation ethic by destroying the essence and the practical application of the environmental ethic. The fact is that the existence of any natural entity or ecological system is only contingently related to the satisfactions of sentient beings. Animals can survive and flourish in habitats that are not their natural homes. Humans, of course, have developed such a multiplicity of artificial enjoyments that there is no real need for the pleasures of the natural world.[18] Now I am not arguing that humans receive no pleasure from the natural environment; my point is that this pleasure is only contingently related to the existence of the natural environment. If the natural environment is only protected, e.g., because it provides humans with aesthetic and recreational satisfactions, then if human interests in aesthetics and recreational activities change (as they seem to be in this increasingly artificial and technological world) there will be no reason to protect the natural environment.[19] The interests of sentient beings cannot provide a secure basis for environmental policies, and thus they cannot be the primary principle of an environmental ethic. The contingent relationship between the existence of the natural environment and the satisfaction or interests of sentient beings prevents the merger of an animal liberation ethic and an environmental ethic. Because an animal liberation ethic only requires the consideration of sentient life, while an environmental ethic requires the preservation of nonsentient entities and systems as well as sentient life, the two systems are basically incompatible.

However, a number of factors serve to modify this bleak picture. First, the environmental ethic here proposed is not based solely on the good of the ecological community as a whole; there is a secondary principle which bases moral evaluation on the good of individual natural entities, including sentient animals. As long as the welfare of the community is not at stake, individual natural entities—including animals—must be protected. Because I have argued for a balanced set of principles as the structure of an environmental ethic, it is possible to save much of an animal liberation ethic. Individual animals (or species of animals) cannot be harmed, unless there is an overriding and serious need on the part of the entire natural community.

A second factor is the problem of domesticated animals. Advocates of an animal liberation ethic, of course, seek many practical changes in human action affecting domesticated animals. Now Callicott, for one, finds this concern to be almost incoherent from the perspective of an environmental ethic. Since domesticated livestock are a human artifact, their effects on the natural environment should be judged as any other human artifact.[20] Sheep grazing in a meadow, for example, may do as much harm to the natural cycles of the region's plant life as the dumping of toxic chemicals. From Callicott's ecological perspective, the fact that the sheep are animals rather than the instruments of human deliberative action would not justify or excuse the harm done to the natural environment. But I do not think that the advocate of an environmental ethic needs to worry about domesticated animals causing ecological damage. *At worst*, domesticated animals, *because they are not part of the natural community*, are simply an irrelevancy from the standpoint of an environmental ethic. Sheep, for example, do not generally graze in natural wilderness areas, but in pasture land that has already been itself domesticated. Their effect on natural ecological cycles is minimal.[21] *At best*, using a two-principle environmental ethic, humans are able to judge the pain and suffering and moral worth of individual domesticated animals as morally significant; as long as questions of environmental health or well-being are not involved, then even domesticated animals can be treated as objects of moral concern.

Finally, it is important to realize that in *practical* terms, a more environmentally appropriate human social policy will greatly benefit animal life. Although from the perspective of ecological theory it may be necessary to sacrifice some animals for the ecological well-being of the natural community, in actual practice more animals are harmed by human actions that *violate* ecological principles. More animals are harmed by humans destroying and degrading ecological communities than by humans attempting to improve them. Adopting principles of an environmental ethic should, in the long run, benefit the lives of animals, for humans will begin to recognize all natural entities as members of a morally relevant natural community.

Notes

1. I take as prime examples of an animal liberation ethic the work of Peter Singer, *Animal Liberation* (New York: New York Review/Random House, 1975), and Tom Regan, "The Moral Basis of Vegetarianism," *Canadian Journal of Philosophy* 5 (1975): 181–214.

2. Aldo Leopold, "The Land Ethic," in *A Sand County Almanac: With Essays on Conservation from Round River* (1949; rpt. New York: Ballantine, 1970), p. 262.

3. J. Baird Callicott, "Animal Liberation: A Triangular Affair," *Environmental Ethics* 2 (1980): 320.

4. Don E. Marietta, Jr., "The Interrelationship of Ecological Science and Environmental Ethics," *Environmental Ethics* 1 (1979): 197.

5. Bryan G. Norton, "Environmental Ethics and Nonhuman Rights," *Environmental Ethics* 4 (1982): 32.

6. Callicott, pp. 332–33.

7. Ibid., p. 327.

8. Lilly-Marlene Russow, "Why Do Species Matter?" *Environmental Ethics* 3 (1981): 103.

9. Joel Feinberg, "The Rights of Animals and Unborn Generations," in *Philosophy and Environmental Crisis*, ed. William T. Blackstone (Athens: University of Georgia Press, 1974), pp. 55–56.

10. Russow, for example, argues that species are important because of the individuals that comprise them.

11. Space limitations prevent a full discussion of the role of species preservation in a system of environmental ethics. Clearly an environmental ethic must recognize that the extinction of species through natural processes—evolutionary defeat by a more successful competitive species—is a morally acceptable event. An environmental ethic does not require humans to prevent naturally occurring extinctions. But of course in reality most of the endangered species that concern environmentalists have been brought to the edge of extinction by human activity, i.e., by human disruption of natural communities. There is thus a duty to attempt to correct our mistakes and to preserve these victims of negligent human actions in the natural environment.

12. Leopold, pp. 237–39.

13. Christopher D. Stone, *Should Trees Have Standing? Towards Legal Rights for Natural Objects* (Los Altos, Calif.: William Kaufmann, 1974), pp. 17–34.

14. For a discussion of intrinsic value see Tom Regan, "The Nature and Possibility of an Environmental Ethic," *Environmental Ethics* 3 (1981): 30–34, and

Evelyn B. Pluhar, "The Justification of an Environmental Ethic," *Environmental Ethics* 5 (1983): 47–61.

15. Kenneth E. Goodpaster, "On Being Morally Considerable," *The Journal of Philosophy* 75 (1978): 308–25.

16. Kenneth E. Goodpaster, "From Egoism to Environmentalism," in *Ethics and Problems of the 21st Century*, ed. K. E. Goodpaster and K. M. Sayre (Notre Dame: University of Notre Dame, 1979), p. 29.

17. Note again that the well-being of individual animals to be sacrificed includes the well-being of human animals. If an environmental ethic limits human projects and activities, then some humans will undoubtedly suffer discomfort, pain, and even death. There may be less energy to be used for recreation or labor-saving devices in the home. Buildings may be colder in the winter and hotter in the summer. Some humans may even die for the sake of environmental well-being: if the mosquito population is not controlled by pesticides, some humans could die from encephalitis, for example.

18. Although some small percentage of the human population may yearn, for example, for the "wilderness experience," it is not clear why this recreational pleasure cannot be satisfied in some other way. As Martin Krieger has argued: "Artificial prairies and wildernesses have been created, and there is no reason to believe that these artificial environments need be unsatisfactory for those who experience them." ("What's Wrong with Plastic Trees?" *Science* 179 [1973]: 453.)

19. For a more detailed discussion of the "human interest" arguments for environmentalism, i.e., the arguments based on the instrumental or utilitarian value of the natural environment, see my "Utilitarianism and Preservation," *Environmental Ethics* 1 (1979): 357–64; Mark Sagoff, "On Preserving the Natural Environment," *Yale Law Journal* 84 (1974): 205–67; Mark Sagoff, "Do We Need a Land Use Ethic?" *Environmental Ethics* 3 (1981): 293–308; Laurence H. Tribe, "Ways Not to Think About Plastic Trees," in *When Values Conflict*, ed. Laurence H. Tribe, Corinne S. Schelling, and John Voss (Cambridge, Mass.: Ballinger, 1976): 61–91; and William Godfrey-Smith, "The Value of Wilderness," *Environmental Ethics* 1 (1979): 309–19.

20. Callicott, p. 330.

21. I realize that the issue of domesticated animals and an environmental ethic cannot be adequately discussed in a brief summary paragraph: it requires an entire essay in itself. All that I wish to suggest is that the animal liberationist's concern for the proper treatment of domesticated animals is neither condemned nor condoned in a theory of environmental ethics. The fate of domesticated animals, as such, is not a subject area of environmental ethics. Of course if domesticated animals begin to intrude upon and harm a natural ecological community, then they would be treated like any other human artifact (machines, chemicals, etc.) that harmed the environment. Or if a human began to kill wild natural animals in order to protect his domesticated sheep he would be violating an environmental ethic, just as if he polluted a stream to "protect"

his recreational pleasure in speedboating. But the vast majority of cases involving domesticated animals—the morality of factory farming, for example—are in a realm of substantive ethics completely removed from the concerns of an environmental ethic. The question of the compatibility or incompatibility of an environmental ethic and an animal liberation ethic when dealing with the treatment of domesticated animals as such is thus unanswerable and misconceived: these are simply two different subject matters.

3

Organism, Community, and the "Substitution Problem"

"Organism, Community, and the 'Substitution Problem'" was originally written for a conference held at the University of Georgia under the auspices of Eugene Hargrove and the journal Environmental Ethics *in October 1984, and was subsequently published in that journal the following year. As far as I know, this essay was the first to analyze the popular idea of "holism" as the basis for an environmental ethic—to show that there were various forms of holistic thinking, and that these different forms (or models) of holism would have differing consequences for ethics and environmental policy. The central argument is that a community model of holism can avoid the negative implications of the organic model, primarily because the community model respects the autonomy, integrity, and identity of the individual members of the holistic system. The argument rests upon a thought experiment called "the substitution problem"—the replacement of individuals or species within a biological system with no negative impact on the well-functioning of the system. Organic holism would seem to permit nonharmful substitutions; the community form of holism does not. Community-based holism maintains the value of the individual members of the system; it respects the identity, integrity, and original genesis of both the system and its constituent parts. This essay is the most detailed statement of my position of modified holism. It also introduces themes that will reappear throughout my essays, such as the problematic status of the imposition of human ideals on natural systems and the moral differentiation of domestic (i.e., human-shaped) species from those that occur naturally.*

I. Introduction

In this essay I examine two basic holistic models of natural systems—organism and community—in order to determine their significance in

33

the formation of an environmental ethic. To develop a convincing, working environmental ethic it is necessary to have a model of the natural environment that is both ecologically and ethically sound. Further, any such model used by philosophers and decision makers must be compatible with current scientific theories concerning ecological systems.[1] Finally, this model must be in accord with basic ethical presumptions regarding environmental policy. An environmental ethic must not violate *basic* environmentalist attitudes.[2]

I suggest here that an environmental ethic based on a holistic model of nature as an organism is unconvincing or unworkable in the light of basic principles or attitudes of environmentalists, that an environmental ethic based on a model of a natural community is in accord with basic environmentalist attitudes, and thus that a community model will be more acceptable to environmentalists and ethical decision makers.

One preliminary warning is in order: I am not directly concerned with any metaethical justification of an environmental ethic, nor do I claim to present any such justification. What interests me is the actual practical operation of an environmental ethic. I want to see if the principles, concepts, and models used in an environmental ethic actually agree with basic intuitions about environmental policy. Obviously, I realize that my intuitions about environmental policy may not be in accord with the intuitions of others; thus, I have tried to present clear cases through which environmentalists of different backgrounds can reach agreement.

II. Leopold's Double Holistic Vision

The holistic orientation of environmental ethics has led to the use of two models of nature—organism and community. It has often been noted that a truly *environmental* or *ecological* ethic cannot be exclusively based on either (a) the interests of the human population or (b) the interests of individual natural entities.[3] Instead, advocates of an environmental ethic must adopt a holistic or "total field" view of natural systems, in which individual natural entities and humans are "conceived as nodes in a biotic web of intrinsically related parts."[4] In an environmental ethic the ecological *system* or the natural environment becomes morally considerable. Don E. Marietta, Jr. writes: "The basic concept behind an ecological ethic is that morally acceptable treatment of the environment is that which does not upset the integrity of the ecosystem as it is seen in a diversity of life forms existing in a dynamic and complex but stable interdependency."[5] The *interdependency* is what counts. The system as a whole—and not merely the individuals in the system—is of primary moral significance. A theory of environmental ethics, thus, takes seriously Aldo Leopold's maxim of moral action: "A thing is right when it tends to preserve the integrity, stability, and beauty of the biotic community. It is wrong when it tends otherwise."[6]

Leopold's maxim is a good place to begin a review of the concepts of organism and community because, despite his use of the term *biotic community*, there is a definite ambivalence in his vision of an environmental ethic, or what he calls the "land ethic." A section of his essay, subtitled "The Community Concept," begins with a straightforward statement about the importance of the idea of community in *any* ethical system: "All ethics so far evolved rest upon a single premise: that the individual is a member of a community with interdependent parts." This premise is also the basis of an environmental ethic because "the land ethic simply enlarges the boundaries of the community to include soils, waters, plants, and animals, or collectively: the land."[7] The source of moral obligations, duties, and rules is the community, extended now to include the entities in the natural world, although human society and individual human beings also remain part of this natural and moral community. "A land ethic changes the role of *Homo sapiens* from conqueror of the land-community to plain member and citizen of it. It implies respect for his fellow-members and also respect for the community as such."[8] Thus, an environmental ethic enlarges the traditional model of a human community as the basis of moral principles. Humanity is part of a broader unit of moral concern and relevance, a broader source of moral value and obligation: humanity is part of the "land," the natural system conceived as a community of interdependent parts.

Leopold, however, does not steadfastly maintain this community model of the land. He also conceives of the land as an organism, modelled after a living individual. For Leopold, an environmental ethic "presupposes the existence of some mental image of land as a biotic mechanism." The reason is that "we can be ethical only in relation to something we can see, feel, understand, love, or otherwise have faith in.'"⁹ Leopold apparently believed that it is impossible to be ethical toward an abstraction, and that nature conceived as a communal system is such an abstraction. If, on the other hand, the natural system is conceived as one biotic entity, it becomes easier to care for its continued life or health, to respect its interests, and to consider it as morally worthwhile. Thus, Leopold describes the "land" as a biotic pyramid, a highly complex organizational structure of various kinds of living and nonliving natural entities. These entities are organized in such a way as to transfer energy throughout the system, "a fountain of energy flowing through a circuit of soils, plants, and animals."¹⁰ Although the land, a biotic pyramid, is a collection of individual entities, it is similar to an individual organism in responding to outside stimuli, adapting to varying conditions, and maintaining its "health" and energy. Leopold also describes it as "a sustained circuit, like a slowly augmented revolving fund of life."¹¹ It is a "collective organism."¹²

It is true that this image of the natural environment as an organism or a biotic mechanism is only a subordinate theme in "The Land Ethic." The idea of land as a new member in an ever broadening moral community is clearly the dominant theme of the essay. Yet, Leopold sometimes thought of the natural environment as a kind of living organism, similar in structure to an individual animal or plant. In an essay published after his death (but written some twenty-five years before "The Land Ethic"), Leopold wrote that "in our intuitive perceptions . . . we realize the indivisibility of the earth—its soil, mountains, rivers, forests, climate, plants, and animals, and respect it collectively not only as a useful servant but as a living being, vastly less alive than ourselves in degree, but vastly greater than ourselves in time and space. . . ."¹³ This organic conception of the natural environment as a vast living being was an integral aspect of Leopold's vision; it was indispensable to his development of a primitive environmental ethic.¹⁴

It is not my purpose in this essay to trace the development of Leopold's thought concerning the establishment of an environmental ethic. Nevertheless, the fact that Leopold used two different models or metaphors in describing the land ethic shows that even in the work of one influential author there can be various kinds of *holistic* accounts of the natural environment. This kind of equivocation can cause problems, moreover, once the implications of the models are brought to bear on ethics. As I show in the following sections, the models of organism and community as applied to natural systems are quite different and yield different and incompatible moral conclusions.

III. Individual Autonomy in Holistic Systems

The crucial difference between the concepts of community and organism as applied to ecological systems lies in the *autonomy* of the individual parts within the holistic system. The model of community implies that there is some autonomy for the individual *members* of the community, while the model of organism implies that the *parts* are not independent beings. Even the terminology is revealing, for each individual in a community can be called a *member* because it exists both in its own right and as a functioning unit of a community. In contrast, the parts within an organism lack the autonomous existence and value of an individual in a community—they are *parts*, nothing more; they are not members, not individuals, but units or elements in an organic whole.

A comparison of a typical organic whole—a human body—and a typical community—a university—clearly demonstrates the distinction. The muscles, liver, the blood, and other parts of the human body are not independent beings with lives or value apart from their organic function. Their existence is due to the continuous functioning of the organic whole of which they are a part. Although various organs of a human body can be removed and transferred to another human body, the organic part is not an independent being in its own right. Organs are not organisms. If an organ is not transferred fairly quickly into another human body—i.e., a similar organic whole—its existence will come to an end.

In a community such as a university, however, the individual members—students, faculty, buildings, laboratory equipment, library materials—have an existence and value both in themselves and as functioning parts in the community. For this collection of entities to function as a university, of course, all the parts must play their roles: students must attend classes, faculty members must teach and do research, the library must update and organize its collections. Yet, all these parts of the university have an autonomous existence that can be separated from their functions in the university system. Members are not organs. Students and faculty have interests that transcend their roles as members of the university. In part, they have lives that are based on *other* communities: a student may have an outside job; a faculty member may also be a scoutmaster. Moreover, they have interests that are valuable outside of a communal context. A student jogs; a professor gambles at the race track. Even the nonliving elements of the university need not be parts of the university to be meaningfully employed. The buildings might be used after school hours by groups not affiliated with the university; the library books bring knowledge to individuals outside the school. In sum, the various entities that make up the university community are not *merely* parts of a holistic system; each has an independent existence. In an organic system, however, the elements are merely parts of the organic whole; each lacks a meaningful independent existence.

The natural ecosystem is more similar to a community like the university than to an organic system like a human body. It is difficult to conceive of humans, plants, and inanimate natural objects as mere parts of one large organism. Although these autonomous entities do participate in an ecological system, they also have independent lives and functions. In addition to the role the entities in an ecological system play in maintaining the natural order, they also perform functions on their own. Evolutionary theory teaches that all species strive for their own survival, but in doing so they contribute to the functioning of the natural system. Bees are attracted to flowering plants for nectar, food for the bees, and as a result, they pollinate plant species, insuring their survival. Natural individuals live and act for and in themselves and as members of a communal system. They pursue their own interests while serving in roles in the community. It is not at all clear that organs in an organism do this.

In addition, consider how individuals can be removed from one particular ecosystem and placed in a different ecosystem. They can be introduced into systems where they do not occur naturally—as "exotics"—and still thrive. They can even be removed from a "natural" ecosystem completely and placed in a zoo. In contrast, the parts of an organism cannot transcend their natural organic role. Organs can be transplanted, but unlike the introduction of exotic species, the organ must be transplanted into a nearly identical organism—they cannot "live" on their own. The ability of natural individual organisms in an ecosystem to be moved (and to move on their own) into new environments shows that they are not simply parts of an organism—they are independent individuals which operate in a flexible system of communal harmony.

An organic model of natural ecosystems is therefore misconceived. J. Baird Callicott, for example, claims that one can differentiate three "orders" of "organic wholes": single-cell organisms, second-order multicell organisms (with "limbs, various organs, myriad cells"), and "biocoenoses," third-order organic wholes such as the natural environment that are "a unified system of integrally related parts."[15] Nothing is gained from this terminology, for it blurs the clear distinction between individual organic bodies and ecological systems composed of individual organic bodies. There are some genuine analogies in the relationship between Callicott's first- and second-order organic wholes and his second- and third-orders: a second-order organic whole is made up of many individual cells, first-order organic wholes; and a third-order organic whole (an ecosystem) is made up of many individual second-order wholes. However, the degree of autonomy in the lives of the individuals in the system is an important disanalogy. The cells that make up a "second-order organism" are not autonomous individuals sharing and creating a common environment, but rather elements of a complex, unified entity. In comparison, the so-called third-order organic whole is not really an organic whole—i.e., an organism—at all. It is a collection of autonomous individuals that function as a system.

Apparently, Callicott and other environmental philosophers[16] conceive or speak of the natural environment or a particular ecosystem as an organic whole in order to emphasize ecological interdependency. As a corrective measure for the common anthropocentric belief that humans exist beyond the realm of natural processes, this organic model may be acceptable—but eventually the organism model *overemphasizes* the *dependency* of the individuals in the system. I am not denying that there is a dependency. However, the value of natural entities should not be based solely on their dependent functioning in the holistic system.[17]

What I have said so far does not show that the community model of the natural environment is better or more plausible than the organism model. I have merely relied on the intuitive appeal of relevant comparisons. I now argue (1) that the organic model leads to moral conclusions that are incompatible with basic environmentalist positions and (2) that the community model is superior, since it does not lead to problematic moral conclusions. As a first step in my argument, I introduce the concepts of intrinsic and instrumental value and examine the relationship between these two kinds of value and the concepts of organism and community.

IV. Intrinsic and Instrumental Value

An entity has intrinsic value if the entity has value in itself, without regard to other entities, without regard to its effect on other entities.

The intrinsic value of an entity is based on its own independent properties. To have intrinsic value it need not have any relationship with another entity; its value, after all, is intrinsic to it.[18] An entity has instrumental value if the value of the entity is a result of some function or use to which it is put. While the function of an entity may depend on its independent, intrinsic properties, the value of the entity is derived from its functional purpose and not its intrinsic properties. It is an instrument to be utilized in some fashion, and nothing more: the effect it has on other entities is the criterion of its value.

In an important sense, then, instrumental value is directly contrary to intrinsic value. An entity valued intrinsically requires no relationships with any other entities. An entity valued instrumentally is dependent on the existence of other entities and the functional relationships between it and these other entities. Instrumental value is not intrinsic but extrinsic. It is a result of interdependent relationships that exist between entities. It is the value an entity has *for* other entities.

Conceived in this manner, these two kinds of value are related to the concepts of organism and community in significant ways. Instrumental value bears a marked similarity to the way in which the parts of an *organism* are related to the whole. Organic parts have no independent value—their value is derived from the entire functioning whole, the organism. The liver, muscles, and blood in a human body are important for what they do *for* the organic whole. They are not valuable in themselves, i.e., intrinsically, but only instrumentally in that they perform functions for other entities. Thus, the parts of the organism have value as *parts* of a system, just as an entity with instrumental value only possesses value through its functional relations with other entities. In a community system, on the other hand, the members have independent existence and value. They may have communal value (i.e., functional value for the community), but they also maintain independent status and value in (conceptual) isolation from the rest of the community. Thus, because a member of a community can be considered as an autonomous individual, it is similar to an entity with intrinsic value; it possesses some value in itself without regard to other entities.

Of course, individual entities possess both kinds of value in different situations and contexts. A member of a community has intrinsic value in itself and instrumental value as a functioning part of a system. As an individual human being, a university student possesses personal characteristics that give him intrinsic value. As a student this individual also serves a function that is valuable for the community of which he is a member: he attends classes, interacts with the faculty, and uses the facilities of the campus. In contrast, it is more difficult to see how parts of an organism can have intrinsic value, for they derive their value only from the role they play as part of a larger organic system. A human liver, in general, has merely instrumental value as a functioning part of an organism.[19]

In sum, the model of community permits the consideration of both intrinsic and instrumental value to a greater extent than the model of organism. Since an organism is primarily concerned with the functions of interdependent parts, it emphasizes instrumental value. A community, on the other hand, which is composed of autonomous members interacting toward a common goal, allows for both kinds of value. The ability of the community model to deal with both, I contend, makes it a better foundation for an environmental ethic than the model of organism. As I show in the next section, the emphasis on instrumental value in the organic model violates the spirit of environmentalism.

V. Intrinsic Value and the Substitution Problem

Other important analyses of the *holistic* structure of an environmental ethic have failed to stress the significance of intrinsic value.[20] In an oft quoted passage, for example, Paul Shepard writes:

> Ecological thinking . . . requires a kind of vision across boundaries. The epidermis of the skin is ecologically like a pond surface or a forest soil, not a shell so much as a delicate interpenetration. It reveals the self ennobled and extended . . . as part of the landscape and the ecosystem, because the beauty and complexity of nature are continuous with ourselves . . . [w]e must affirm that the world is a being, a part of our own body.[21]

Shepard's metaphor that the natural world is part of my body, and similarly, that my body is part of the organic structure of the natural world, is clearly an organic conception. This concentration on the organic unity of the entities in the natural environment results in an emphasis on the instrumental value of entities in the organic system instead of on the intrinsic value of the entities in themselves. Even Holmes Rolston, who is sympathetic to both kinds of value, argues that when one considers natural systems the idea of intrinsic value tends to blur or fade into the idea of instrumental value: the idea that an entity can be evaluated "'for what it is in itself' . . . becomes problematic in a holistic web." The concept of intrinsic value ignores "relatedness and externality."[22] Within a natural system, "things do not have their separate natures merely in and for themselves, but they face outward and co-fit into broader natures."[23] This "fit into broader natures" is the instrumental value that an entity has; its significance is determined by its effects on the external entities with which it is related, not merely on its own "separate nature," its own individual properties and intrinsic status.

The emphasis on the organic model for natural systems—with the resulting overemphasis on instrumental value—leads to a particular interpretation of the primary rule of action in an environmental ethic: the good for the natural system as a whole is the primary consideration. Callicott interprets Leopold's maxim—"A thing is right when it tends to preserve the integrity, stability, and beauty of the biotic community"—to mean that "the effect upon ecological systems is the decisive factor in the determination of the ethical quality of action."[24] This concern for systemic good tends to downgrade or even to ignore the intrinsic value of individual entities. Thus, Callicott criticizes the advocates of animal rights for focusing on the intrinsic evil of pain. He argues that it is not a proper consideration in the treatment of animals in natural ecological systems. Even if pain were an intrinsic evil, it is irrelevant from the point of view of systemic good. "Pain and pleasure seem to have nothing at all to do with good and evil if our appraisal is taken from the vantage point of ecological biology."[25] Pain and pleasure are intrinsically related to an entity in itself; they contribute nothing directly to the overall functioning of the natural system. The existence of intrinsic values in individuals, moreover, can be ignored in the evaluation of the overall good for the natural system, since the instrumental functional value of entities contributing to systemic well-being is given ethical priority. What is evil for individuals might be, and often is, a systemic functional good, and in this sense is acceptable.

This organic model of the natural environment and its overemphasis on instrumental value leads to an unacceptable conclusion involving a serious moral problem which I call "the substitution problem." If an entity in a system is valued for its instrumental function and not its intrinsic value, then it can be replaced by a substitute entity as long as the function it performs remains undisturbed. In other words, if an entity is considered valuable because of its functional role in the system, then what is really important is the role, and if an adequate substitute can be found, then the entity itself can be destroyed or replaced without loss of value. None of the overall good of the system is lost. As long as the system is maintained, the precise character or intrinsic worth of the particular individuals performing its functions is irrelevant.

The substitution problem arises as a result of human action in the environment. It is ethically significant only as a consequence of human activity. There is nothing problematic about substitutions or modifications that result from natural evolutionary processes. Since only human beings—and human institutions—are moral *agents* only their actions can be considered to be morally correct or not. Although nature and its inhabitants may be conceived of as moral patients—the recipients of moral considerability—it is meaningless to attribute moral responsibility to nonrational beings and systems. Thus, the substitution problem involves the "artificial" replacement of one natural entity or species with something else—usually a different natural entity or species—that performs the function of the original entity.

Although there are no perfect or "pure" cases of the substitution problem, in which one species or entity is substituted for another with no other changes in the natural system, this kind of substitution is a logical possibility, and provides the basis for a useful thought experiment. From time to time, something like the substitution problem occurs in nature, since ecological competition concerns the conflict of species over particular ecological niches in the system. One species drives out another with little or no change in the overall functioning of the natural environment. The ecological niche is filled by a different species which assumes the role of its defeated competitor. The natural system is maintained unchanged. Our human knowledge of ecology might eventually reach the point where nonnatural substitutions of natural species could also be made with little or no damage to the natural system. While these substitutions are morally acceptable policies of action in accordance with any organic model, they clearly violate the spirit of environmentalism, for destroying and replacing a natural entity is not what environmental protection is all about.

There are related examples of the problem that are not merely theoretical. Lilly-Marlene Russow and John Passmore, for example, each discuss the possibility of modifying an existing ecosystem by increasing its diversity. Russow is interested in criticizing any environmental ethic that is based on a holistic principle such as the overall good of the natural community. This kind of argument seems to allow "changes which do not affect the system, or which result in the substitution of a richer, more complex system for one that is more primitive or less evolved."[26] The institution of "changes which do not affect the system" is quite similar to the "substitution problem." The idea of creating more complex systems is simply another version of the problem. Russow cites the introduction of new species in isolated areas (such as New Zealand and Australia) that replace the indigenous species and create a new, workable ecosystem.[27] An environmental ethic based on the good of the natural ecosystem cannot prohibit this modification of nature, provided we know with certainty that the new ecosystem will be successful, and that the life of the natural entities in the system will continue in a normal or improved state. But surely there is something wrong with this kind of modification.

Passmore considers whether ecological diversity can be a moral criterion. Should the enrichment of an ecosystem by human action be given more weight in moral decisions? Passmore—arguing from an admittedly human-centered perspective—notes that increasing or decreasing species diversity can be either good or bad depending on the factual circumstances. Although environmentalists are usually concerned about the loss of diversity caused by the extinction of species, not all such extinctions are considered moral evils. The elimination of the smallpox virus, for example, was not condemned as a loss of ecological diversity.[28] Passmore considers the possibility of eradicating disease-bearing mosquitoes if this could be achieved without any ecological damage to the rest of the ecosystem.[29] In such a situation, the preservation of a mosquito species just for the sake of diversity appears to be a mistake. Similarly, the addition of species, increasing diversity, can either be correct or incorrect. Passmore cites the introduction of the elm and oak in Britain, where the increased diversity led to a more beneficial and stable environment.[30] Depending on the circumstances, therefore, the increase or decrease in diversity can have good or bad consequences for an ecological system. Thus, an environmental ethic cannot blindly employ the principle of diversity for adjudicating cases. Passmore concludes that "there is no general argument from a principle of diversity to preservationist conclusions."[31]

Granting that the overall system is not harmed, why do certain kinds of cases involving diversity strike an environmentalist as inappropriate? Why is the elimination of a thriving species or the artificial diversification of an ecosystem considered bad? The answer involves the ideas of identity, integrity, or intrinsic value applied to individual organisms and species. This set of ideas provides the key to understanding the "substitution problem." Artificial diversification of a natural system violates the "naturalness" of the system. It alters the system in a way that is not the outgrowth of natural evolutionary change. In a sense it imposes a human ideal on the operations of a nonhuman natural system. Passmore, for example, also thinks that a wilderness without flies would be better than a wilderness with flies. A hypothetical wilderness experience without bug bites would be more pleasurable and just as (spiritually) enriching as the wilderness experience as it actually is today.[32] Nevertheless, there is something terribly wrong with this kind of modification. The best way I can express this is to say that human modifications harm the intrinsic value of the entities contained within natural systems. Individuals within natural systems have intrinsic value (among other reasons) by virtue of their existence in the *natural* world. Forcing these entities to conform to a human ideal, a human value, of what nature ought to be, would harm this intrinsic value. Thus, the modification of natural systems—even when the result is an increase in systemic well-being—is a violation of the intrinsic value of natural entities.

In other words, what I am suggesting is that *part* of what we mean by the intrinsic value of natural entities is their source or origin—what caused them to be what they are. A natural entity possesses intrinsic value to some extent because it is *natural*, an entity that arose through processes that are not artificially human. This "naturalness" is one of the properties that gives it its value. Robert Elliot makes this same point about natural entities by comparing them to works of art. A technically perfect reproduction of a work of art lacks the value that the original has because of its "causal genesis."[33] Art reproductions are, in fact, a fine analogue to instances of the substitution problem. A technically perfect art reproduction *functions* as well as the original; what it lacks is the intrinsic value of the original, because it is a copy, a fake, a forgery; it is not the product of the original artist's creative process. The same is true for natural entities: a technically adequate functional substitute, because it is not an outgrowth of the original natural processes of the system, does not possess the same intrinsic value as the original entity.

Moreover, the violation of individuals' intrinsic value ultimately affects the integrity or value of the system as a whole. When the individuals are changed as substitutions are made, the system becomes different. Consider a case involving a human system. A school administrator wants to increase the overall reading level of his school. Rather than hire more remedial reading tutors, he simply transfers into his district several dozen students who are much better than average readers. To make room for these students, he suspends some of his worst students for a semester. Something is wrong with this "artificial substitution" of individuals. Although the reading scores go up, although the system is improved, there has been a violation of individual and systemic intrinsic value and integrity.

Finally, consider the preservation of rare and endangered species. Russow notes that the preservation of rare species—particularly those that have been removed almost entirely from their natural habitats— cannot be justified by an appeal to ecological well-being, to the functional value these individuals provide the ecosystem.[34] Such individuals are no longer really part of an ecological system. They have no instrumental value, since the ecological system seems to function quite well without them.[35] Thus, if they are to be preserved or protected, as environmentalist policies universally dictate, it must be because of their intrinsic value. What makes this conclusion interesting is that cases of rare and endangered species can be considered to be instances of the substitution problem, so to speak, in midstream. A species becoming extinct was once a functional member of the natural system; because it occupied an ecological niche in the system, it had instrumental value. Its present endangered state is a result of some kind of substitution—either it lost an evolutionary-biological battle with a more competitive species that is replacing it or it has been displaced by artificial human modifications of the environment. The fact that the completion of the substitution process—extinction—is viewed by environmentalists as a wrong to be prevented shows clearly that the intrinsic value of species is a prime consideration in environmental decision making.

At the core of the "substitution problem" lies the idea of intrinsic value in a natural system. To take a well-functioning ecological system and replace one entity or species with another, to substitute one element of a system for another, to increase or decrease the diversity of the ecological structure, to fail to prevent or even to aid the extinction of the species—all these actions compromise the intrinsic value of the entities in the system. An environmentally conscious moral decision maker cannot merely consider the instrumental value, the functional operation of the entities in the ecological system; he must also consider the integrity and identity of the entities in the system, i.e., their intrinsic value.

VI. Conclusion

Consideration of the substitution problem suggests that the community model of the natural environment is superior to the organic model as the guiding metaphor of an environmental ethic. If an environmental ethic uses the model of organism, it will be unable to account for the intrinsic value of the individuals in the system, and will fall prey to the substitution problem. Because an organic model overemphasizes the functional dependency of all the entities in the system, it can only consider the instrumental value that the parts of the organism have for the whole. The substitution of one part for another, one natural entity or species for another, will be morally and environmentally acceptable, as long as the overall functioning of the organic system continues.

An environmental ethic that considers the natural environment to be a community of autonomous but interdependent entities can, however, contain both instrumental and intrinsic value. It can consider both the contribution each member makes to the system and its independent existence and value. The consideration of both kinds of value enables a community-based environmental ethic to avoid the consequences of the substitution problem. Such an ethic will be able to explain why a functionally appropriate substitute for a natural entity (or species) is environmentally and ethically incorrect. The substitution of one entity for another violates the intrinsic value of the entity—ultimately, it violates the integrity of the system—despite the maintenance of the functional value of the system. Because the community model is flexible enough to consider both instrumental and intrinsic value, it does not violate environmentalist principles by permitting substitutions.

Let me conclude with the words of Leopold: "A land ethic changes the role of *Homo sapiens* from conqueror of the land-community to plain member and citizen of it. It implies respect for his fellow-members and also respect for the community as such."[36] We must take Leopold quite seriously on this point. An environmental ethic must take into account the good for the community as a whole, and the good for each and every member of the community as an individual. The community model of nature can do this, and thus it results in a modification of a *purely holistic* ideal. A practical and meaningful environmental ethic thus requires a definite formula for the balancing of instrumental and intrinsic value criteria relative to *individuals* in a *system*. This is a task that remains to be done; but it cannot even be considered from the organic holistic perspective.[37]

Notes

1. I do not mean to raise the spectre of the fact/value problem. This problem is pervasive throughout the literature on environmental ethics, and I can-

not address it here. See E. M. Adams, "Ecology and Value Theory," *Southern Journal of Philosophy* 10 (1972): 3–6; Thomas B. Colwell, Jr., "The Balance of Nature: A Ground for Human Value," *Main Currents in Modern Thought* 26 (1969): 46–52; Holmes Rolston, Ill, "Is There an Ecological Ethic?" *Ethics* 85 (1975): 93–109, and "Are Values in Nature Subjective or Objective?" *Environmental Ethics* 4 (1982): 125–51; and J. Baird Callicott, "Hume's *Is/Ought* Dichotomy and the Relation of Ecology to Leopold's Land Ethic," *Environmental Ethics* 4 (1982): 163–74. What I am saying here is much simpler. A workable environmental ethic cannot violate scientific laws about the operation of ecological systems. An environmental ethic that prescribed pollution (scientifically described) would be absurd.

2. I mean *basic* attitudes. Obviously, there are many different kinds of environmentalists, with different ideas about the use and preservation of the natural environment. I make no dogmatic assumptions about what constitutes an environmentalist. I do assume, however, that the careful use and protection of natural resources, the control of pollution, and the preservation of endangered species are the broad heart of the position. In this light, the differences between Garret Hardin, Barry Commoner, David Brower, and Edward Abbey—to name just a few—are matters of degree.

3. This literature is too vast to be noted completely. For the general character of an environmental ethic, see Rolston and Colwell in note 1. See also Don E. Marietta, Jr., "The Interrelationship of Ecological Science and Environmental Ethics," *Environmental Ethics* 1 (1979): 195–207, and J. Baird Callicott, "Animal Liberation: A Triangular Affair," *Environmental Ethics* 2 (1980): 311–38. An environmental ethic cannot be based on human interests because of the contingent relationship between human interests and the welfare of the natural environment. For a discussion of this point see Martin H. Krieger, "What's Wrong with Plastic Trees?" *Science* 179 (1973): 446–55; Laurence H. Tribe, "Ways Not to Think About Plastic Trees," *Yale Law Journal* 83 (1974): 1315–48; Mark Sagoff, "On Preserving the Natural Environment," *Yale Law Journal* 84 (1974): 205–67, and "Do We Need a Land Use Ethic?" *Environmental Ethics* 3 (1981): 293–308; Christopher Stone, *Should Trees Have Standing? Towards Legal Rights for Natural Objects* (Los Altos, Calif.: William Kaufmann, 1974); William Godfrey-Smith, "The Value of Wilderness," *Environmental Ethics* 1 (1979): 308–19; and my "Utilitarianism and Preservation," *Environmental Ethics* 1 (1979): 357–64. An environmental ethic cannot be based on the interests of individual natural beings because many natural entities worth preserving are not clearly the possessors of interests. These nonliving and nonsentient beings acquire moral standing through membership in a holistic system. See Kenneth E. Goodpaster, "On Being Morally Considerable," *The Journal of Philosophy* 75 (1978): 308–25, and "From Egoism to Environmentalism," in *Ethics and Problems of the 21st Century*, ed. K. E. Goodpaster and K. M. Sayre (Notre Dame: University of Notre Dame, 1979), pp. 21–35; Bryan G. Norton, "Environmental Ethics and Nonhuman Rights," *Environmental Ethics* 4 (1982): 17–36; and my

"Is There a Place for Animals in the Moral Consideration of Nature?" *Ethics and Animals* 4 (1983): 74–87.

4. Godfrey-Smith, "Value of Wilderness," p. 316. He cites Arne Naess, "The Shallow and the Deep, Long-Range Ecology Movement: A Summary," *Inquiry* 16 (1973): 95–100.

5. Marietta, "Ecological Science and Environmental Ethics," p. 197.

6. Aldo Leopold, "The Land Ethic," in *A Sand County Almanac* (New York: Ballantine, 1970), p. 262.

7. Ibid., p. 239.

8. Ibid., p. 240.

9. Ibid., p. 251.

10. Ibid., p. 253.

11. Ibid., p. 253. The full discussion is on pp. 251–61.

12. Ibid., p. 261.

13. Aldo Leopold, "Some Fundamentals of Conservation in the Southwest," *Environmental Ethics* 1 (1979): 140.

14. ". . . a rereading of 'The Land Ethic' in the light of 'Some Fundamentals' reveals that Leopold did not entirely abandon the organic analogy in favor of the community analogy." Callicott, "Animal Liberation," p. 322, note 26.

15. Ibid., p. 321, and note 25.

16. See, for example, Paul Shepard, "Ecology and Man—A Viewpoint," in *The Subversive Science,* ed. Paul Shepard and Daniel McKinley (Boston: Houghton Mifflin, 1969), pp. 2–3. Shepard is discussed below in the text.

17. In reviewing an earlier version of this paper, Callicott was severely critical of the preceding section of the argument. As a means of making the argument clearer, I will attempt a brief summary of Callicott's criticisms and an answer to them. Callicott has two major complaints regarding my contrast of the models of organism and community, and the subsequent comparison of community and natural ecosystems. First, he claims that I misrepresent the model of organism by focusing on the parts of an organism as organs rather than cells. If we consider a "cellular model" of organism, the parts of the organism gain a substantial amount of autonomy. Cells can be more easily transferred than organs. Now I agree that the cells in an organism are more autonomous than organs—but this only makes the "cellular-model" of organism more akin to a community model. As I see it, Callicott's cellular view of organic parts is simply another form of community, and it gains its plausibility from its affinity with a communal model. Second, Callicott claims that my argument is only plausible because I have limited my discussion to "micro" holistic systems—a university instead of society per se, a natural ecosystem instead of the global biosphere. An organ cannot exist outside an organism; a person cannot exist outside of all society; a natural entity cannot exist outside the global biosphere. These "macro" comparisons suggest to Callicott an organic approach. Yet, even on this large scale there are differences. An organic part must be transplanted into a nearly identical being—a human liver into a

human body. But a social individual can be transferred into many different kinds of society. Although a twentieth-century social being might perish if cut off from all society, he might still survive in an assortment of social frameworks: with Bedouins, monks in Tibet, the elite in Hollywood, or even a family of baboons. Members of a community—unlike organic parts—have a greater freedom to move and change their systemic places. This freedom is their autonomy, their difference from organic parts. Finally, it is my intuition that the "larger" these models get the more implausible both of them seem to be. The entire biosphere is neither one organism nor one community. To consider it to be either seems to result in a vague generalization—similar to the "brotherhood of man"—that does nothing to advance environmental ethics.

18. I exclude from consideration the relationship between the entity and the perceiver of value (i.e., the consciousness aware of the intrinsic value). Although consciousness *may* be necessary for the existence of value (I leave this question open and do not address it here), it is still the case that consciousness can value an entity for what it is in itself, intrinsically. Note also that I am not arguing that intrinsic value is a psychological state of an individual, as a Benthamite would. I do not know what intrinsic value is, and I do not specifically define it here. The precise characterization of intrinsic value awaits further study. All that I claim is that intrinsic value, whatever it is, is based on the entity's own properties. See for more discussion, Andrew Brennan, "The Moral Standing of Natural Objects," *Environmental Ethics* 6 (1984): 35–56, and the references in note 20 below.

19. One might want to argue that a human liver is aesthetically beautiful, and that if beauty is an intrinsic value, that the liver thus possesses intrinsic value. But I think this kind of example is farfetched. Although *any* existing thing could have intrinsic value based on its own individual properties, the predominant value associated with organic parts is instrumental value.

20. Those that do stress intrinsic value (for example, Tom Regan, "The Nature and Possibility of an Environmental Ethic," *Environmental Ethics* 3 [1981]: 19–34, and Lilly-Marlene Russow, "Why Do Species Matter?" *Environmental Ethics* 3 [1981]: 101–12) tend to abandon the holistic conceptions of an environmental ethic.

21. Shepard, "Ecology and Man," pp. 2–3.

22. Rolston, "Are Values in Nature Subjective or Objective," p. 146.

23. Ibid., p. 147. See also Holmes Rolston, III, "Values Gone Wild?" *Inquiry* 26 (1983): 181–207, for a further discussion of the blending of intrinsic and instrumental value.

24. Callicott, "Animal Liberation," p. 320.

25. Ibid., p. 332.

26. Russow, "Why Do Species Matter?" p. 107.

27. Ibid., p. 108.

28. But see David Ehrenfeld, *The Arrogance of Humanism* (New York: Oxford, 1978), pp. 207–11, where he does condemn this loss. The implication of my

essay is that the loss of the smallpox virus would be a moral wrong, for it is a loss of intrinsic value.

29. John Passmore, *Man's Responsibility for Nature* (New York: Scribner's, 1974), p. 119.

30. Ibid., p. 120.

31. Ibid., p. 121.

32. Ibid., p. 107. Passmore writes: "But it is not at all clear that to sustain this [wilderness] experience the wild country needs to be a wilderness in the full sense of the word: were it, for example, to be purged of flies, I, for one, would not find the refreshment diminished. It is much easier to state a case for the preservation of humanised wildernesses as places of recreation than for the preservation of wildernesses proper."

33. Compare Robert Elliot, "Faking Nature," *Inquiry* 25 (1982): 81-93. Elliot considers the "forgery" of natural ecological systems in an analogy with art works.

34. Russow, "Why Do Species Matter?" p. 107. For another discussion of the difficulty in justifying the preservation of rare species, see Alastair S. Gunn, "Why Should We Care About Rare Species?" *Environmental Ethics* 2 (1980): 17–37. Gunn demonstrates the impossibility of utilitarian (i.e., instrumental) arguments for preservation of rare species, and suggests the importance of intrinsic value.

35. Note that I am not discussing rare endangered species that are biologically important to an ecosystem. There are obvious reasons for preserving those kinds of endangered species. What interests me is why we should preserve species that are *not* biologically important.

36. Leopold, "The Land Ethic," p. 240.

37. I have attempted to balance the communal (instrumental) and the individual (intrinsic) moral criteria in an environmental ethic in "Is There a Place for Animals in the Moral Consideration of Nature?" See also Evelyn B. Pluhar, "Two Conceptions of an Environmental Ethic and Their Implications," *Ethics and Animals* 4 (1983): 110–27.

4

Buffalo-Killing and the Valuation of Species

This essay was written for a conference with the theme "Values and Moral Standing" held at Bowling Green State University in April 1986. Since a primary focus of the field of environmental ethics has been the development of acceptable criteria for the moral consideration of natural entities and systems, this conference appeared to be a perfect venue for a detailed reexamination of several individualistic and holistic justifications of environmental value. In this essay, my central concern is the value that can be attributed to rare and endangered species, a problematic case that seems to challenge both individualistic and holistic forms of an environmental ethic. Rare and endangered species play little or no part in a natural system, so it is difficult to find holistic value in their continued existence. But individuals qua individuals are never rare or endangered—any individualistic criterion of moral value (such as the ability to feel pain, as in Peter Singer's version of "animal liberation") would apply equally to members of both endangered and plentiful species. Thus neither kind of theory can account for the environmentalist intuition (and policy) that rare and endangered species ought to be protected and preserved. In "Buffalo-Killing and the Valuation of Species" I suggest that the debate between individualism and holism has overlooked a crucial aspect of the issue—temporality and history. The destruction of species—of the individual members of a species—cannot be viewed as an isolated single act, but rather must be viewed as a historical process, with different moral evaluations arising at different times. The temporal context is an integral part of our moral evaluation of an act of destruction—indeed, of any action. Considering the history of the destruction of a natural species permits us to introduce the ideas of justice and reparations as key components in environmental ethics and policy.

In his now classic article, "The Tragedy of the Commons," Garrett Hardin briefly discusses the morality of killing the American bison. "A hundred and fifty years ago a plainsman could kill an American bison, cut out only the tongue for his dinner, and discard the rest of the animal. He was not in any important sense being wasteful. Today, with only a few thousand bison left, we would be appalled at such behavior."[1] Perhaps because this remark is tangential to the main theme of Hardin's argument it has not received the attention it deserves. But philosophers interested in the ethics of environmental issues should be concerned, for Hardin's moral intuition about the value of dead bison raises important questions about the valuation of species and the individuals that comprise them—questions rarely raised in the literature of environmental ethics.[2]

My first intuition about that rotting, tongueless buffalo carcass is that it was as wasteful *then* as it would be *now*. At best, a defender of Hardin's view might claim that our moral *perception* about the bison-killing has changed—but that would in no way change the moral character of the act itself. But that is only my *initial* intuition. A closer examination of the case leads me to temper my categorical rejection of Hardin's evaluation. There is *some* truth in what he says about the buffalo, but I am not sure why. This kind of case—the human-induced extinction of a natural species—is exceedingly complex. It raises a set of fundamental questions rarely considered by moral philosophers: Does the valuation of species or natural individuals depend in some way on *when* the evaluation takes place? Can the value moral decision makers ascribe to a species or an individual depend, not on any of its intrinsic features, but rather on the temporal situation of both the species and the moral evaluator? In short, does the reason *why* we value a species depend upon the *when*? This is the bewildering issue raised by the buffalo-killing.[3]

Explanations of the value of natural species fall roughly into two categories: those based on the properties of the individual entities and those based on the holistic system in which the species plays a functional role. In this essay I refer to these positions as "individualism" and "holism," respectively. Much of the debate in environmental ethics has concerned the clash between these differing viewpoints, and recently a few attempts have been made to effect a compromise.[4] Nevertheless, the theories appear radically different in their basic conceptions, and in their implications for moral policy.

Individualism claims that there are intrinsic properties of each individual entity which render the entity valuable. The species itself is not valuable, despite the presumed fact that all the individual members have the same relevant properties. At best, the species has a kind of derivative value because it is made up of valuable individuals. As a public policy, we attempt to preserve the species from extinction because the continued existence of the species will produce more of the valuable individuals.

The appeal of individualism lies in the similarity between the evaluation of nonhumans and humans; after all, we value human beings as individuals, i.e., because of properties that each unique individual possesses. But the major problem of this view lies in determining exactly what properties of the individual confer the value: from what characteristics of an entity does value derive? This question has not been conclusively answered in the realm of human life—as the recent debates over malformed fetuses, abortion, and euthanasia have shown. Even more problematic then is the ascription of value to nonhuman individuals. None of the traditional criteria—rationality, consciousness, sentience, or even life—match our intuitions about the value of all nonhuman entities.

Because of these difficulties, philosophers concerned with the moral treatment of the environment have proposed that the value of natural individuals is not intrinsic to them, not based on their individual characteristics, but instead is a result of the functions of their species in a holistic system. Natural species serve roles, they occupy ecological niches, in well-functioning ecological systems. The species and its individual members are valuable instrumentally. They perform a function that is valuable for the system.

What motivates this view of natural value is the environmentalists' concern for *environments*, for whole systems of entities co-existing in a complex interaction. Individual entities are not really significant from a holistic environmental perspective: the death, decay, and re-cycling of individual entities is normal procedure for the natural system. But this indifference to individual value is, of course, the source of major problems for holism. First, holistic evaluation is not applicable to human individuals. Human beings are not normally sacrificed for, or subsumed under, the good of the larger system or community. So this method of valuation, even if valid for natural nonhuman entities, would not be a comprehensive theory. Second, and more importantly, advocates of holistic valuation must explain *why* functional roles in a system confer value. Why indeed are *systems* valuable? If systems are considered to be valuable because of *their* intrinsic properties, then the same problems of individualistic valuation arise: which properties, and why?

A consideration of Hardin's buffalo can shed some light on the problems surrounding these two methods of valuation when applied to rare species. An individualistic evaluation would clearly agree with my initial intuition about the case. If an individual bison has some properties that make it valuable—e.g., sentience—then it has those properties now and in the past. As an objective fact it would have had the same value then as it has now. The plainsman kills the bison because he has not developed the moral awareness of the bison's value. But that value—common to all individuals of the bison species—does not change over time.

This initial negative reaction to Hardin's view of the case is plausible; however, it encounters problems. First, does it make sense to say that the plainsman was doing something wrong although he did not know it? Is it reasonable for us to blame him? His guilt as an individual agent might be mitigated by his ignorance of the future development of the bison species, yet we would still hold up his action as an example of immoral, irresponsible, or insensitive environmental behavior. Is this a reasonable way to interpret the morality of the situation?

I think not. Consider the (all too plausible) possibility that 150 years from now the amount of clean drinking water will be very limited. In the 22nd century fresh water is only used for drinking, cooking, cleaning, and agriculture—never for recreation, sanitation, or non-agricultural gardening. Under these circumstances, would a moral philosopher in 2135 be judging reasonably if he condemned our profligate use and waste of water in 1985? Could he say that we are actually performing immoral actions when we flush our toilets and water our lawns? Could he say that it is only our lack of knowledge about the conditions of future water supplies that excuses us from complete moral guilt in our water use activities?

To clarify the relevance of this future water case to the bison, let me remind you of the possible alternatives. If Hardin's view of the bison is correct, then the future moral philosopher cannot condemn us, for we, like the plainsman of the 1830s, are doing nothing wrong in our present time. It will only be in the changed world of the future that the action is perceived as morally wrong. If, however, the individualistic evaluation of the bison is correct, and if this evaluative principle is generalized, then the future moral philosopher can condemn our use of water, for the moral character of the properties of the action/entity do not change over time. What is wrong now is also wrong then, and vice versa.

Faced with this dilemma, I find that I cannot choose either alternative. The future moral philosopher is in one sense, right to condemn us, and in another sense, wrong—just as we are both right and wrong to condemn the buffalo-shooting plainsman. What is of crucial importance in deciding the issue is the amount of knowledge possessed by the moral agent. Can the moral agent be expected to be aware of the foreseeable effects of his action? Should he be expected to know the long-range consequences of his action? Should he be morally blamed for not taking them into account? The answer, I think, is yes—and thus a moral decision in these cases rests on our interpretation of the state of the agent's knowledge: to paraphrase a famous political question, "How much did the agent know, and when did he know it?"

Although it may seem like a strange conclusion, it is correct to say that in a sense we commit a moral wrong when we use water (wastefully) to water our lawns. It is wrong to the extent that we can foresee the problem of chronic water shortages in the future. Since we know that these shortages are a good possibility, and indeed, are causally related to our present wasteful behavior, our actions meet the knowledge criterion of moral culpability. Or if we acted in ignorance of the possibility of future water shortages, we might still be open to moral blame—for we irresponsibly and insensitively failed to see the consequences of our ignorance. However, there may be good reason not to judge the plainsman as harshly: it is unlikely that the possibility of species extinction was well-known in that time. The foreseeable consequences of the bison-killing did not include the eradication of the buffalo species. On this empirical claim alone rests the moral defense of the buffalo-killing plainsman.

These considerations, then, suggest one reason to reject the theory of individualism. The moral value of an entity does not entirely depend on some temporally invariable property of the entity. The moral value instead is dependent in some sense on the knowledge available to the agent about the foreseeable consequences of his action on the entity. The agent's knowledge may obviously change with time, while the individualistic properties of the entity do not; but the only way to explain our moral intuitions in cases like the buffalo-killing or the water shortage is to acknowledge the way in which moral evaluations change over time.[5]

Let me briefly note a second reason to reject the theory of individualism as applied to the buffalo: the rarity of the individuals in a species
contributes to the value we ascribe to them. I am not sure why this is
so; nor am I sure if this factor can be justified as part of the evaluation
process. But it is undeniably part of the human meaning and consciousness of value. Rarity adds to the value of an entity—whether the
entity is a living being, a gemstone, or a work of art. The rarity of the
American bison *now* thus adds to its moral value, and this particularly
corroborates Hardin's view of the change in moral evaluation. But rarity cannot be explained by individualism. Rarity is not an intrinsic
property of an individual; it is meaningless to say that an individual is
rare, for the individual is what it is, without regard to similar entities.
Rarity makes sense only as a relational property. It signifies a factor
both in the relationship between an entity and other similar entities
and in the relationship between that class of entities and the universe
as a whole. The concept of rarity requires a holistic perspective on valuation, for the relational properties involved transcend the characteristics of the individual in itself.

My preliminary conclusion then is that Hardin cannot be proven
wrong from the perspective of individualism. Individualism fails to
explain the case of the buffalo-killing. But this does not, of course,
make Hardin's view correct. It is at least wrong in one respect, for
moral agents can be held responsible for what they can reasonably
foresee as the consequences of their actions. The plainsman is not, as
Hardin's view implies, morally pure and innocent. He is morally cul-
pable to the extent that he should have known the long-range effects
of his wasteful action. The amount of moral guilt is unclear. In any
particular situation the extent of guilt will depend on the empirical
question about the available knowledge.

Hardin's bison also presents a problem for holism. A holistic moral
evaluation based on the functional contribution of an entity to the overall ecological system would, at first, tend to agree with Hardin's view
of the bison-killing. From the standpoint of ecological function, one
bison more or less is not going to affect the well-being of the ecosystem
of the American plains. Whether the bison is killed by a human or a
natural predator, and whether the carcass is eaten or "wasted" by
merely decaying into basic ecological nutrients is all irrelevant. The
individual bison, as Hardin's view suggests, is not the least bit important. What matters is the continued ecological function of the bison
species.

Unfortunately, the issue is not so clear-cut. Although the holistic evaluation may be able to explain why the plainsman can morally kill the bison, it fails completely to explain why it is *now* wrong for *us* to kill it. The depressing fact is that the American bison today—as well as any other seriously threatened species—plays little or no role in the continued functioning of the ecosystem. The natural ecosystem of which the bison was once an integral member no longer exists—in part because of the near extinction of the bison species. Thus, ecological functioning cannot be the reason why we ascribe value to individuals that comprise a rare, endangered species. Their very rarity precludes an important ecological significance.

So I am not sure why Hardin believes the killing of the bison *today* is so appalling. From an ecological holistic perspective there would be only one precise moment when the killing of an individual would be morally wrong. At some point in the downward path from "flourishing" to "extinction" there would be a threshold beyond which the species would no longer be a constructive member of the ecological community. Around that threshold point the continued survival of each individual in the species would be quite significant, for the loss of just one individual would seriously alter the ecological function of the species. Only then could an individual be valued from a holistic perspective. Once below the threshold, the death of individuals or even the extinction of the species would be irrelevant to the continued existence of the "new" ecosystem. So in general the holistic perspective fails to justify the ascription of moral value to individuals—even individual members of rare and endangered species.

Hardin's bison thus presents a serious challenge to both models of moral evaluation in the field of environmental ethics. No view of the morality of bison-killing can be completely explained by either of the theories. This suggests that there is something wrong with the debate between individualism and holism. Either a compromise must be reached to save the best parts of both theories, or a completely new theory of the moral evaluation of individual natural entities and species must be developed.

Elsewhere I have tried to effect a compromise between individualism and holism.[6] Here I would like to make some tentative suggestions regarding the development of a new theory. The preceding discussion has revealed that there is more to the valuation of natural entities than an analysis of specific properties. Value is not determined merely by looking at *what* a specific entity is—either in itself or in a larger system. Nor are questions of value in environmental ethics likely to be answered by debates over *what kind* of entity—individuals or systems—is the main focus of moral consciousness. There are fairly good reasons why we actually do value all kinds of natural entities—individuals, species, ecosystems. The traditional criteria such as beauty, life, sentience, consciousness, ecological function, etc., are all extremely plausible, and that is why they all have their adherents in the literature. But each of these standards has the problem that it is not comprehensive. No one criterion explains common moral intuitions in all problematic cases, and despite some convoluted philosophical gymnastics, none seems likely to do so. Hence, the issue that should be addressed by moral philosophers is when the varying criteria are each appropriate. *What* natural entities we value, and *why* we value them are questions that are relatively clear: the interesting question is *when*, according to the several accepted standards, we ought to value them.

I call this question the problem of the temporality of valuation: how the weight of differing evaluative criteria shifts over time. It rears its ugly head quite clearly in the case of Hardin's bison, for only if we consider the temporal point of the moral evaluation can we make sense of our moral intuitions. When considered atemporally, the traditional criteria—such as sentience or ecological function—fail to account for all the moral judgments philosophers make.

But the best features of the traditional value criteria and the doctrines of individualism and holism can be saved once we begin to view moral evaluation from the perspective of time. Such a strategy seems particularly appropriate in the field of environmental ethics, for here we are concerned with entities that develop and exist over long periods of history. Our moral evaluations concern not only individuals but also species and ecosystems that continue to exist beyond the limits of individual human life. And there are two obvious ways in which our value judgments can be temporally related. First, as noted above, our moral evaluations must be based on the amount of predictive knowledge possessed by moral agents at the time of action. I cannot fully evaluate a bison or a mosquito or a whooping crane or a gallon of water merely by looking at their intrinsic properties in the world *now*. An adequate moral evaluation must include the foreseeable consequences—the continuing life history—of these entities and their kind. One aspect of the value of that dead bison in 1830—an aspect obviously overlooked by the plainsman—was the continuing role that bison *should have played* in the ecosystem of the North American plains. One aspect of the value of fresh water today is its probable increasing scarcity and importance in the world of the future. The properties of the entity considered valuable are determined by the temporal use of knowledge: the consideration of future consequences.

A second way of introducing temporality into moral valuation is more subtle. Those committed to environmental values such as the preservation of rare endangered species are often accused of being impractical romantic dreamers—or worse. There seems to be no valid reason now why humans should spend vast sums of money and great amounts of time preserving the remnants of moribund natural species. From an atemporal perspective these accusations appear quite cogent. But once we begin to view the elimination of a species as a negative historical process in which humans often played a crucial descriptive role, then the romanticism of the preservationist becomes justified. The temporally based reason why rare species are valuable is that humans *owe reparations* to the species and to nature itself for the past "crimes" of humanity. As a matter of simple justice, to correct past wrongs, we are morally obligated to value and to protect the entities of nature.

I offer these ideas of temporal valuation as a suggestion for a different outlook on problems in environmental ethics. At least, they help to explain my revised, reflective intuitions about the case of Hardin's bison. There is some truth in Hardin's determination of the morality of the bison-killing: the actions occurring at different times should be evaluated differently. But I am unwilling to let that intrepid plainsman escape all moral guilt. He can be blamed to some degree for lacking the foresight to see the consequences of his wasteful act. And his fellow plainsmen can be blamed for later killings that occurred near to the threshold point on the road to extinction. Today, however, we ascribe value to the solitary bison not because of its intrinsic properties nor because of its ecological function, but because we are repaying the debt created for us by that plainsman and his brethren. As compensation for the past behavior of causing the near extinction of the bison species, we have a moral duty to preserve the remnants. This is the only reason that explains our current interest in the preservation of rare species without leading to other problematic conclusions. For if we view Hardin's bison from the perspective of individualism, the bison *then* and *now* has the same moral value—but that cannot be correct, since its present rarity makes a contemporary killing worse than a killing in 1830. But if we view the bison from a perspective of ecological holism, there seems to be no reason to protect it, for its ecological role has vanished. In sum, the traditional criteria for moral evaluation of natural entities fail to explain the case of Hardin's bison; but new temporally based criteria suggest plausible, unproblematic reasons for the valuations.

It should now be clear why I have tried to avoid a direct discussion or justification of the traditional value criteria such as sentience, rationality, or ecological function. The case of Hardin's bison is a serious challenge to these traditional criteria because it raises the issue of temporal relevance in value ascription. The advocates of both individualistic and holistic valuation must begin to transcend their favorite *a*temporal criteria. They must develop a theory that can account for the different valuations present at different times in the history of a natural species, entity, or ecosystem. In short, they must develop a theory that explains the *when*, as well as the *why*, of moral value. If environmental philosophers cannot accomplish this task, then their theories will never escape the ghosts of buffalo on the North American plains.[7]

Notes

1. Garrett Hardin, "The Tragedy of the Commons," *Science* 162 (1968): 1243–48.

2. In this essay I will be using the term "valuation" in two senses: (1) as the ascription of value to an *entity*, such as a *bison* or the bison *species*, and (2) as the judging of an *action* that concerns an entity, such as the killing of a bison. It is a working assumption of my essay that values in sense (2) are dependent in some crucial way on values in sense (1); i.e., we judge the morality of a bison-kiling by some value possessed by the bison, among other reasons. This assumption can be challenged. Many environmental philosophers deny that there is value in sense (1) for nonhuman entities. They thus claim that value (2) depends on other aspects of the situation—e.g., benefits for the human community. These "human interest" arguments for environmental ethics have been discussed extensively in the literature, and I believe that they have been decisively refuted—at the very least, they are uninteresting. For a discussion, see Martin H. Krieger, "What's Wrong with Plastic Trees?" *Science* 179 (1973): 446–55; Laurence H. Tribe, "Ways Not to Think About Plastic Trees," *Yale Law Journal* 83 (1974): 1315–48; Mark Sagoff, "On Preserving the Natural Environment," *Yale Law Journal* 84 (1974): 205–67, and "Do We Need a Land Use Ethic?" *Environmental Ethics* 3 (1981): 293–308; Christopher Stone, *Should Trees Have Standing? Towards Legal Rights for Natural Objects* (Los Altos, Calif.: William Kaufmann, 1974); William Godfrey-Smith, "The Value of Wilderness," *Environmental Ethics* 1 (1979): 308–19; Alastair S. Gunn, "Why Should We Care About Rare Species?" *Environmental Ethics* 2 (1980): 17–37; and Eric Katz, "Utilitarianism and Preservation," *Environmental Ethics* 1 (1979): 357–64.

3. Let me note that this essay is not a commentary on or a criticism of Garrett Hardin's major philosophical doctrines about the environment, population, or pollution. Although I shall continue to label the position expressed in the first paragraph as "Hardin's view," I am not concerned whether Hardin ever held

or now holds that position. Nor am I interested in the relationship between that view and Hardin's general theme of the tragedy of the commons as a moral paradigm for understanding ethical and social issues. My sole concern is the problem of *temporality* as it relates to the ascription of value to species and individuals in the natural environment. The quotation by Hardin merely serves to bring this problem into focus.

4. The literature on individualism and holism is vast. Good examples of individualism are Tom Regan, "The Nature and Possibility of an Environmental Ethic," *Environmental Ethics* 3 (1981): 19–34, and Lilly-Marlene Russow, "Why Do Species Matter?" *Environmental Ethics* 3 (1981): 101–12. One of the most provocative justifications of holism is J. Baird Callicott, "Animal Liberation: A Triangular Affair," *Environmental Ethics* 2 (1980): 311–38. Attempts to combine individualism and holism can be found in Evelyn B. Pluhar, "Two Conceptions of an Environmental Ethic and Their Implications," *Ethics and Animals* 4 (1983): 110–27, and Eric Katz, "Is There a Place for Animals in the Moral Consideration of Nature?" *Ethics and Animals* 4 (1983): 74–87.

5. One attempt to save an individualistic model of value would be to accept, initially, the claim that the killing of the individual buffalo (in 1835) was not too serious, but to argue further that the killing of individual buffalo adds up to a collective harm as more and more buffalo are killed. The harmful consequences of the buffalo-killing are *felt* collectively, even though the harms themselves befall individuals. So on this interpretation, the plainsman does perform a moral wrong by killing the buffalo, for he is contributing, in an incremental way, to a future collective harm; and similarly, when I water my lawn I am performing an individualistic wrongful act that is felt as a collective harm (in the future).

I believe that this view of the buffalo-killing would force us to consider the whole range of problems dealing with collective decision making and free-riders; and that in the end, it would still *not* save the individualistic position regarding natural entities. On this view, the value of the individual buffalo (or the water used for my lawn) would depend not on the properties of the entity but on the actual occurrence of the collective harm. If counterfactually, the buffalo species had not been nearly exterminated, then the killing of the individual buffalo could not be conceived as an immoral act. An atemporal ascription of value to individuals will not explain the morality of the buffalo-killing, for the killing only *becomes* immoral through a temporal perspective on the action and entity. For more discussion, see the text below.

6. Eric Katz, "Organism, Community, and 'The Substitution Problem,' *Environmental Ethics* 7 (1985): 241–56.

7. I would like to thank Holmes Rolston for his helpful comments on an earlier version of this essay.

5

Searching for Intrinsic Value: Pragmatism and Despair in Environmental Ethics

"Searching for Intrinsic Value" was written in response to an essay by Anthony Weston, "Beyond Intrinsic Value: Pragmatism in Environmental Ethics," Environmental Ethics *7 (1985): 321–39. Weston had criticized the role that the concept of "intrinsic value" plays in the development of an environmental ethic. According to Weston, the search for intrinsic value was a misdirected attempt to derive an absolute foundation for the moral consideration of natural entities. Instead, he suggested a "pragmatic shift" toward a plurality of values based on the entire range of human experiences with nature. I criticize Weston for two basic reasons. As a methodological point, Weston overemphasized the role of intrinsic value in the establishment of an environmental ethic—probably because he focused on individualistic accounts of an environmental ethic. More importantly, Weston's pragmatic derivation of values is completely anthropocentric, as it is based on human experiences with the natural world. Nevertheless, I am quite sympathetic to the pragmatic approach to applied ethics and social policy. I too support value pluralism: from within my modified community-based holism, there is a clear plurality of values, respecting both individual autonomy and communal integrity and identity. But I reject the tendency toward subjectivism that is a central part of pragmatic ethics. Obligations to protect the natural environment cannot be based on the "feelings" that humans have when they interact with the natural world. "Searching for Intrinsic Value" drew a further response from Weston and a rebuttal by me, both appearing in* Environmental Ethics *10 (1988): 285–88. The entire Weston–Katz exchange, with a commentary by*

Andrew Light, has been reprinted in Environmental Pragmatism, *ed. Andrew Light and Eric Katz (London and New York: Routledge, 1996), pp. 285–338.*

I. Introduction

What role does the concept of intrinsic value play in the development of an environmental ethic? Must the principles of an environmental ethic be *grounded* on the existence and recognition of self-sufficient, abstract, and independent value in natural entities? Or is the concern over the existence and explanation of intrinsic value in nature a mistake, a misdirection, a dead end in the field of environmental ethics? In a recent article in *Environmental Ethics*, "Beyond Intrinsic Value: Pragmatism in Environmental Ethics,"[1] Anthony Weston argues that the allure of "intrinsic value" is fundamentally misguided, that rather than provide a ground for environmental ethics it dooms the development of a plausible moral argument for environmental protection. Weston claims that even environmental philosophers who base their arguments on the need for intrinsic value recognize the near impossibility of justifying such a theory of moral value. But we can do better than this (he claims). All we need to do is turn to the pragmatic conception of value and apply it to the development of an environmental ethic. This will remove the dualisms of traditional value theory—means/ends, intrinsic/instrumental—that are conceptual obstacles to the real practical understanding of both ethics in general and environmental ethics in particular. We will thus discover that the principles of an environmental ethic are part of the constellation (or web) of interrelated pluralistic values that pragmatists tell us is the heart of ethical theory.

Weston's challenge to the *structure* of the debate in environmental ethics is a powerful one; indeed, I share many of his concerns. Nonetheless, his suggestion for a solution to the "sorry state" of environmental ethics is far from acceptable. A pragmatic value theory and ethics—even if justifiable in itself—would produce an environmental ethic that is irredeemably anthropocentric and subjective. A workable environmental ethic will share many fundamental concepts with pragmatism—e.g., the emphasis on the concrete situation—but it cannot ultimately rest on the values of pragmatism, for these values are inextricably bound up with human desires and interests.

II. Intrinsic Value and Pragmatism in Environmental Ethics

How important is the concept of intrinsic value in environmental ethics? Is it really the foundation upon which all ethical obligations regarding the natural environment depend? Weston paints a picture of despair and futility as he surveys the attempts of environmental philosophers to justify the value of natural entities: like Tom Regan, they end in the positing of dubious nonnatural ontological properties, or like Thomas Hill, Jr., Mark Sagoff, or Bryan Norton, they end in a "second best" appeal to human virtues and ideals.[2] No one, it seems, can give a plausible account and justification of the intrinsic value of non-human natural entities.[3] This despairing failure leads Weston to conclude that environmental ethics is "in a sorry state indeed" (p. 327).

But the difficulties encountered by environmental ethics are not *primarily* the result of the attempted justification of intrinsic value. Weston overemphasizes the importance of this concept in the literature. Environmental philosophers undoubtedly talk a great deal about the concept of intrinsic value—I have been guilty of this myself[4]—but their use of the concept is not as Weston suggests (pp. 322–23). Intrinsic value is not sought as the *ground* of an environmental ethic. Its explication is not pursued as the justification of environmental policies—and thus the failure to articulate it does not lead to the failure of environmental ethics.

The primary justifications for an environmental ethic are instrumental: they attempt to reveal the purposes behind environmental protection, and to show why these purposes are beneficial and moral. But not all instrumental values are acceptable to an environmental ethicist; one major goal of an environmental ethic is to show that exclusively human-centered goals are not capable of justifying environmental policies. Within this project of justification, the intrinsic value of natural entities can be used to limit or to map out the range of appropriate instrumental values. The basic goal of developing a nonanthropocentric justification for environmental policies is *aided* by the existence of nonhuman intrinsic value. Human purposes, desires, and interests will not be the only possible justifications of action. This supportive function of the concept of nonhuman intrinsic value is a far cry from the central or primary justification of an environmental ethic. Environmental ethics, in short, does not rest on the development of a theory of a nonhuman natural intrinsic value; it merely uses this intrinsic value to clarify appropriate instrumental values.

I am here making a claim that is primarily about the *methodology* of environmental ethics, not about its substantive content. Such a claim can only be justified by a detailed examination of the literature—a task obviously beyond the scope of this essay. It may, however, be supported by briefer considerations: (1) a close rereading of Holmes Rolston—who is mentioned quite prominently in Weston's essay—and of J. Baird Callicott on the nature of intrinsic value in environmental ethics; and (2) an examination of the dialectical assumptions of the argument for an environmental ethic supposedly based on intrinsic value.

(1) Although Weston correctly criticizes Rolston for using the concept of "intrinsic value" in a place where it is not needed (p. 336),[5] this particular use is not typical of Rolston's work as a whole. Rolston is much more concerned with the various kinds of *instrumental* value that are provided by wild nature—thus, he prepares elegant taxonomies of natural value.[6] Even more importantly, on the theoretical level, Rolston has argued for a dissolving of the distinction between instrumental and intrinsic value. The entire notion of intrinsic value loses its meaning from the perspective of ecological holism, because each natural entity performs some function in the ecological system. "Things do not have their separate natures merely in and for themselves, but they face outward and cofit into broader natures. Value-in-itself is smeared out to become value-in-togetherness."[7] A pragmatist interested in resolving conceptual dualisms could not ask for more!

Similarly, Callicott has tried to break down and to reinterpret the concept of natural intrinsic value. In a recent series of papers[8] he has developed an axiology based on a model of Humean/Darwinian bioempathy, and he has further indicated how this model agrees with recent discussions in quantum physics. In brief, Callicott challenges the entire distinction between subject and object, and with it the existence of purely objective properties and purely subjective values for natural entities. The existence of ontologically discrete entities is an illusion, as well as the existence of independent intrinsic properties and values. Callicott claims to have "transformed" or "truncated" the traditional concept of intrinsic value because it is no longer entirely independent; it requires the existence of a valuing consciousness.[9]

It is not my purpose here to endorse any specific view of the conceptual structure of intrinsic and instrumental value. More specifically, I am not myself trying to dissolve the categories of "intrinsic" and "instrumental" as Rolston, Callicott—and indeed, Weston—have attempted. My point, again, is formal and methodological: it is about the *use* of the concept of "intrinsic value" in environmental ethics. This brief review of the main ideas of two prominent environmental philosophers—Rolston and Callicott—shows that the concept of intrinsic value is not (as Weston supposes) the ultimate ground upon which all ethical obligation concerning the environment depends; it plays a much more complicated and subtle role in the development of an environmental ethic.

It might be objected that my methodological claim rests on a wilful disregard of *other* environmental philosophers who do employ a concept of intrinsic value in the kind of basic way that Weston supposes— such as Tom Regan and Paul Taylor.[10] But this objection is without merit. (i) First, it is my contention that Weston has misconstrued the nature of the debate in environmental ethics, that he has misidentified the purpose of the concept of intrinsic value. The existence of philosophers who do employ a concept of intrinsic value does not damage my claim, as long as I can show that there are important environmental philosophers who do not use the concept of intrinsic value in the manner suggested by Weston. I have done this in my brief review of Rolston and Callicott. (ii) A more controversial reason for ignoring environmental philosophers like Regan and Taylor is that their fundamental value assumptions lead to impractical or incomplete versions of environmental ethics. Regan places value in the subjects of a continuous conscious life; Taylor's biocentric view emphasizes the value of living entities. Neither view is broad enough to include the holistic systems and nonliving entities that a comprehensive environmentalism wishes to preserve.

(2) Indeed, this brief criticism of Regan and Taylor leads directly to the second consideration supporting my methodological claim about environmental ethics. Weston, again, is concerned that the search for intrinsic value is the primary focus of an environmental ethic; but his concern is misdirected. The search for natural intrinsic value is not the ultimate ground of an environmental ethics. Nor *could* it be, for any argument for an environmental ethic based on an articulation of natural intrinsic value would be fundamentally mistaken.

The concept of intrinsic value fails as the source of an environmental ethic for two basic reasons: it implies that individual entities—and not whole systems—are the bearers of value; and it tends to focus attention on anthropocentric values such as sentience and rationality. Weston himself mentions this latter point: "The implicit demand to reduce intrinsic value to a single common denominator may incline us . . . toward the anthropocentric-sentientist end of the range of possible environmental ethics" (p. 325). More directly, Richard Sylvan argues against the notion of intrinsic value as developed by "deep ecologists" such as Arne Naess—i.e., the idea of "self-realization." The idea of developing one's highest potential—whether one be a human, animal, or plant—skews the notion of value not only toward *living* entities, but also toward those that are analogues of human beings.[11] We human philosophers, in short, seem to find that the essential nature of value lies in some aspect of human experience. We can understand this kind of value as intrinsic to our own lives, and thus we suppose it is valuable for nonhuman entities also. But this articulation of a concept of intrinsic value is nothing but a disguised anthropocentrism, and cannot be the basis of a real environmental ethic.[12]

The search for intrinsic value also biases an environmental ethic toward the perspective of individualism. The entire notion is directed toward the independent properties of discrete individuals.[13] But the most defensible forms of an environmental ethic (e.g., those of Rolston and Callicott) are essentially *holistic*. An environmental ethic, because it deals with environments, must focus its moral concern on the interdependent functioning of the entire ecological system, not merely on the (conceptually) isolated individuals who make up the system. The idea of intrinsic value loses its sense in a holistic system. An emphasis on intrinsic value, indeed, would preclude the development of a holistic environmental ethic. As Rolston notes, ". . . the 'for what it is in itself' facet of *intrinsic* becomes problematic in a holistic web. It is too internal and elementary; it forgets relatedness and externality."[14]

These considerations suggest that the creation of a nonindividualistic and nonanthropocentric environmental ethic cannot be based on the search for an intrinsic value that will serve as the ground of moral obligation. But this conclusion is nothing new. Environmental philosophers such as Rolston and Callicott have realized this for quite some time—their methodology, the primary methodology of environmental ethics, is not the methodology that Weston criticizes.

This means that Weston's call for a pragmatic shift in value orientation is pointed in the wrong direction—toward an atypical, individualistic, environmental philosopher.[15] But that alone does *not* invalidate many of his observations. There is a good deal of truth in a pragmatic conception of value as applied to environmental ethics—we may be dealing here with a mere terminological dispute, for once we see that environmental ethics is primarily concerned with the *instrumental* values of environmental protection—and not, as Weston supposes, the intrinsic value of natural individuals—then many pragmatic elements of moral theory come into play.

Evidence that Weston's critique of intrinsic value and his subsequent "pragmatic shift" is nothing more than a dispute over terms can be found in his discussion of Rolston's value of "sourcehood." Rolston has argued that nature should not be treated as a mere resource to be used, but rather as a *source* of what we value. "One is not so much looking to *resources* as to *sources*, seeking relationships in an elemental stream of being with transcending integrities."[16] For Rolston, nature as a source of value is then itself intrinsically valuable—but Weston thinks that this second claim adds nothing to our understanding and valuation of wild nature. What really matters, Weston says, is that we see nature as a *source* of value and valuable experiences (p. 336). Rolston, however, is saying the same thing! Weston is only disputing the form of Rolston's expression; he agrees with the *content*. Because he is overly concerned with the illusory importance of the concept of intrinsic value, Weston finds it necessary to distance himself from any *terminological* use of the concept of "intrinsic value." He is looking at allies and seeing enemies.

Once clear of this terminological morass, Weston's form of pragmatic value theory coheres very well with the dominant form of instrumental-holistic environmental ethics. First, Weston emphasizes that value for the pragmatist is pluralistic and relational: there are many values found in nature and these values interact in various ways with other values, interests, and desires that we possess. But an adequate environmental ethic does not deny this. It claims that there are many kinds of value found in holistic ecological systems—e.g., diversity, stability, beauty—and that all these contribute to arguments for environmental preservation. No *one abstract* comprehensive "intrinsic" value is sought by philosophers wishing to justify environmental protection. A plurality of practical—albeit ecological—values are articulated by philosophers and environmental scientists: the values that contribute to the well-functioning of the ecological system.

Second, pragmatic value is irrevocably tied to specific concrete situations: there is no good in itself; there are only good situations in the real world. Thus, Weston denies meaning to the question "Why preserve wilderness?" As a question of practical policy it is too abstract. For the pragmatist the real question is "Why preserve *this* wilderness?"—what is it about this particular natural region which interacts with our pluralistic set of interrelating values (pp. 337–38)? But any workable environmental ethic does the same. Because an articulation of precise ecological values is a necessary requirement for protectionist policy, the environmental philosopher must examine specific environmental systems to determine their degree of worth. Environmental philosophy must be informed by ecological science. This science is not one of abstract principles; it specifically analyzes concrete problems.[17]

In this way, certain key elements of pragmatic value do fit within a certain kind of environmental ethic. Nevertheless, environmental ethics does not require—as Weston supposes—a *shift* toward pragmatism, for the most adequate and justifiable forms of an environmental ethic already make use of many pragmatic elements. What I have argued so far is that Weston's criticism of "intrinsic value" employs a distorted picture of the methodology—the formal argumentative structure—of environmental ethics. Once beyond that distorted picture one can see the basic similarities between an adequate environmental ethic and a pragmatic ethic. But as I argue in the concluding section, environmental ethics cannot be subsumed under pragmatism per se. Despite compelling and comforting analogies, pragmatism and environmental ethics must part company over the role of *human interests* in the determination of value.

III. Pragmatism and Humanity

Weston explicitly denies that pragmatism is committed to a "crude anthropocentrism," but despite his denial, he ties pragmatic value to "a certain kind of desiring," and he adds, "possibly only humans desire in this way" (p. 327). Further on, he begins his "defense of environmental values" by focusing on the "feelings" awakened by the experience of nature as "essential starting points" (p. 334). And the entire pragmatic project is designed to "articulate . . . the relation of [environmental] values to other parts of our system of desires . . . and to the solution of concrete problems" (p. 335).

The human desire for certain kinds of natural experience, and indeed, certain kinds of human experiences of nature, thus become the *ground* of a pragmatic environmental ethic. But this is clearly shaky ground. The interrelated web of desires, values, and experiences that make up each individual human life is not common to all humans. There is, in short, *no common ground* for the start of rational negotiation. Weston's dogmatic insistence that there are not really cases where people "do not care less" about wilderness, and that "common ground remains" is the hollow echo of an empty position (p. 338). He clearly misses the fact that some people do *not* care at all about the experience of nature.

And why must we insist that they do? Why must an ethics of the environment—or any ethics, for that matter—be based on a certain kind of favorable experience? The ethical obligation to tell the truth is not based on the subjective experience of truth telling, nor on the avoidance of the experience of lying. One need not experience adultery to know that it is ethically incorrect. Why then must the ethical obligation to protect the natural environment—*if such an obligation exists*—be based on favorable natural experiences? If environmental protection is morally correct, it is so regardless of the experiences produced by interacting with nature. If some people do not respond to nature in a "positive" environmentalist way, that is no excuse for them to violate the obligation to protect the environment. Similarly, the dislike of monogamous marriage does not justify promiscuous adultery; the dislike of truth telling does not justify telling a lie. Ethical obligations do not derive their force from favorable experiences.

The insistence that an environmental ethic is grounded on the experiences felt in interacting with nature leads inevitably to a kind of subjective relativism: those agents who do not feel the "awe" and "respect" and "wonder" of nature will have no good reason—no reason at all?!—to protect it. This is not a question of needing a "careful phenomenology" of human experiences regarding nature, as Weston suggests (p. 337). The fact is that some people do not experience nature in a positive way. They *do* want their motorboats and hibachis and condos to go everywhere.[18] As Weston admits, many people hold "deeply different, probably irreconcilable, visions of the ideal world" (p. 339). But rather than this being a source of strength for pragmatism—rather than it being an expression of Deweyan moral autonomy—it condemns it to the swamp of subjective relativism. Whatever the individual agent experiences as useful to himself is valuable, is morally obligatory— even the destruction of wild natural entities and systems.

Weston anticipates this subjectivist criticism of a pragmatic environmental ethic, for he begins his article with a brief claim distinguishing "subjectivism" from "subject-centrism." Pragmatism, he admits, is *subjective*—it "makes valuing an activity of subjects, possibly only of human subjects" (p. 321). But that does not mean it is subject-centrist: subjects—human beings—are not necessarily "the sole or final objects of valuation" (p. 322). Human subjects can recognize value that is "world-directed"; i.e., values external to human beings. "Subjectivism," Weston concludes, "does not imply . . . subject-*centrism*."

Weston is undoubtedly correct about the distinction between subjectivism and subject-centrism, but unfortunately, that does not mitigate my criticism of pragmatism. It is good old-fashioned subjectivism that is the problem here. Pragmatism places the value of the natural environment squarely on the *experiences* of human beings interacting with nature: the desires and feelings of human subjects. Pragmatic valuers may be "world-directed" instead of self-interested, but all that means is that they value experiences, desires, and feelings that arise in external relations, interactions beyond their immediate selves. The pragmatic value of nature—as with all pragmatic value—is irrevocably tied to human experiences. This kind of value cannot be the basis for a stable environmental ethic, for different human beings are going to value different objects, experiences, and feelings in nature. Pragmatism may not rest on a "crude anthropocentrism" of value, but it will result in a *relativism* of value—not everyone will value the "correct" environmentalist experience of the natural world.

The key point here is that human desires, interests, or experiences cannot be the source of moral obligations to protect the environment. Human desires, interests, and experiences are only contingently related to the continued existence of wild nature as such.[19] If environmental policy is based on an "articulation" of human desires and experiences related to a plurality of human values, then it becomes extremely important *who* is articulating the values: *whose* desires and experiences are being used as the source of moral obligations? Environmental policy will depend on the "feelings" of the decision makers at the particular time the policy is established. The ever-changing flux of human feelings concerning the natural environment does not appear to me to be a secure or reliable "common ground" for establishing an environmental ethic.

These criticisms of the use of human experiences in the development of an environmental ethic do not, of course, apply only to pragmatism—they apply with equal force to any environmental ethic based on human interests (e.g., certain kinds of utilitarianism). But what is particularly distressing in the case of pragmatism is that many of the nonanthropocentric elements of the value theory agree with a workable environmental ethic—it is only the emphasis on human interests that destroys pragmatism's effectiveness. Although an environmental ethic must be based on a plurality of instrumental natural values and on a specific analysis of concrete ecological systems, it cannot be grounded on the ever-changing subjective feelings of humans as they experience nature.

There are many reasons for despair when one surveys the field of environmental ethics; there are many reasons to believe that "we are in a sorry state indeed." Given the present state of twentieth-century metaethics, the possibility of any justification for substantive applied ethics seems remote. Justification of environmental values inevitably raises the problem of reconciling facts with values. A workable environmental ethic must incorporate detailed scientific information about the operations of natural systems; yet, little interdisciplinary dialogue between scientists and philosophers has been successful. Finally, a truly environmental ethic must reorient our value systems away from individuals and toward species, systems, and communities; it requires a radical transformation of ethical vision.

However, one problem that is not a cause for despair is the pursuit of the concept of intrinsic value for natural entities. This concept is not the ground of all environmental obligation. Intrinsic value plays only a small role in the formation of an environmental ethic—it serves to limit the exclusive reliance on anthropocentric instrumental values. The existence of intrinsic value needs to be acknowledged, to serve as the limit to anthropocentric instrumentalism; but this value need not be totally articulated or justified, for it is not the ground of all obligation. The problem of intrinsic value in nature is a problem that does not require a solution; it is enough to know that some kind of nonanthropocentric value exists, even if the description of this value remains unclear. What is clear, nevertheless, is that we cannot accept the solution offered by anthropocentric pragmatism. Basing our environmental obligations on the human "system of desires" offered us by the pragmatic theory of value would doom an environmental ethic to the contingent feelings of people who "experience nature" in the "correct" manner. *That* method of justifying ethical obligations is a prescription for real despair in the development of an environmental ethic.

Notes

1. Anthony Weston, "Beyond Intrinsic Value: Pragmatism in Environmental Ethics," *Environmental Ethics* 7 (1985): 321–39. All page references in the text are from this article.

2. Weston refers specifically to one article by each of these philosophers: Thomas Hill, Jr., "Ideals of Human Excellence and Preserving Natural Environments," *Environmental Ethics* 5 (1983): 211–24; Mark Sagoff, "On Preserving the Natural Environment," *Yale Law Journal* 84 (1974): 205–67; and Bryan G. Norton, "Environmental Ethics and Weak Anthropocentrism," *Environmental Ethics* 6 (1984): 131–48.

3. It is of some interest that Weston omits discussing the work of J. Baird Callicott, one of the leading writers on the concept of "intrinsic value" in envi-

ronmental ethics. Is it because Callicott "dissolves" the problem of intrinsic value in a way that undermines Weston's argument? See the text below for more discussion.

4. See, e.g., "Organism, Community, and the 'Substitution Problem,' " *Environmental Ethics* 7 (1985): 241–56.

5. The reference is to Holmes Rolston, III, "Values Gone Wild," *Inquiry* 26 (1983): 181–83.

6. See, e.g., Holmes Rolston, III, "Can and Ought We to Follow Nature?" *Environmental Ethics* 1 (1979): 7–30, and "Valuing Wildlands," *Environmental Ethics* 7 (1985): 23–48.

7. Holmes Rolston, III, "Are Values in Nature Objective or Subjective?" *Environmental Ethics* 4 (1982): 147.

8. J. Baird Callicott, "Hume's *Is/Ought* Dichotomy and the Relation of Ecology to Leopold's Land Ethic," *Environmental Ethics* 4 (1982): 163–74; "Nonanthropocentric Value Theory and Environmental Ethics," *American Philosophical Quarterly* 21 (1984): 299–309; "On the Intrinsic Value of Nonhuman Species," in Bryan G. Norton, ed., *The Preservation of Species* (Princeton: Princeton University Press, 1986), pp. 138–72; and "Intrinsic Value, Quantum Theory, and Environmental Ethics," *Environmental Ethics* 7 (1985): 257–75.

9. J. Baird Callicott, "On the Intrinsic Value of Nonhuman Species," pp. 142–43.

10. See, e.g., Tom Regan, "The Nature and Possibility of an Environmental Ethic," *Environmental Ethics* 3 (1981): 19–34; and Paul W. Taylor, "The Ethics of Respect for Nature," *Environmental Ethics* 3 (1981): 197–218.

11. Richard Sylvan, "A Critique of Deep Ecology," *Radical Philosophy* 40 (Summer 1985): 11.

12. Compare the argument of John Rodman, "The Liberation of Nature?" *Inquiry* 20 (1977): 83–131.

13. In one of the best treatments of intrinsic value in nature, Andrew Brennan discusses the possibility of attributing intrinsic value to systems as well as to individuals. See his "The Moral Standing of Natural Objects," *Environmental Ethics* 6 (1984): 35–56. Weston fails to mention this article in his critique.

14. Rolston, "Are Values in Nature Objective or Subjective?" p. 146.

15. Again let me emphasize that it is a serious mistake for Weston to use the work of Tom Regan as paradigmatic of environmental ethics as a discipline. Regan simply is *not* a "mainstream" environmental philosopher. He has a different agenda; the moral treatment of animals (indeed, the *higher* animals). Perhaps Weston has a distorted view of the methodology of environmental ethics because he focuses on the wrong philosopher. A good critical discussion of Regan's treatment of environmental ethics can be found in J. Baird Callicott's review of Tom Regan, *The Case for Animal Rights*, in *Environmental Ethics* 7 (1985): 365–72.

16. Rolston, "Values Gone Wild," p. 183.

17. There is always a danger, however, in being too concrete. Focusing only

on specific situations may lead to a kind of ad hoc, contingent, moral thinking. Moral judgment, if it is to be at all defensible, must be based on some commonly accepted general principles—in the case of environmental protection, these might include beauty, diversity, and stability. These principles then must be applied to the specific situation—or at least, they must be found there— before a judgment about a particular situation can be made.

18. See the penetrating discussion by Mark Sagoff, "Do We Need a Land Use Ethic?" *Environmental Ethics* 3 (1981): 293–308.

19. Eric Katz, "Utilitarianism and Preservation," *Environmental Ethics* 1 (1979): 357–64.

6

Defending the Use of Animals by Business: Animal Liberation and Environmental Ethics

Despite its title, this essay is not a full-fledged defense of the treatment of animals by the industrial, scientific, and agricultural communities. Written for a national conference on "Business, Ethics, and the Environment" held at the Center for Business Ethics at Bentley College in October 1989, the essay uses the commercial and scientific treatment of animals as a starting point for an argument advocating ecological holism. I review the arguments in favor of the moral consideration of animals and show that environmental ethics is basically incompatible with an ethic of animal liberation. I return to several themes presented in earlier essays, such as the plurality of values in a community-based holism, and the difference between domesticated and wild species of animals. In one sense, "Defending the Use of Animals by Business" represents a turning point in the growth of my environmental philosophy. By the time it was written (in 1989) the development of my theoretical position of a modified community holism was essentially complete. I believed that there was no longer anything to be gained by repeating theoretical arguments in favor of an environmental ethic. Now was the time to begin applying my vision of an ethic based on ecological community to practical issues in environmental policy. This essay was published in Business, Ethics and the Environment: The Public Policy Debate, *ed. W. Michael Hoffman, Robert Frederick, and Edward S. Petry, Jr. (New York: Quorum Books, 1991), pp. 223–32, and is reprinted with permission of Greenwood Publishing Group, Inc., Westport, Conn. Copyright © 1990 by the Center for Business Ethics at Bentley College.*

In recent years much attention has been focused on the proper treatment of animals by business. Among those who care about animals,
two concerns seem paramount: that animals are being used for the
wrong purposes and that animals are being mistreated or abused,
whether or not the purposes are justifiable. Thus, arguments are made
against the use of animals for fur, food, or experimentation in the cos-
metics industry; additionally, arguments are made against the treatment of animals in laboratories, on factory farms, and in zoological
parks. In part, the role of business in the misuse and treatment of animals has received attention as a spillover from the organized protests
against the use of animals in scientific and medical research.[1] Also in
part, business has been scrutinized because of environmental concerns;
the annual Canadian baby seal hunt and, more recently, the Exxon oil
spill in Alaska draw attention to the killing and abuse of wild animals.
But more directly, business has come under increasing attack from
those who advocate the general principle that animals deserve moral
consideration, that animals have both legal and moral rights, that animals should be "liberated" from the oppression and domination of
humanity.

The animal liberation movement descends from the animal welfare
or humane movement of the late nineteenth and early twentieth centuries, but its purposes and tactics clearly differ. The goals of animal
liberation go far beyond urging the benevolent care of pets and animals used for labor. Animal liberation seeks to end all unnecessary
cruelty and suffering that humans perpetrate on animal life, especially
the use of animals in scientific experimentation, in industrial product
testing, and in food production. Animal liberation thus advocates vegetarianism and alternative methods of research and experimentation.
Most animal liberationists use traditional tactics for effecting social
change: lobbying, boycotts, and philosophical and political arguments.
But some elements of the movement have resorted to acts of violence,
coercion, and terrorism. In 1989 demonstrators at Saks Fifth Avenue in
New York protested the sale of furs and harassed wearers of fur coats
who passed by the store. One splinter group, the Animal Liberation
Front, is considered a terrorist organization by the FBI. Recently national attention was focused on this group because of the alleged bombing attempt of a surgical supply company that practiced vivisection
in the sales demonstrations of its surgical tools.[2]

And so business is faced with the task of defending its treatment of
animals from the moral arguments and political tactics of the animal
liberation movement. In this essay I present a method—or at least, sev-

eral arguments—that business can employ to blunt these attacks. I suggest that the adoption by business of a more conscious environmentalism can serve as a defense against the animal liberation movement. This strategy may seem paradoxical: how can business defend its use of animals by advocating the protection of the environment? But the paradox disappears once we see that animal liberation and environmentalism are incompatible practical moral doctrines.

Arguments in favor of the direct moral consideration of animals follow two major lines of thought.[3] First, it is argued that no morally relevant criterion can be applied to all human beings to differentiate them from nonhuman animals. Traditional criteria such as rationality, autonomy, or linguistic capability are not possessed by all humans. Other criteria, such as the possession of an immortal soul, are problematic at best. Thus, the animal liberationist argues that a moral preference for humans over animals, insofar as it is based on mere species membership, is an irrational prejudice analogous to racial or sexual bias. Animal liberationists often label such arguments "speciesist."[4] Like racism or sexism, speciesism is a groundless bias in favor of one's own kind.

This first argument is essentially negative. It demonstrates the absence of a significant difference between humans and other animals in the establishment of moral consideration. The second argument for the moral consideration of animals is positive. It claims that moral standing is derived from the ability to feel pleasure and pain or, as it is commonly termed in the literature, sentience. As Peter Singer writes, "If a being suffers there can be no moral justification for refusing to take that suffering into consideration. . . . If a being is not capable of suffering, or of experiencing enjoyment or happiness, there is nothing to be taken into account."[5] Any moral agent must consider the pain and pleasure that result from his or her actions. This is the minimum requirement of morality. Since most animals experience pain and pleasure, a moral agent must take these experiences into account. Animals must be given moral standing, moral consideration. The capacity to suffer, to undergo experiences of pain and pleasure, is the primary moral similarity between human and nonhuman animals. Sentience, then, is the nonarbitrary, nonspeciesist basis of moral value.

These two lines of argument are generally combined to form the strongest case for the moral consideration of animals. Yet the two arguments are actually quite different; they derive from totally different philosophical roots. The second argument, with its focus on pain and pleasure, is an outgrowth of classical Benthamite utilitarianism. It is a consequentialist doctrine, in which pain and pleasure are the only two determinants of moral value.[6] The first argument, with its focus on rights, uses a deontological model of thought. Within this model, the central problem in normative ethics becomes the search for a moral criterion that is not directly connected to the results of an action. The possession of rights is not determined by the consequences of action but by the inherent qualities of the possessor. The differing supports for the moral consideration of animals suggest the possibility of differing critical attacks. Each line of thought can be subjected to a unique criticism that weakens the case for animal liberation and points in the direction of a more comprehensive doctrine of environmentalism.

The utilitarian criterion of sentience is problematic for at least two reasons. First, how far down the scale of animal life can one safely assume the experience of pain and pleasure? Is the kind of experience required for animal suffering (and hence for the moral consideration of animals) limited to the so-called higher animals—mammals, birds, and so on? One author suggests that insects have the requisite nervous system for the possible experience of pain.[7] Insects then would be serious candidates for moral consideration. Does this possibility suggest that the utilitarian basis of an animal liberation ethic can be pushed too far, offering a reductio ad absurdum of the position? Or does it place limits on the operational application of the concept of sentience, rendering only higher animals morally considerable? Both alternatives are problematic. The first case includes too many animals under the purview of moral consideration. The second presents a new, more subtle form of speciesism: only animals that resemble humans, who experience pain and pleasure in ways recognizable to us, gain entry into the moral kingdom.[8]

To a certain extent, this criticism is a theoretical quibble. Except for insects killed by pesticides, almost all animals used in business meet the minimum standards of sentient experience. Animals that are used in scientific research, that are hunted, or that are raised for food clearly do feel pain. Neverthelesss, this mere theoretical criticism tends to demonstrate that the arguments in favor of the moral consideration of animals are not consistent. There are implications, weak points, and even holes in the arguments that are not addressed by advocates of animal liberation.

The second problem with the criterion of sentience is the contextual significance of pain. The utilitarian advocate of animal consideration contends that pain is an intrinsic evil, but the argument focuses on an abstract concept of pain separated from natural reality. In its concrete natural existence pain has an instrumental function in organisms: a warning of internal stress or external danger. Understood in context, pain is not an evil at all; it is an essential part of a successful organic life. An organism that does not feel pain cannot survive. It cannot reproduce itself, condemning its species to extinction. Once one adopts a more contextual environmental perspective, one can understand the role of pain in organic life. In the natural world pain serves a crucial positive function. But the hallmark of utilitarian animal liberation—the absolute, abstract denial of pain—ignores this context. It proscribes the infliction of any and all pain. Such a denial is both practically impossible and conceptually meaningless.[9]

The deontological concern for animal rights fares no better as a moral argument. The advocates of animal moral consideration claim that the denial of animal rights without a specific moral criterion shows a preference for human beings that is analogous to racism or sexism. The absence of a nonarbitrary moral criterion that distinguishes all humans from all nonhuman animals leaves no justifiable defense of preferential treatment for human beings. This animal rights argument rests on the claim that "marginal" cases of humanity—the severely retarded, the insane, comatose humans, newborns with severe birth defects, fetuses—are treated as normal or typical humans from the moral point of view. The crucial point is that even though marginal humans do not meet standards of moral consideration such as rationality or linguistic capability, they are given a full moral standing that is denied to animals—even when the animals are not inferior to the marginal humans. The moral consideration of marginal humans thus shows the speciesist bias in our treatment of animals.

This argument is empirically false. No observer of the contemporary world, or the history of humanity, could possibly believe that marginal humans are given full moral consideration. The cases obviously differ, but all in all, these humans are clearly deemed to have less moral value because of their reduced capacities. It is true, as animal rightists claim, that we do not eat retarded humans or babies. But we do perform scientific and medical experiments on marginal humans, and we generally find it easier to sacrifice their lives. The factual moral truth, however depressing as it might be, is that the hierarchy of moral value exemplified in the human treatment of animals is echoed and repeated in the human treatment of other humans. The animal rightist claim about human speciesism is hollow, for it assumes the equal treatment of all humans, a treatment that is superior to all animals.[10] There is not an arbitrary speciesist preference for humans. There is the imperfect application of ambiguous criteria such as rationality, autonomy, and linguistic capability. These criteria are used, not altogether consistently, to determine the moral considerability of various classes of humans and nonhumans alike. A recognition of this picture of moral thinking softens the sharpest attack of the animal rights advocates.

Defenders of the use of animals by business and industry thus can raise several problems for questioning the moral consideration of animals. These criticisms are supplemented by the adoption of an "environmental ethic," that is, a direct concern for the moral consideration of nature and natural processes.

The term *environmental ethic* has been used extensively since the mid-1970s to denote a more benign relationship between humanity and the natural world. Within academic philosophy the term has developed in several overlapping, but often contradictory, directions.[11] This is not the proper place for a review of these various formulations. Instead I will merely suggest that the most useful environmental ethic for business to adopt as a countermeasure to animal liberation is ecological holism. This ethic uses the normal functioning of natural ecological systems as the baseline for human decisions that affect the environment. The primary and direct ethical focus is on the continuation of environments, natural ecological systems, not the lives or experiences of individual natural entities. As Also Leopold wrote over forty years ago, "A thing is right when it tends to preserve the integrity, stability, and beauty of the biotic community. It is wrong when it tends otherwise."[12] Consequently the way animals live in and through natural ecological systems would be the model for their treatment by humans. Business, or any other human institution, would look to the operations of natural ecological systems as a guide to the proper behavior regarding animals and other natural beings.[13]

As a countermeasure to animal liberation, ecological holism reinforces the proper role of pain in organic life. Since pain is as necessary as pleasure in a successful organic life, it cannot, and should not, be considered a moral evil. Pain, and even death, are crucial aspects in the operation of natural systems. Pain is a warning to individual natural organisms. It is an instrumental good for the preservation of individual life. The death of individuals in nature is a means for reusing and redirecting the energy in the system. In being eaten by a predator, an organism "donates" its energy to another individual in the system. Its corpse decays into basic organic elements, donating its energy to the rest of the system. From an ecological point of view, it is thus a mistake to consider pain and death as merely intrinsic evils that must be eliminated.

Indeed, advocates of animal liberation have trouble with the basic natural process of predation. A utilitarian concerned with the lessening of pain in the world would be forced to prevent predation in the wild. The advocate of animal rights would also, it seems, consider the rights of the prey to be violated in the act of predation.[14] But the prevention of predation seems an absurd position to advocate; if the moral consideration of animals implies the implementation of such a moral policy, then animals cannot be morally considerable.

An environmental perspective acknowledges predation as a basic fact of natural existence. Killing other animals for food serves the interests of the individual carnivore by sustaining its life. Predation serves the interests of the carnivore species by preserving its function or niche in the ecological system. In addition, the killing of prey, often the weakest members of the herd, helps preserve and strengthen the species that is preyed upon. In sum, there is no ecological reason to attempt an elimination of pain, killing, and death in the animal kingdom.

Here the advocate of animal moral considerability can offer a serious objection: the use and mistreatment of animals by humans is not normally an act of predation in the wild. Indeed, the few humans who need to hunt for a food supply may be permitted to do so.[15] However, most of the harm inflicted on animals by humanity takes place through factory farming, scientific experimentation, and industrial testing. So, the objection goes, the beneficial instrumental value of pain in the wild is an irrelevant consideration. The pain of animals in slaughterhouses or research laboratories serves no useful natural function.

The answer to this objection lies in a consciously radical environmentalism. From the perspective of ecological holism, the pain of animals in factory farms, slaughterhouses, and research laboratories is not natural pain. The animals suffering the pain are domesticated animals. They are themselves irrelevant to a comprehensive environmental ethic.

This radical environmentalism is based on the fact that most domesticated species of animals are essentially human artifacts. For thousands of years they have been bred for the development of traits important for human life and human use. Recent advances in the technology of agriculture and recombinant DNA research only make this fact clearer. Consider the injection of antibiotics into beef cattle or the genetically altered Harvard mice that are susceptible to forms of cancer.[16] Thus, the animals used by business and industry are human creations designed to fulfill a specific human need. They are artifacts, living artifacts to be sure, but they are no more natural than the wooden table I am using to write this essay. To consider them the moral equals of wild animals—who, analogously to autonomous humans, pursue their own goals in a natural system—is a serious category mistake.[17]

Nevertheless, there are proper and improper ways to treat human artifacts. Humans may be required to grant direct moral consideration to some artifacts. Works of art seem to be a paradigm example.[18] So the defender of the business use of animals may be led to a kind of moral pluralism in which various kinds of natural and artificial entities, human and nonhuman organisms, natural individuals and collectives, are each determined to have differing amounts of moral value. Adopting a serious environmental ethic may involve remapping the entire landscape of our moral obligations, so that we take into account wild and domestic animals, marginal humans, plants, ecosystems, nonliving natural entities, species, and even future generations. This remapping is clearly a formidable task, but I believe that it will yield more moral truth than the overly easy utilitarian and rights-based arguments proposed by the advocates of animal liberation.[19]

One possible direction for the development of moral pluralism is an emphasis on the context of moral decision making. I criticized the utilitarian consideration of animal pain as being too abstract. The value or disvalue of pain can be understood only in the exact context of an organism's life. This contextual approach to ethical decision making should be generalized to include all practical moral thought. An emphasis on context is inseparable from moral pluralism. This ethical viewpoint implies that there is no one objective overall moral standard. Various criteria—such as sentience, rationality, life, beauty, integrity—are applicable in varying situations. In one situation it may be morally obligatory to treat a dog better than a human; at a different time or situation the human would come first. The point is that no moral decision can be made abstracted from the context of real life. The concrete situation determines the proper moral outcome.

I conclude by returning to the defense of business in its use of animals for food, fur, and research. The argument presented here suggests that business can blunt the criticisms of the animal liberation movement if it adopts an ethic of ecological holism and moral pluralism. Business must stress that the primary value to be promoted in the human interaction with the animal kingdom is the natural fit with ecological processes.[20] Pain and death are not absolute or intrinsic evils. They serve important instrumental functions in the preservation of individuals, species, and systems. They need not be avoided at all costs. As long as animals are used in ways that respect their natural integrity or their natural functions in ecological systems, then they are being treated with the proper moral consideration. Human beings, as natural omnivores, are not acting directly against moral value when they raise and kill animals for food.[21] The human use of domestic animals falls outside the realm of environmental ethics; domestic animals are nothing more than living human artifacts. This conclusion does not deny that there are proper and improper ways of treating animals bred for human purposes; however, these moral constraints are not the absolutes proposed by animal liberationists. Consequently business should argue for a contextual approach to the human treatment of animals. Harms and benefits, value and disvalue, can be determined only in concrete situations. Before making a moral decision, the complex relationship between human and animal, society and nature, individual and species must be understood.

I have consciously avoided presenting specific proposals. I recommend a general approach to applied ethics that eschews the determination of specific ethical commands abstracted from actual situations. Nevertheless, this defense of the use of animals by business and industry does not imply approbation of current practices. Many of the specific techniques of factory farming, to cite one example, cause pain and suffering that is unnecessary from even a perspective of ecological holism. Although I have argued that pain is not an absolute evil and that it is a mistake to consider it as an evil abstracted from a concrete situation, I am not suggesting that it is never an evil in specific contexts. It can be unnecessary. Humans can reform their practices so that they gain the benefits of using animals without mistreating them. Business and industry ought to modify existing technologies in the raising, harvesting, and slaughtering of animals, even as they defend themselves against the critical attacks of animal liberation.

A final impetus for reform would be the sincere adoption of environmentalist attitudes. An ethic of ecological holism would require major revisions in human activities regarding wildlife and the natural environment. Industry would be compelled to develop alternative technologies with low impact on natural evolutionary processes, such as solar power and organic pesticides. These reforms would affect the animal kingdom in positive ways, for reducing air and water pollution benefits all organic life. However, the reforms required by an attitude of environmentalism are minuscule compared to the reforms demanded by the animal liberation movement. That prudential reason alone should be enough to convince business to adopt an environmental ethic.

Notes

I thank Michal McMahon for helpful comments on an earlier version of this essay.

1. One medical researcher gave up fourteen years of research because of protests against animal use. See Sarah Lyall, "Pressed on Animal Rights, Researcher Gives Up Grant," *New York Times*, November 22, 1988, sec. 2, p. 1.

2. The antifur demonstration was reported in Carole Agus, "The Fur and the Fury," *Newsday*, February 21, 1989, pt. 2, pp. 16–18. For more on fur protests see James Hirsch, "Animal-Rights Groups Step Up Attacks on Furriers," *New York Times*, November 27, 1988, sec. 1, p. 50. In the last year, the *New York Times* has printed several articles on the "animal rights" movement—a sure sign of public acceptance of the merits of the debate. See Kirk Johnson, "Arrest Points Up Split in Animal-Rights Movement," *New York Times*, November 13, 1988, sec. 2, p. 40; Robert A. Hamilton, "Advocates of Animal Rights See Influence Grow in State," *New York Times*, November 27, 1988, sec. 23, p. 1; Katherine Bishop, "From Shop to Lab to Farm, Animal Rights Battle Is Felt," *New York Times*, January 14, 1989, sec. 1, p. 1; Barnaby J. Feder, "Research Labs Look Away from Laboratory Animals," *New York Times*, January 29, 1989, sec. 4, p. 24. The Trutt bombing case was originally reported by Robert D. McFadden, "A Bombing Is Thwarted in Norwalk," *New York Times*, November 12, 1988, sec. 1, p. 29, and McFadden, "Norwalk Bomb Inquiry: Did Suspect Have Help?" *New York Times*, November 14, 1989, sec. 2, p. 3.

3. These two lines are represented by Tom Regan, *The Case for Animal Rights* (Berkeley: University of California Press, 1983), and Peter Singer, *Animal Liberation: A New Ethics for Our Treatment of Animals* (New York: Avon Books, 1977).

4. Singer attributes the term *speciesism* to Richard Ryder, author of *Victims of Science* (London: Davis-Poynter, 1975); see *Animal Liberation*, pp. 7, 25.

5. Singer, *Animal Liberation*, p. 8.

6. Hedonistic utilitarianism, the moral doctrine that judges human action by the resulting pleasure and pain, derives from Jeremy Bentham: "Nature has placed mankind under the governance of two sovereign masters, *pain and pleasure.*" *An Introduction to the Principles of Morals and Legislation* (1789; rpt. *The Utilitarians*, Garden City, N.Y.: Anchor, 1973), p. 17. Bentham extends the moral significance of pain and pleasure to the animal kingdom; in an oft-quoted passage, he writes: "The French have already discovered that the blackness of the skin is no reason why a human being should be abandoned without redress to the caprice of a tormentor. It may come one day to be recognized, that the number of the legs, the villosity of the skin, or the termination of the *os sacrum*, are reasons equally insufficient for abandoning a sensitive being to the same fate. What else is it that should trace the insuperable line? Is it the faculty of reason, or, perhaps, the faculty of discourse? But a full-grown horse or dog is beyond comparison a more rational, as well as a more conversable animal, than an infant of a day, or a week, or even a month, old. But suppose the case

were otherwise, what would it avail? The question is not, Can they *reason?* nor, Can they *talk?* but, Can they *Suffer?" Utilitarians,* p. 381.

7. Jeffrey A. Lockwood, "Not to Harm a Fly: Our Ethical Obligations to Insects," *Between the Species* 4 (3) (1988): 204–11.

8. See John Rodman, "The Liberation of Nature?" *Inquiry* 20 (1977): 83–131, esp. 90–91.

9. One of the most important criticisms of the animal liberationist use of pain can be found in J. Baird Callicott, "Animal Liberation: A Triangular Affair," *Environmental Ethics* 2 (1980): 311–38, esp. 332–33. Another movement in ethics that emphasizes context is feminist ethics, although many feminists advocate vegetarianism and other nonharmful treatment of animals. I argue that a proper attention to context permits the use and eating of animals. For feminist ethics in general see Carol Gilligan, *In a Different Voice: Psychological Theory and Women's Development* (Cambridge: Harvard University Press, 1982). For a feminist perspective on environmental issues, see Jim Cheney, "Ecofeminism and Deep Ecology," *Environmental Ethics* 9 (1987): 115–45; for a feminist perspective on animals, see Cora Diamond, "Eating Meat and Eating People," *Philosophy* 53 (1978): 464–79.

10. Many animals are treated better than humans. I provide my pet dog, for example, with a better life than millions of humans in the world. His nutritional and medical needs are met to a higher level (I am guessing) than any individual in the entire homeless population of New York City or in the famine regions of the Third World. Since we do not normally condemn this "preferential" treatment of pet animals, we can see that we are not speciesists.

11. The large literature on environmental ethics cannot be cited here. Some of the best book-length treatments of the subject are Mark Sagoff, *The Economy of the Earth* (Cambridge: Cambridge University Press, 1988), Holmes Rolston, III, *Environmental Ethics: Duties to and Values in the Natural World* (Philadelphia: Temple University Press, 1988), and Paul Taylor, *Respect for Nature: A Theory of Environmental Ethics* (Princeton: Princeton University Press, 1986). Two excellent anthologies are Donald Scherer and Thomas Attig, eds., *Ethics and the Environment* (Englewood Cliffs, N.J.: Prentice-Hall, 1983), and Donald VanDeVeer and Christine Pierce, eds., *People, Penguins and Plastic Trees: Basic Issues in Environmental Ethics* (Belmont, Calif.: Wadsworth, 1986). Current debates in the field appear in the journal *Environmental Ethics*, ed. Eugene Hargrove, Department of Philosophy, University of North Texas. I have published an annotated bibliography of recent titles in the field: "Environmental Ethics: A Select Annotated Bibliography, 1983–1987," *Research in Philosophy and Technology* 9 (1989): 251–85.

12. Aldo Leopold, *A Sand County Almanac* (1949; rpt., New York: Ballantine, 1970), p. 262.

13. Rolston, *Environmental Ethics*, pp. 45–125.

14. For more on predation, see Steve F. Sapontzis, "Predation," *Ethics and Animals* 5 (2) (June 1984): 27–38, and J. Baird Callicott's review of Tom Regan's *The Case for Animal Rights* in *Environmental Ethics* 7 (1985): 365–72.

15. So argues Peter Wenz, despite his concern for the moral consideration of animals. See his *Environmental Justice* (Albany: SUNY Press, 1988), pp. 324–31.

16. The creation and patenting of the so-called Harvard mice is reported in "U.S. Plans to Issue First Patent on Animal Today," *New York Times*, April 12, 1988, sec. 1, p. 21, and Keith Schneider, "Harvard Gets a Mouse Patent, a World First," *New York Times*, April 13, 1988, sec. 1, p. 1.

17. See Callicott, "Animal Liberation," pp. 329–36, and Rodman, "Liberation of Nature?" pp. 93–118, for more on domestication and its significance for animal and environmental ethics.

18. For discussion, see Alan Tormey, "Aesthetic Rights," *Journal of Aesthetics and Art Criticism* 32 (1973): 163–70, and a reply by David Goldblatt, "Do Works of Art Have Rights?" *Journal of Aesthetics and Art Criticism* 35 (1976): 69–77.

19. The idea of a morally pluralistic system of ethical value is being discussed seriously in the literature. See Christopher Stone, *Earth and Other Ethics: The Case for Moral Pluralism* (New York: Harper & Row, 1987); Wenz, *Environmental Justice*, esp. pp. 310–43; Callicott, "Animal Liberation and Environmental Ethics: Back Together Again," *Between the Species* 4 (3) (1988): 163–69; and my two articles, "Organism, Community and 'The Substitution Problem,'" *Environmental Ethics* 7 (1985): 241–56, and "Buffalo-Killing and the Valuation of Species," in *Values and Moral Standing*, ed. L. W. Sumner (Bowling Green, Ohio: Bowling Green State University Press, 1986), pp. 114–23.

20. See Rolston, *Environmental Ethics*.

21. But they may be acting indirectly against their interests and the overall health of the biosphere. Meat production is one of the most inefficient means of converting biomass to protein. There would be more food for the human population of the earth if we ceased meat production and shifted to a basic vegetarian diet.

Part II

Restoration and Domination

7

The Big Lie: Human Restoration of Nature

"The Big Lie" is the first in a series of four essays that focus on the human attempt to modify, manipulate, and control the processes of the natural environment. If we are required by an environmental ethic to respect the autonomous development of the natural community, then human intervention into natural processes must be severely limited. To illustrate this practical consequence of an environmental ethic I closely examine the field of ecological restoration and redesign, and in particular, the arguments of a professional forester and environmentalist, Chris Maser. Maser claims that it is possible to plan and design a sustainable forest, so that we humans can enjoy the benefits of the forest—wood production, protection of wildlife, maintenance of watersheds—while at the same time preserving the natural environment. I argue that the imposition of human plans—human ideals, goals, and designs— converts natural processes into human artifacts. The natural environment cannot be redesigned or restored and remain natural. My argument further develops a comparison between the natural environment and the creation of artwork originally proposed by Robert Elliot in "Faking Nature," Inquiry 25 *(1982): 81–93.*

"The Big Lie" has a complicated history. Written for a conference on "Moral Philosophy in the Public Domain" at the University of British Columbia in June 1990, it was originally published in Research in Philosophy and Technology 12 *(1992). Before its publication, it was shown in manuscript form (without my knowledge) to Bill Jordan, the editor of* Restoration and Management Notes, *the official journal of the Society for Ecological Restoration. Jordan was anxious to have the membership of his society read the essay, so a slightly modified version, with a new introduction and addi-*

tional material on the work of restorationist Steve Packard, was published as "Restoration and Redesign: The Ethical Significance of the Human Intervention in Nature" in Restoration and Management Notes *9:2 (Winter 1991): 90–96. In the version of the essay in this collection I have inserted the additional material on Packard's restoration of the tallgrass savanna that did not originally appear in "The Big Lie."*

> *The trail of the human serpent is thus over everything.*
>   —William James, *Pragmatism*

I

I begin with an empirical point, based on my own random observations: the idea that humanity can restore or repair the natural environment has begun to play an important part in decisions regarding environmental policy. We are urged to plant trees to reverse the "greenhouse effect." Real estate developers are obligated to restore previously damaged acreage in exchange for building permits.[1] The U.S. National Park Service spends $33 million to "rehabilitate" 39,000 acres of the Redwood Creek watershed.[2] And the U.S. Forest Service is criticized for its "plantation" mentality: it is harvesting trees from old-growth forests rather than "redesigning" forests according to the sustainable principles of nature. "Restoration forestry is the only true forestry," claims an environmentally conscious former employee of the Bureau of Land Management.[3]

These policies present the message that humanity should repair the damage that human intervention has caused the natural environment. The message is an optimistic one, for it implies that we recognize the harm we have caused in the natural environment and that we possess the means and will to correct these harms. These policies also make us feel good; the prospect of restoration relieves the guilt we feel about the destruction of nature. The wounds we have inflicted on the natural world are not permanent; nature can be made "whole" again. Our natural resource base and foundation for survival can be saved by the appropriate policies of restoration, regeneration, and redesign.

It is also apparent that these ideas are not restricted to policymakers, environmentalists, or the general public—they have begun to pervade the normative principles of philosophers concerned with developing an adequate environmental ethic. Paul Taylor uses a concept of "restitutive justice" both as one of the basic rules of duty in his biocentric ethic and as a "priority principle" to resolve competing claims.[4] The basic idea of this rule is that human violators of nature will in some way repair or compensate injured natural entities and systems. Peter Wenz also endorses a principle of restitution as being essential to an adequate theory of environmental ethics; he then attacks Taylor's theory for not presenting a coherent principle.[5] The idea that humanity is morally responsible for reconstructing natural areas and entities— species, communities, ecosystems—thus becomes a central concern of an applied environmental ethic.

In this essay I question the environmentalists' concern for the restoration of nature and argue against the optimistic view that humanity has the obligation and ability to repair or reconstruct damaged natural systems. This conception of environmental policy and environmental ethics is based on a misperception of natural reality and a misguided understanding of the human place in the natural environment. On a simple level, it is the same kind of "technological fix" that has engendered the environmental crisis. Human science and technology will fix, repair, and improve natural processes. On a deeper level, it is an expression of an anthropocentric world view, in which human interests shape and redesign a comfortable natural reality. A "restored" nature is an artifact created to meet human satisfactions and interests. Thus, on the most fundamental level, it is an unrecognized manifestation of the insidious dream of the human domination of nature. Once and for all, humanity will demonstrate its mastery of nature by "restoring" and repairing the degraded ecosystems of the biosphere. Cloaked in an environmental consciousness, human power will reign supreme.

II

It has been eight years since Robert Elliott published his sharp and accurate criticism of "the restoration thesis."[6] In an article entitled "Faking Nature," Elliott examined the moral objections to the practical environmental policy of restoring damaged natural systems, locations, and landscapes. For the sake of argument, Elliott assumed that the restoration of a damaged area could be recreated perfectly, so that the area would appear in its original condition after the restoration was completed. He then argued that the perfect copy of the natural area would be of less value than the original, for the newly restored natural area would be analogous to an art forgery. Two points seem crucial to Elliott's argument. First, the value of objects can be explained "in terms of their origins, in terms of the kinds of processes that brought them into being."[7] We value an art work in part because of the fact that a particular artist, a human individual, created the work at a precise moment in historical time. Similarly, we value a natural area because of its "special kind of continuity with the past." But to understand the art work or the natural area in its historical context we require a special kind of insight or knowledge. Thus, the second crucial point of Elliot's argument is the co-existence of "understanding and evaluation." The art expert brings to the analysis and evaluation of a work of art a full range of information about the artist, the period, the intentions of the work, and so on. In a similar way, the evaluation of a natural area is informed by a detailed knowledge of ecological processes, a knowledge that can be learned as easily as the history of art.[8] To value the restored landscape as much as the original is thus a kind of ignorance; we are being fooled by the superficial similarities to the natural area, just as the ignorant art "appreciator" is fooled by the appearance of the art forgery.

Although Elliot's argument has had a profound effect on my own thinking about environmental issues, I believed that the problem he uses as a starting point is purely theoretical, almost fanciful.[9] After all, who would possibly believe that a land developer or a strip mining company would actually restore a natural area to its original state? Elliot himself claims that "the restoration thesis" is generally used "as a way of undermining the arguments of conservationists."[10] Thus it is with concern that I discover that serious environmentalist thinkers, as noted above, have argued for a position similar to Elliot's "restoration thesis." The restoration of a damaged nature is seen not only as a practical option for environmental policy but also as a moral obligation for right-thinking environmentalists. If we are to continue human projects which (unfortunately) impinge on the natural environment (it is claimed), then we must repair the damage. In a few short years a "sea-change" has occurred: what Elliot attacked as both a physical impossibility and a moral mistake is now advocated as proper environmental policy. Am I alone in thinking that something has gone wrong here?

Perhaps not enough people have read Elliot's arguments; neither Taylor nor Wenz, the principal advocates of restitutive environmental justice, list this article in their notes or bibliographies. Perhaps we need to re-examine the idea of re-creating a natural landscape; in what sense is this action analogous to an art forgery? Perhaps we need to push beyond Elliot's analysis, to use his arguments as a starting point for a deeper investigation into the fundamental errors of restoration policy.

III

My initial reaction to the possibility of restoration policy is almost entirely visceral: I am outraged by the idea that a technologically created "nature" will be passed off as reality. The human presumption that we are capable of this technological fix demonstrates (once again) the arrogance with which humanity surveys the natural world. Whatever the problem may be, there will be a technological, mechanical, or scientific solution. Human engineering will modify the secrets of natural processes and effect a satisfactory result. Chemical fertilizers will increase food production; pesticides will control disease-carrying insects; hydroelectric dams will harness the power of our rivers. The familiar list goes on and on.

The relationship between this technological mind-set and the environmental crisis has been amply demonstrated, and need not concern us here.[11] My interest is narrower. I want to focus on the creation of artifacts, for that is what technology does. The re-created natural environment that is the end result of a restoration project is nothing more than an artifact created for human use. The problem for an applied environmental ethic is the determination of the moral value of this artifact.

Recently, Michael Losonsky has pointed out how little we know about the nature, structure, and meaning of artifacts. "[C]ompared to the scientific study of nature, the scientific study of artifacts is in its infancy."[12] What is clear, of course, is that an artifact is not equivalent to a natural object; but the precise difference, or set of differences, is not readily apparent. Indeed, when we consider objects such as beaver dams, we are unsure if we are dealing with natural objects or artifacts. Fortunately, however, these kinds of animal-created artifacts can be safely ignored in the present investigation. Nature restoration projects are obviously human. A human built dam is clearly artifactual.

The concepts of function and purpose are central to an understanding of artifacts. Losonsky rejects the Aristotelian view that artifacts (as distinguished from natural objects) have no inner nature or hidden essence that can be discovered. Artifacts have a "nature" that is partially comprised of three features: "internal structure, purpose, and manner of use." This nature, in turn, explains why artifacts "have predictable lifespans during which they undergo regular and predictable changes."[13] The structure, function, and use of the artifacts determine to some extent the changes which they undergo. Clocks would not develop in a manner which prevented the measurement of time.

Natural objects lack the kind of purpose and function found in artifacts. As Andrew Brennan has argued, natural entities have no "intrinsic functions," as he calls them, for they were not the result of design. They were not created for a particular purpose; they have no set manner of use. Although we often speak as if natural individuals (for example, predators) have roles to play in ecosystemic well-being (the maintenance of optimum population levels), this kind of talk is either metaphorical or fallacious. No one created or designed the mountain lion as a regulator of the deer population.[14]

This is the key point. Natural individuals were not designed for a purpose. They lack intrinsic functions, making them different from human-created artifacts. Artifacts, I claim, are essentially anthropocentric. They are created for human use, human purpose—they serve a function for human life. Their existence is centered on human life. It would be impossible to imagine an artifact not designed to meet a human purpose. Without a foreseen use the object would not be created. This is completely different from the way natural entities and species evolve to fill ecological niches in the biosphere.

The doctrine of anthropocentrism is thus an essential element in understanding the meaning of artifacts. This conceptual relationship is not generally problematic, for most artifacts are human creations designed for use in human social and cultural contexts. But once we begin to redesign natural systems and processes, once we begin to create restored natural environments, we impose our anthropocentric purposes on areas that exist outside human society. We will construct so-called natural objects on the model of human desires, interests, and satisfactions. Depending on the adequacy of our technology, these restored and redesigned natural areas will appear more or less natural, but they will never be natural—they will be anthropocentrically designed human artifacts.

A disturbing example of this conceptual problem applied to environmental policy can be found in Chris Maser's *The Redesigned Forest*. Maser is a former research scientist for the United States Department of Interior Bureau of Land Management. His book attests to his deeply felt commitment to the policy of "sustainable" forestry, as opposed to the short-term expediency of present-day forestry practices. Maser argues for a forestry policy that "restores" the forest as it harvests it; we must be true foresters and not "plantation" managers.

Nonetheless, Maser's plans for "redesigning" forests reveal several problems about the concepts and values implicit in restoration policy. First, Maser consistently compares the human design of forests with Nature's design. The entire first chapter is a series of short sections comparing the two "designs." In the "Introduction," he writes, "[W]e are redesigning our forests from Nature's blueprint to humanity's blueprint."[15] But Nature, of course, does not have a blueprint, nor a design. As a zoologist, Maser knows this, but his metaphorical talk is dangerous. It implies that we can discover the plan, the methods, the processes of nature, and mold them to our purposes.

Maser himself often writes as if he accepts that implication. The second problem with his argument is the comparison of nature to a mechanism that we do not fully understand. The crucial error we make in simplifying forest ecology—turning forests into plantations—is that we are assuming our design for the forest mechanism is better than nature's. "Forests are not automobiles in which we can tailor artificially substituted parts for original parts."[16] How true. But Maser's argument against this substitution is empirical: "A forest cannot be 'rebuilt' and remain the same forest, but we could probably rebuild a forest similar to the original if we knew how. No one has ever done it. . . . [W]e do not have a parts catalog, or a maintenance manual. . . ."[17] The implication is that if we did have a catalog and manual, if nature were known as well as artifactual machines, then the restoration of forests would be morally and practically acceptable. This conclusion serves as Maser's chief argument for the preservation of old-growth and other unmanaged forests: "We have to maintain some original, unmanaged old-growth forest, mature forest, and young-growth forest as parts catalog, maintenance manual, and service department from which to learn to practice restoration forestry."[18] Is the forest-as-parts-catalog a better guiding metaphor than the forest-as-plantation?

This mechanistic conception of nature underlies, or explains, the third problem with Maser's argument. His goal for restoration forestry, his purpose in criticizing the short-term plantation mentality, is irredeemably anthropocentric. The problem with present-day forestry practices is that they are "exclusive of all other human values except production of fast-grown wood fiber."[19] It is the elimination of other human values and interests that concerns Maser. "We need to learn to see the forest as the factory that produces raw materials. . . ." to meet our "common goal[:] . . . a sustainable forest for a sustainable industry for a sustainable environment for a sustainable human population."[20] Restoration forestry is necessary because it is the best method for achieving the human goods which we extract from nature. Our goal is to build a better "factory-forest," using the complex knowledge of forest ecology.

What is disturbing about Maser's position is that it comes from an environmentalist. Unlike Elliot's theoretical opponents of conservation, who wished to subvert the environmentalist position with the "restoration thesis," Maser advocates the human design of forests as a method of environmental protection and conservation for human use. His conclusion shows us the danger of using anthropocentric and mechanistic models of thought in the formulation of environmental policy. These models leave us with forests that are "factories" for the production of human commodities, spare-parts catalogs for the maintenance of the machine.

But Maser's view can be considered an extreme version of restoration thinking. Is Steve Packard's work with The Nature Conservancy a better expression of the underlying principles and values of restoration policy?[21] Is Packard's work more aligned with natural processes? Is it less technological, artifactual, and anthropocentric? Unfortunately not: even this more benign and less interventionist project of ecological restoration is based on problematic assumptions about the management of nature.

Packard describes the research and actions undertaken to rediscover and restore the tallgrass savanna or oak opening community of the Midwest. As he relates, the rediscovery of the savanna was an accidental by-product of a different project, the restoration of prairie landscapes which included a bur oak edge. Involving seven small sites with degraded "prairies," the project entailed the enlargement of the areas by clearing brush and planting prairie species in its place. "Our objective was clear," he writes. "It was to restore these tracts to their original natural condition."

But how was this goal achieved? Packard asserts that he wanted to use "natural forces" such as fire to clear the brush; but this methodology is soon abandoned: "the question was, did we have enough determination and patience to give natural processes two or three hundred years to work themselves out? Or could we find something quicker?" Thus, he writes, "we decided to leapfrog the persistent brushy border and to recut our fire lines. . . ." Although Packard is using the natural force of fire, he is employing it in an artificially accelerated manner to achieve the desired results more quickly. A similar process is used when the "seeding process" begins: naturally occurring seeds are used, but the process involves the preparation of a "savanna mix," and human decisions regarding the placement and release of the seeds.

Although I have nothing but admiration for Packard's work, and I sincerely applaud his success, the significant philosophical lesson from his restoration project is that even such a "benign" and minimal intervention compromises the natural integrity of the system being restored. Despite his goal of restoring an original natural condition, Packard is actually creating an artifactual substitute for the real savanna, one based on human technologies and designed for human purposes: a pure and grand vision of the old Midwest. The most telling passage in his chronicle of the savanna restoration is his report of the "farsighted" 1913 law which established the Forest Preserve District," a law whose statement of purpose "emboldened" Packard to accelerate the burning process. He quotes the law, with emphasis added: "to *restore*, restock, protect and preserve the natural forests and said lands . . . as nearly as may be, in their natural state and condition, for the purpose of the education, pleasure, and recreation of the public." Note that the purpose of the preservation and restoration is the production of human goods; as with all artifacts, the goal is a human benefit. Packard calls this a "noble statement." Clearly the aim of restoration is the creation of environments that are pleasing to the human population. If the restoration is done well, as in the case of Packard's savannas, the area may appear natural; but it will not be natural, since it is the result of a technological acceleration of natural forces.

I began this section with a report of my visceral reaction to the technological re-creation of natural environments. This reaction has now been explained and analyzed. Nature restoration projects are the creations of human technologies, and as such, are artifacts. But artifacts are essentially the constructs of an anthropocentric world view. They are designed by humans for humans to satisfy human interests and needs. Artifactual restored nature is thus fundamentally different from natural objects and systems which exist without human design. It is not surprising, then, that we view restored nature with a value different from the original.

IV

To this point, my analysis has supported the argument and conclusions of Elliot's criticism of "the restoration thesis." But further reflection on the nature of artifacts, and the comparison of forests to well run machines, makes me doubt the central analogy which serves as the foundation of his case. Can we compare an undisturbed natural environment to a work of art? Should we?

As noted in Section II, Elliot uses the art/nature analogy to make two fundamental points about the process of evaluation: (1) the importance of a continuous causal history; and (2) the use of knowledge about this causal history to make appropriate judgments. A work of art or a natural entity which lacks a continuous causal history, as understood by the expert in the field, would be judged inferior. If the object is "passed off" as an original, with its causal history intact, then we would judge it to be a forgery or an instance of "faked" nature.

I do not deny that this is a powerful analogy. It demonstrates the crucial importance of causal history in the analysis of value. But the analogy should not be pushed too far, for the comparison suggests that we possess an understanding of art forgery that is now simply being applied to natural objects. I doubt that our understanding of art forgery is adequate for this task. L. B. Cebik argues that an analysis of forgery involves basic ontological questions about the meaning of art. Cebik claims that it is a mistake to focus exclusively on questions of value when analyzing art forgeries, for the practice of forgery raises fundamental issues about the status of art itself.[22]

According to Cebik, an analysis of forgeries demonstrates that our understanding of art is dominated by a limiting paradigm— "production by individuals." We focus almost exclusively on the individual identity of the artist as the determining factor in assessing authenticity. "Nowhere . . . is there room for paradigmatic art being fluid, unfinished, evolving, and continuous in its creation." Cebik has in mind a dynamic, communally based art, an ever-changing neighborhood mural or music passed on for generations.[23] Another example would be classical ballet, a performance of which is a unique dynamic movement, different from every other performance of the same ballet.

These suggestions about a different paradigm of art show clearly, I think, what is wrong with the art/nature analogy as a useful analytical tool. Natural entities and systems are much more akin to the fluid evolving art of Cebik's alternative model than they are to the static, finished, individual artworks of the dominant paradigm. It is thus an error to use criteria of forgery and authenticity that derive from an individualistic, static conception of art for an evaluation of natural entities and systems. Natural entities and systems are nothing like static, finished objects of art. They are fluid, evolving systems which completely transcend the category of artist or creator. The perceived disvalue in restored natural objects does not derive from a misunderstanding over the identity of the creator of the objects. It derives instead from the misplaced category of "creator"—for natural objects do not have creators or designers as human artworks do. Once we realize that the natural entity we are viewing has been "restored" by a human artisan it ceases to be a natural object. It is not a forgery; it is an artifact.

We thus return to artifacts, and their essential anthropocentric nature. We cannot (and should not) think of natural objects as artifacts, for this imposes a human purpose or design on their very essence. As artifacts, they are evaluated by their success in meeting human interests and needs, not by their own intrinsic being. Using the art/nature analogy of forgery reinforces the impression that natural objects are similar to artifacts—artworks—and that they can be evaluated using the same anthropocentric criteria. Natural entities have to be evaluated on their own terms, not as artworks, machines, factories, or any other human-created artifact.

V

But what are the terms appropriate for the evaluation of natural objects? What criteria should be used? To answer this question we need to do more than differentiate natural objects from artifacts; we need to examine the essence or nature of natural objects. What does it mean to say that an entity is natural (and hence, not an artifact)? Is there a distinguishing mark or characteristic that determines the descriptive judgment? What makes an object natural, and why is the standard not met through the restoration process?

The simple answer to this question—a response I basically support—is that the natural is defined as being independent of the actions of humanity. Thus, Taylor advocates a principle of noninterference as a primary moral duty in his ethic of respect for nature. "[W]e put aside our personal likes and our human interests. . . . Our respect for nature means that we acknowledge the sufficiency of the natural world to sustain its own proper order throughout the whole domain of life."[24] The processes of the natural world that are free of human interference are the most natural.

There are two obvious problems with this first simple answer. First, there is the empirical point that the human effect on the environment is, by now, fairly pervasive. No part of the natural world lies untouched by our pollution and technology. In a sense, then, nothing natural truly exists (anymore). Second, there is the logical point that humans themselves are naturally evolved beings, and so all human actions would be "natural," regardless of the amount of technology used or the interference on nonhuman nature. The creation of artifacts is a natural human activity, and thus the distinction between artifact and natural object begins to blur.

These problems in the relationship of humanity to nature are not new. Mill raised similar objections to the idea of "nature" as a moral norm over a hundred years ago, and I need not review his arguments.[25] The answer to these problems is twofold. First, we admit that the concepts of "natural" and "artifactual" are not absolutes; they exist along a spectrum, where various gradations of both concepts can be discerned. The human effect on the natural world is pervasive, but there are differences in human actions that make a descriptive difference. A toxic waste dump is different from a compost heap of organic material. To claim that both are equally non-natural would obscure important distinctions.

A second response is presented by Brennan.[26] Although a broad definition of "natural" denotes independence from human management or interference, a more useful notion (because it has implications for value theory and ethics) can be derived from the consideration of evolutionary adaptations. Our natural diet is the one we are adapted for, that is "in keeping with our nature." All human activity is not unnatural, only that activity which goes beyond our biological and evolutionary capacities. As an example, Brennan cites the procedure of "natural childbirth," that is, childbirth free of technological medical interventions. "Childbirth is an especially striking example of the wildness within us . . . where we can appreciate the natural at first hand. . . ." It is natural, free, and wild not because it is a nonhuman activity—after all, it is human childbirth—but because it is independent of a certain type of human activity, actions designed to control or to manipulate natural processes.

The "natural" then is a term we use to designate objects and processes that exist as far as possible from human manipulation and control. Natural entities are autonomous in ways that human-created artifacts are not; as Taylor writes, "to be free to pursue the realization of one's good according to the laws of one's nature."[27] When we thus judge natural objects, and evaluate them more highly than artifacts, we are focusing on the extent of their independence from human domination. In this sense, then, human actions can also be judged to be natural—these are the human actions that exist as evolutionary adaptations, free of the control and alteration of technological processes.

If these reflections on the meaning of "natural" are plausible, then it should be clear why the restoration process fails to meet the criteria of naturalness. The attempt to redesign, recreate, and restore natural areas and objects is a radical intervention in natural processes. Although there is an obvious spectrum of possible restoration and redesign projects which differ in their value—Maser's redesigned sustainable forest is better than a tree plantation—all of these projects involve the manipulation and domination of natural areas. All of these projects involve the creation of artifactual natural realities, the imposition of anthropocentric interests on the processes and objects of nature. Nature is not permitted to be free, to pursue its own independent course of development.

The fundamental error is thus domination, the denial of freedom and autonomy. Anthropocentrism, the major concern of most environmental philosophers, is only one species of the more basic attack on the preeminent value of self-realization. From within the perspective of anthropocentrism, humanity believes it is justified in dominating and molding the nonhuman world to its own human purposes. But a policy of domination transcends the anthropocentric subversion of natural processes. A policy of domination subverts both nature and human existence; it denies both the cultural and natural realization of individual good, human and nonhuman. Liberation from all forms of domination is thus the chief goal of any ethical or political system.

It is difficult to awaken from the dream of domination. We are all impressed by the power and breadth of human technological achievements. Why is it not possible to extend this power further, until we control, manipulate, and dominate the entire natural universe? This is the illusion that the restoration of nature presents to us. But it is only an illusion. Once we dominate nature, once we restore and redesign nature for our own purposes, then we have destroyed nature—we have created an artifactual reality, in a sense, a false reality, which merely provides us the pleasant illusory appearance of the natural environment.

VI

As a concluding note, let me leave the realm of philosophical speculation and return to the world of practical environmental policy. Nothing I have said in this essay should be taken as an endorsement of actions that develop, exploit, or injure areas of the natural environment and leave them in a damaged state. I believe, for example, that Exxon should attempt to clean up and restore the Alaskan waterways and land that was harmed by its corporate negligence. The point of my argument here is that we must not misunderstand what we humans are doing when we attempt to restore or repair natural areas. We are not restoring nature; we are not making it whole and healthy again. Nature restoration is a compromise; it should not be a basic policy goal. It is a policy that makes the best of a bad situation; it cleans up our mess. We are putting a piece of furniture over the stain in the carpet, for it provides a better appearance. As a matter of policy, however, it would be much more significant to prevent the causes of the stains.

Notes

1. In Islip Town, New York, real-estate developers have cited the New York State Department of Environmental Conservation policy of "no-net loss" in proposing the restoration of parts of their property to a natural state, in exchange for permission to develop. A report in *Newsday* discusses a controversial case: "In hopes of gaining town-board approval, Blankman has promised to return a three-quarter-mile dirt road on his property to its natural habitat. . . ." Katti Gray, "Wetlands in the Eye of a Storm," Islip Special, *Newsday*, April 22, 1990, pp. 1, 5.

2. *Garbage: The Practical Journal for the Environment*, May/June 1990, rear cover.

3. Chris Maser, *The Redesigned Forest* (San Pedro, Calif.: R. & E. Miles, 1988), p. 173. It is also interesting to note that there now exists a dissident group within the U.S. Forest Service, called the Association of Forest Service Employees for Environmental Ethics (AFSEEE). They advocate a return to sustainable forestry.

4. Paul Taylor, *Respect for Nature: A Theory of Environmental Ethics* (Princeton: Princeton University Press, 1986), pp. 186–92, 304–6, and chapt. 4 and 6 generally.

5. Peter S. Wenz, *Environmental Justice* (Albany: SUNY Press, 1988), pp. 287–91.

6. Robert Elliot, "Faking Nature," *Inquiry* 25 (1982): 81–93; reprinted in Donald VanDeVeer and Christine Pierce, eds., *People, Penguins, and Plastic Trees: Basic Issues in Environmental Ethics* (Belmont, Calif.: Wadsworth, 1986), pp. 142–50.

7. Ibid., p. 86 (VanDeVeer and Pierce, p. 145).

8. Ibid., p. 91 (VanDeVeer and Pierce, p. 149).

9. Eric Katz, "Organism, Community, and the 'Substitution Problem,' *Environmental Ethics* 7 (1985): 253–55.

10. Elliot, p. 81 (VanDeVeer and Pierce, p. 142).

11. See, for example, Barry Commoner, *The Closing Circle* (New York: Knopf, 1971) and Arnold Pacey, *The Culture of Technology* (Cambridge: MIT Press, 1983).

12. Michael Losonsky, "The Nature of Artifacts," *Philosophy* 65 (1990): 88.

13. Ibid., p. 84.

14. Andrew Brennan, "The Moral Standing of Natural Objects," *Environmental Ethics* 6 (1984): 41–44.

15. Maser, *The Redesigned Forest*, p. xvii.

16. Ibid., pp. 176–77.

17. Ibid., pp. 88–89.

18. Ibid., p. 174.

19. Ibid., p. 94.

20. Ibid., pp. 148–49.

21. Steve Packard, "Just a Few Oddball Species: Restoration and the Rediscovery of the Tallgrass Savanna," *Restoration and Management Notes* 6:1 (Summer 1988): 13–22.

22. L. B. Cebik, "Forging Issues from Forged Art," *Southern Journal of Philosophy* 27 (1989): 331–46.

23. Ibid., p. 342.

24. Taylor, p. 177. The rule of noninterference is discussed on pp. 173–79.

25. J. S. Mill, "Nature," in *Three Essays on Religion* (London: 1874).

26. Andrew Brennan, *Thinking About Nature: An Investigation of Nature, Value, and Ecology* (Athens: University of Georgia Press, 1988), pp. 88–91.

27. Taylor, p. 174.

8

The Call of the Wild: The Struggle Against Domination and the Technological Fix of Nature

Originally written for a meeting of the Society for Philosophy and Technology held at the Universityy of Puerto Rico in Mayaguez in March 1991, "The Call of the Wild" is a continuation of the ideas first developed in "The Big Lie." My criticism of ecological restoration showed that a central idea within any practical environmental ethic would be a workable differentiation of the "natural" from the "artificial." Humanity cannot avoid intervention in the processes of nature, but when do these activities change the value of a wild and autonomous natural world? Why is the wild natural world valuable? Why is it worthy of moral respect and consideration? How is the value of the wild natural world different from the value of human technological artifacts? Using my personal experiences with the wild deer population of Fire Island, I discuss the significance of free and uncontrolled natural entities. If we are to take seriously the idea that humans and natural entities exist together in a moral community, we must resist our desire to dominate our fellow members and partners in the communal natural system. As in "The Big Lie," I am here bringing together ideas in the philosophy of technology concerning the essential character of artifacts with ideas in environmental philosophy concerning the moral respect for the natural community as a holistic system.

I

During the summer I live with my family on Fire Island, a barrier beach off the coast of Long Island. Most mornings, if I wake up early,

I can look out my window and watch white-tailed deer munching their breakfast of flowers and leaves from the trees surrounding my house. The deer are rather tame; they have become accustomed to the transient human population that invades the island each summer. A few years ago, if they had heard me walking onto the deck, they would have jumped and run off into the thicker underbrush. Now, if they hear me, they might look up to see if I have a carrot; more likely still, they will simply ignore me and continue foraging. My experiences with these deer are the closest encounters I have with what I like to call the "wild."

Using the adjective *wild* to describe these deer is obviously a distortion of terminology. These are animals that live in and around a fairly dense human community; they consume, much to the dismay of many residents, the cultivated gardens of flowers and vegetables; they seek handouts from passing humans—my daughters often feed them breadsticks and pretzels. Yet, seeing them is different than my experience with any other animal, surely different than seeing white-tailed deer in the zoo, on a petting farm, or in a nature documentary film on television. The mornings when I find them in my yard are something special. If I walk close to one, unaware, at night, my heart beats faster. These animals are my connection to "wild nature." Despite their acceptance of the human presence, they embody something untouched and beyond humanity. They are a deep and forceful *symbol* of the wild "other." The world—my world—would be a poorer place if they were not there.

In this essay, I explore this "call of the wild"—our *attraction to value* that exists in a natural world outside of human control. To understand this value, we must understand the relationship between technology and the natural world, the ways in which humanity attempts to "fix" and mold nature to suit human purposes. Thomas Birch has described this project as the "control of otherness,"[1] a form of domination that includes the control of nature and all such outsiders of human society. Here I bring together several ideas about the philosophy of technology and the nature of artifacts, and combine them with themes raised by Birch. I argue that value exists in nature to the extent it avoids the domination of human technological practice. Technology can satisfy human wants by creating the artifactual products we desire, but it cannot supply, replace, or restore the "wild."

II

One promise of the technological enterprise is the creation of "new worlds." This optimistic view of the ability of technology to improve the human condition is based on the belief that humanity has the power to alter the physical structure of the world. Consider the words of Emmanuel Mesthene:

> We . . . have enough . . . power actually at hand to create new possibilities almost at will. By massive physical changes deliberately induced, we can literally pry new alternatives out of nature. The ancient tyranny of matter has been broken, and we know it. . . . We can change it and shape it to suit our purposes.[2]

No longer limited by the physical necessities of the "given" natural world, our technological power enables us to create a new world of our dreams and desires. Nature can be controlled; its limitations overcome; humanity can achieve its highest potential. For Mesthene, "our technical prowess literally bursts with the promise of new freedom, enhanced human dignity, and unfettered aspiration."[3]

I admit to being mesmerized by the resonances of meaning in the concept of the "new world." The technological promise of a new dignity and freedom, a limitless opportunity, an unchained power, sounds suspiciously like the promise envisioned in the new political and social conditions of the New World of the European discovery, our homeland, the Americas. But the "new world" of the European discovery was not, in fact, a *new* world; indeed, it was a very *old* world, the world of a wild untamed nature, with a minimal human presence that was itself quite old. The freedom, dignity, and benefits of the new human population were achieved, to some degree, at the expense of the older natural world. For the new world to be useful to humanity, it had to be developed and cultivated.[4] The New World had to cease being wild.[5]

The comparison between the taming of the American wilderness and the technological control of brute physical matter is disturbing. I do not believe that the technological control of nature is a desirable end of human activity. The control of nature is a dream, an illusion, a hallucination. It involves the replacement of the wild natural environment with a human artifactual environment. It creates a fundamental change in the value of the world. This change in value, in turn, forces a reexamination of the ethical relationship between humanity and the natural environment.

III

It is a commonplace to refer to the improvements of technology as a "technological fix." It is supposed that the advanced technology of the contemporary world can "fix" nature. The term *fix* is used here in two complementary ways: it implies either that something is broken or that it can be improved. Thus, the technological fix of nature means that natural processes can be "improved" to maximize human satisfaction and good; alternatively, damage to the environment can be repaired by the technological reconstruction of degraded ecological systems. Humans use nature to create benefits for humanity, and we can restore natural environments after they have been damaged by use. The only new aspect of this technological activity is its increased scope and power. The practical control of natural processes has increased to such an extent that we no longer acknowledge the impossibility of doing anything; nature can be improved and restored to any extent that we wish.

Both processes—the improvement-use and the restoration of nature—lead to serious questions about value and moral obligation. The idea that nature ought to be used (and improved, if necessary) for human benefit is the fundamental assumption of "resource environmentalism"—arguably the mainstream of the American conservation movement. Under this doctrine, environmental policies are designed to maximize human satisfactions or minimize human harms. The pollution of the atmosphere is a problem because of the health hazards to human beings. The extinction of a species is a problem because the extinct species may be useful to humans, or the resulting instability in the ecosystem may be harmful. The greenhouse effect is a problem because the changes in climate may have dramatic impacts on agriculture and coastal geography. With all environmental problems, the effects on humanity are the primary concern.[6]

These "human interest" resource arguments for environmental protection have been criticized by thinkers in several disciplines concerned with environmental philosophy and environmental ethics. A full inventory of the arguments against so-called anthropocentric environmental ethics is clearly beyond the scope of this discussion.[7] Here I focus on one particular implication of the anthropocentric resource view, i.e., the creation of an artificial world that more adequately meets the demands of human welfare. As Martin Krieger has written:

> Artificial prairies and wildernesses have been created, and there is no reason to believe that these artificial environments need be unsatisfactory for those who experience them. . . . What's wrong with plastic trees? My guess is that there is very little wrong with them. Much more can be done with plastic trees and the like to give most people the feeling that they are experiencing nature.[8]

Krieger thus argues for "responsible interventions" to manage, manipulate, and control natural environments for the promotion of human good. "A summum bonum of preserving trees has no place in an ethic of social justice."[9] Because human social justice, the production and distribution of human goods, is the primary policy goal, the manipulation of natural processes and the creation of artificial environments is an acceptable (and probably required) human activity.

Krieger's vision of a "user-friendly" plasticized human environment is chilling; it is not a world view that has many advocates. Nevertheless, the point of his argument is that a primary concern for the human uses of the natural environment leads inevitably to a policy of human intervention and manipulation in nature, and the subsequent creation of artificial environments. If humanity is planning to "fix" the natural environment, to use it and improve it to meet human needs, wants, and interests, the conclusion of the process is a technologically created "new" world of our own design. "Wild" nature will no longer exist, merely the controlled nature that offers pleasant experiences.

The restoration of nature, the policy of repairing damaged ecosystems and habitats, leads to similar results. The central issue is the *value* of the restored environments. If a restored environment is an adequate replacement for the previously existing natural environment, then humans can use, degrade, destroy, and replace natural entities and habitats with no moral consequences whatsoever. The value in the original natural entity does not require preservation.

The value of the restored environment, however, is questionable. Robert Elliot has argued that even a technologically perfect reproduction of a natural area is not equivalent to the original.[10] Elliot uses the analogy of an art forgery, in which even a perfect copy loses the value of the original artwork. What is missing in the forgery is the causal history of the original, the fact that a particular human artist created a specific work in a specific historical period. Although the copy may be as superficially pleasing as the original, the knowledge that it is not the work created by the artist distorts and disvalues our experience. Similarly, we value a natural area because of its "special kind of continuity with the past." This history, Eugene Hargrove argues, provides the authenticity of nature. He writes: "Nature is not simply a collection of natural objects; it is a process that progressively transforms those objects. . . . When we admire nature, we also admire that history."[11] Thus, a restored nature is a fake nature; it is an artificial human creation, not the product of a historical natural process.

The technological "fix" of repairing a damaged and degraded nature is an illusion and a falsehood; elsewhere, I have called it "the big lie."[12] As with all technology, the product of nature restoration is a human artifact, not the end result of a historically based natural process. Artifacts, of course, can have positive or negative value. However, what makes the value in the artifactually restored natural environment questionable is its ostensible claim to be the original.

Both forms of technological intervention in the natural world thus lead to the same result: the establishment of an artifactual world rather than a natural one. When our policy is to use nature to our best advantage, we end up with a series of so-called responsible interventions that manipulate natural processes to create the most pleasant human experiences possible. When our policy is to restore and repair a degraded natural environment, we end up with an unauthentic copy of the original. The technological "fix" of nature merely produces artifacts for the satisfaction of human interests.

IV

The issue of *value* now has a sharper focus. We can ask, "What is the value of artifacts and what are the moral obligations that derive from that value?" More precisely, "How is the value of the artifacts, and the derivative moral obligations, different from the value and moral obligations concerning 'wild' nature?" Framed in this manner, the answer to the problem is clear: artifacts differ from natural entities in their anthropocentric and instrumental origins. Artifacts are products of the larger human project of the domination of the natural world.

The concepts of function and purpose are central to an understanding of artifacts.[13] Artifacts, unlike natural objects, are created for a specific purpose. They are essentially anthropocentric instruments, tools or objects, that serve a function in human life. The existence of artifacts is centered on human life. It is impossible to imagine an artifact that is not designed to meet a human purpose, for without a foreseen use the object would not have been created.

The anthropocentric instrumentality of artifacts is completely different from the essential characteristics of natural entities, species, and ecosystems. Living natural entities and systems of entities evolve to fill ecological niches in the biosphere; they are not designed to meet human needs or interests. Andrew Brennan thus argues that natural entities have no "intrinsic functions": they are not created for a particular purpose; they have no set manner of use. We may speak as if natural individuals (e.g., predators) have roles to play in ecosystemic well-being (the maintenance of optimum population levels), but this talk is either metaphorical or fallacious. No one created or designed the mountain lion as a regulator of the deer population.[14]

From a moral point of view, the difference between purposely designed artifacts and evolving natural entities is not generally problematic. The anthropocentric instrumentality of artifacts is not a serious moral concern, for most artifacts are designed for use in human social and cultural contexts. Nevertheless, the human intervention into "wild" nature is a different process entirely. Hargrove notes how human intervention alters the aesthetic evaluation of nature: "To attempt to manipulate nature, even for aesthetic reasons, alters nature adversely from an aesthetic standpoint. Historically, manipulation of nature, even to improve it, has been considered subjugation or domination."[15] This domination resulting from human intervention can be generalized beyond aesthetic valuations; it leads to more than just a loss of beauty. The management of nature results in the imposition of our anthropocentric purposes on areas that exist outside human society. We intervene in nature to create so-called natural objects and environments based on models of human desires, interests, and satisfactions. In doing so, we engage in the project of the human domination of nature: the reconstruction of the natural world in our own image, to suit our purposes.

Need we ask why domination is a moral issue? In the context of human social and political thought, domination is the evil that restricts, denies, or distorts individual (and social) freedom and autonomy. In the context of environmental philosophy, domination is the anthropocentric alteration of natural processes. The entities and systems that comprise nature are not permitted to be free, to pursue their own independent and unplanned course of development. Even Hargrove, who emphasizes the aesthetic value of nature, judges this loss of freedom the crucial evil of domination: it "reduces [nature's] ability to be creative."[16] Wherever it exists, in nature or in human culture, the process of domination attacks the preeminent value of self-realization.

Is the analysis of domination appropriate here? Does it make sense to say that we can deny the autonomy, the self-realization, of natural nonhuman entities? The central assumption of this analysis is that natural entities and systems have a value in their own right, a value that transcends the instrumentality of human concerns, projects, and interests. Nature is not merely the physical matter that is the *object* of technological practice and alteration; it is also a *subject*, with its own proc-

ess and history of development independent of human intervention
and activity. Nature thus has a value that can be subverted and destroyed by the process of human domination. In this way, human domination, alteration, and management are issues of moral concern.

V

But does the "wild" have a moral claim on humanity? The answer to
this question determines the moral status of the human domination of
nature. Does the wilderness, the world of nature untouched by the
technological alteration of humanity, possess a moral value worth preserving? Is the creation of a technological "new world" morally harmful? Does it destroy the value of the original New World of the European discovery of America, the untamed and "wild" wilderness? How
do we discern a method for answering these questions?

It is at this point that my thoughts return to my encounters with the
white-tailed deer on Fire Island. They are not truly wild, for they are
no longer afraid of the human presence on the island. They seem to
realize that the summer residents are not hunters. These humans come
with pretzels, not rifles. Nevertheless, there are some human residents
who are deeply disturbed by the existence of the deer. The deer carry
ticks that are part of the life cycle of Lyme disease. They eat the flowers
and vegetables of well-tended gardens. They are unpredictable, and
they can knock a person down. A considerable portion of the human
community thus wants the deer hunted and removed from the island.

Just the thought of losing these deer disturbs me—and until recently
I did not understand why. In my lucid rational moments, I realize that
they are not "wild," that they have prospered on Fire Island due to an
unnatural absence of predators; their population could be decreased
with no appreciable harm to the herd or the remaining natural ecosystem of the barrier beach. Nevertheless, they are the vestiges of a truly
wild natural community; they are reminders that the forces of domination and subjugation do not always succeed.

Birch describes the process of wilderness preservation as "incarceration" by "the technological imperium"—i.e., by the primary social-po-
litical force of the contemporary world.[17] The entire process of creating
and maintaining wilderness reservations by human law is contradictory, for the wildness is destroyed by the power of the human-techno-
logical system:

Wilderness reservations are not meant to be voids in the fabric of domination where "anarchy" is permitted, where nature is actually liberated. Not at all. The rule of law is presupposed as supreme. Just as wilderness reservations are created by law, so too they can be abolished by law. The threat of annihilation is always maintained.[18]

The domination of natural wildness is just one example of the system of power. "The whole point, purpose, and meaning of imperial power, and its most basic legitimation, is to give humans control over otherness."[19]

It is here that Birch sees the contradiction in the imperial technological domination of wild nature. "The wildness is still there, and it is still wild," and it maintains its own integrity.[20] The wildness, the otherness of nature, remains, I suggest, because the forces of the imperial power require its existence. If there is no "other" recognized as the victim of domination, then the power of the imperium is empty. There would be nothing upon which to exercise power. But maintaining the existence of the wild other, even in the diminished capacity of wilderness reservations managed by the government, lays the seeds for the subversion of the imperial domination of technology.

Birch thus recommends that we view wilderness, wherever it can be found, as a "sacred space" acting as "an implacable counterforce to the momentum of totalizing power." Wilderness appears anywhere: "old roadbeds, wild plots in suburban yards, flower boxes in urban windows, cracks in the pavement. . . . "[21] And it appears, in my life, in the presence of the white-tailed deer of Fire Island. My commitment to the preservation of the deer in my community is part of my resistance to the total domination of the technological world.

This resistance is based on yet a deeper moral commitment: the deer themselves are members of my moral and natural community. The deer and I are partners in the continuous struggle for the preservation of autonomy, freedom, and integrity. This shared partnership creates obligations on the part of humanity for the preservation and protection of the natural world. This is the *call of the wild*—the moral claim of the natural world.

We are all impressed by the breadth of human technological power. Why is it not possible to extend this power further, until we control the entire natural universe? This insidious dream of domination can only end by respecting freedom and self-determination, wherever it exists, and by recognizing the true extent of the moral community in the natural world.

Notes

1. Thomas H. Birch, "The Incarceration of Wildness: Wilderness Areas as Prisons," *Environmental Ethics* 12 (1990): 18.

2. Emmanuel G. Mesthene, "Technology and Wisdom," in *Philosophy and Technology: Readings in the Philosophical Problems of Technology,* ed. Carl Mitcham and Robert Mackey (New York: Free Press, 1983), p. 110.

3. Ibid., p. 111.

4. One of the best examples of this attitude from a historical source contemporaneous with the period of European expansion is the discussion of property by John Locke, *Second Treatise on Government,* chap. 5, especially, secs. 40–43. Locke specifically mentions the lack of value in American land because of the absence of labor and cultivation.

5. For my purposes, it is irrelevant to raise the question, whether North America ever really was wild. It existed then, and now, as a *symbol* of nature uncontrolled by human civilization. Of course, it may have been altered and modified through fire and hunting by Native American populations. Such practices, however, do not change its *significance* as wild and untamed. First, the control of the natural world by Native Americans was definitely limited compared to the new European attempt of total cultivation. Second, the issue here is *not* the purity of the wild in frontier America, but rather the ethical significance of the Western belief that value only arises in nature with human intervention and modification. To discuss that issue, the New World of the Western discovery is useful, because it was relatively uncontrolled and uncultivated, i.e., wild.

6. There are sound political and motivational reasons for arguments that outline the threat to human interests caused by environmental degradation. These arguments have been the rallying cry of popular conservationists from Rachel Carson, *Silent Spring* (New York: Houghton Mifflin, 1962), to Barry Commoner, *The Closing Circle: Nature, Man, and Technology* (New York: Knopf, 1971), to Bill McKibben, *The End of Nature* (New York: Random House, 1989). My philosophical criticisms of these views do not diminish my respect for the positive social and political changes these works have inspired.

7. A complete listing of the relevant literature is impossible. One of the best early works is David Ehrenfeld, *The Arrogance of Humanism* (New York: Oxford University Press, 1978). Other major representative works of nonanthropocentric strands in environmental ethics are Holmes Rolston, III, *Environmental Ethics: Duties to and Values in the Natural World* (Philadelphia: Temple University Press, 1988), J. Baird Callicott, *In Defense of the Land Ethic* (Albany: SUNY Press, 1989), Paul Taylor, *Respect for Nature: A Theory of Environmental Ethics* (Princeton: Princeton University Press, 1986), Arne Naess, *Ecology, Community and Lifestyle,* trans. and ed. David Rothenberg (Cambridge: Cambridge University Press, 1989). For a discussion of enlightened anthropocentric views, see Bryan G. Norton, *Why Preserve Natural Variety?* (Princeton: Princeton Uni-

versity Press, 1987), Eugene C. Hargrove, *The Foundations of Environmental Ethics* (Englewood Cliffs, N.J.: Prentice-Hall, 1989), and Mark Sagoff, *The Economy of the Earth: Philosophy, Law, and the Environment* (Cambridge: Cambridge University Press, 1988).

8. Martin H. Krieger, "What's Wrong with Plastic Trees?" *Science* 179 (1973): 453.

9. Ibid.

10. Robert Elliot, "Faking Nature," *Inquiry* 25 (1982): 81–93, specifically, p. 86.

11. Hargrove, *The Foundations of Environmental Ethics*, p. 195.

12. Eric Katz, "The Big Lie: Human Restoration of Nature," *Research in Philosophy and Technology*, 12 (1992): 231–41.

13. The argument of this section is based on Katz, "The Big Lie." For a further discussion, see Michael Losonsky, "The Nature of Artifacts," *Philosophy* 65 (1990): 81–88.

14. Andrew Brennan, "The Moral Standing of Natural Objects," *Environmental Ethics* 6 (1984): 41–44.

15. Hargrove, *The Foundations of Environmental Ethics*, p. 195.

16. Ibid.

17. Birch, "The Incarceration of Wildness," p. 10.

18. Ibid.

19. Ibid., p. 18.

20. Ibid., pp. 21–22.

21. Ibid., pp. 24–25.

9

Artifacts and Functions: A Note on the Value of Nature

The third essay in the series on the human control of nature, "Artifacts and Functions" focuses more directly on the distinction between human-made objects and naturally evolving entities. The crucial distinction is that artifacts are always the result of a human plan or design, while natural entities are not. Artifacts are thus anthropocentric in a fundamental ontological sense— their value is conditioned on the satisfaction of some human purpose. The distinction between artifacts and natural entities, I argue, is more important for environmental ethics than the distinction between living and nonliving entities. From the perspective of an environmental ethic, nonliving natural entities, such as rivers and mountains, are more significant than living artifacts, such as domesticated animals. The design of artifacts, their creation and manipulation by humans, ties directly into the ideas of autonomy and domination. Natural entities, processes, and systems can be truly autonomous, while artifacts cannot. Once we plan or control natural processes, we turn Nature into an artifact, an entity that is no longer subject to its own development. "Artifacts and Functions" can be read as a companion piece to "The Call of the Wild," emphasizing the theoretical elements of the distinction between nature and the artifactual world. Earlier versions of the essay were read at the Boston University Colloquium for the Philosophy of Science in April 1993 and a meeting of the Society for Philosophy and Technology in Peñíscola, Spain, in May 1993.

I

Consider the character of artifacts as human creations. Artifacts are conceived and designed to meet the demands of human need or pur-

121

pose; they are tools for the achievement of human tasks. Not all artifacts actually fulfill the purposes for which they were intended; often,
artifacts designed for one purpose are used in unforeseen or different
contexts. Nevertheless, the artifact would not exist at all if some purpose had not been forseen for it; artifacts are created to meet a specific
human need.

Artifacts thus stand in a necessary *ontological* relationship with
human purpose. The existence of a human purpose, a human intention, is a *necessary* condition for the existence of the artifact. Human
purpose and intention are clearly not *sufficient* conditions for the characterization of an entity as an artifact, for some things are the result of
human intentions although we would hesitate to call them artifacts.
Human infants, for example, may be the result of intention and purpose. Interhuman relationships—for example, my friendship with
John—may also be intentional.

However, although human creations other than artifacts may exhibit
intentionality, natural entities do not. Natural entities, insofar as they
are natural, are not the result of human intentions. The necessary ontological relationship with human purpose serves to distinguish artifacts
from natural entities. In this essay I examine the nature of this distinction and its normative implications.

II

An anthropocentric worldview places humanity and human interests
at the center of value. From the perspective of anthropocentrism, the
world exists for humanity; the world is the complex of objects and
systems that form the material for human achievements. Technology—
the design and creation of artifacts—is a central project in the development of this anthropocentric world; technology shapes the material of
the world to meet human concerns, to satisfy human desires, wants,
and needs. Broadly conceived, technology is any social or cultural artifact used by humans for the organization and control of nature and
the world.[1]

Technological products—artifacts—are thus fundamentally anthropocentric, by which I mean that their existence, purpose, and meaning
all derive from the concerns of human agents, either as individual persons or as social institutions. A proper understanding of artifacts is
tied inextricably to an analysis of function and purpose. Artifacts are

instruments or tools for the betterment of human life. They can only be understood as anthropocentric instruments.

The anthropocentric instrumentality of artifacts is completely different from the basic characteristics of natural entities, species, and ecosystems. Natural entities exist independently from human purpose or design. Living natural entities and systems of entities evolve to fill ecological niches in the biosphere, not to meet human needs or interests. More clearly, nonliving natural entities such as rock formations, rivers, canyons, soils (and so on) simply *exist*, without any evolutionary "fit" at all. Nonliving natural entities, although subject to change, do not "evolve" or adapt to changing conditions in their local ecosystems. It is thus difficult even to ascribe the notion of function or purpose to natural entities.

The consideration of function and the comparison of artifacts and natural entities leads Andrew Brennan to argue that natural entities are "intrinsically functionless." Natural entities were not created for a particular purpose, nor did they evolve for a specific reason, design, or plan; natural entities have no set manner of use, no role to play in natural ecosystems. We often speak as if natural individuals and species (e.g., predators) have roles or functions to perform in the maintenance of ecosystemic well-being (e.g., preserving the equilibriums of optimum population levels), but such talk is either metaphorical or fallacious. No one created or designed the mountain lion as a regulator of the deer population.[2] Natural entities are not instruments, although we humans may use them instrumentally. When we do, we graft our designs, so to speak, on to the naturally functionless entity. But outside considerations of human use, the natural entity has no purpose; since it is not an artifact, since it is not the result of a design or plan, it has no "intrinsic function."

It may be objected that the preceding analysis of the difference between humanly created artifacts and natural entities reinforces the very separation between humanity and nature that environmental philosophy (and an enlightened environmental policy) seeks to overcome. For too long, humanity has apparently believed that it can exist independently of natural processes. But humans are part of the natural system, and require a well-functioning natural environment to survive. Humans are themselves the products of natural evolution, the objection continues, so that human artifacts are likewise natural.

Although this objection introduces a valid concern into the proper basis of environmental policy—the interdependence of humanity and nature—an overemphasis on this useful hortatory rhetoric of the environmental movement only tends to obscure a clear analysis of the differences between the results of human action in the environment and the outcomes produced by natural processes. Humanity itself is a product of evolution, but the primary sphere of human activity is the realm of culture, the complex system of social arrangements and artifacts that was created by humanity for the furtherance of human ends. Although human cultural artifacts may exist along a continuous spectrum with natural evolving entities—my steel hammer is related to the bone, stick, or rock used by a chimpanzee in the wild—there is indeed a distinction to be made between human artifacts—machines, institutions, ideas—and the natural evolving entities of the biosphere. Human artifacts do not evolve. To say that I am using a third-generation personal computer to write this essay, and that this PC evolved from earlier PCs or indeed from Turing's idea of a thinking machine, is to speak in metaphors. Real evolution only occurs in biological systems and entities, not in artifacts. Humans may use evolutionary principles as they "redesign" living artifacts, such as food crops, but here again the distinction between a process driven by human intention and one driven by natural selection is clear. Humans are in some sense natural beings; humanity requires a functioning nature to survive; but not everything humans do or make is natural. It is thus important to understand how and why human creations or artifacts are different from natural entities. Without a proper understanding of the distinction, we will lack a basis for a moral environmental policy.

III

Since artifacts are designed for a human purpose, while natural entities evolve with no design or purpose, the lack of what Brennan terms "intrinsic function" is the distinguishing characteristic that separates natural entities from artifacts. An example from practical environmental policy can begin to demonstrate the significance of this distinction for an ontological and axiological understanding of nature. The comparison between artifacts and natural entities reveals the foundation of natural value; the comparison explains the value of nature.

Consider the policy of sustainable forestry.[3] As its name implies, sustainable forestry is a land-management policy that advocates the wise use and restoration of forests as sustainable and renewable resources. It is thus opposed to the short-term expediency of present-day forestry practices. Current policies often involve a maximum harvest with little regard for the restoration or maintenance of the forest as an ecosystem. Forests are treated as if they were agricultural products, tree plantations. Advocates of sustainable forestry seek to remodel the practice of forest management along the lines of natural evolution, restoration, and ecosystemic development.

From the perspective of environmentalists, sustainable forestry would appear to be a good policy, well worth advocating as a corrective to an exploitative and disrespectful misuse of natural ecosystems. But a deeper examination shows that sustainable forestry is not an appropriate improvement over short-term development, for both policies treat the forest as an artifact, an instrument for the furtherance of human interests. An analysis of sustainable forestry only reveals the wide gulf between natural entities and human-centered artifacts.

The artifactual treatment of nature within sustainable forestry policy is clearly demonstrated in Chris Maser's *The Redesigned Forest*.[4] Maser, a former research scientist for the United States Department of Interior Bureau of Land Management, argues that we must redesign forests according to natural ecological principles, so that we become true foresters and not "plantation managers." Maser's position is instructive precisely because it exhibits the tension between a policy based on natural evolutionary principles and a policy based on short-term human interests. Unlike the "forest-plantation manager," Maser attempts to create a forest policy that respects natural processes. Nevertheless, his argument and language are disturbing; the text is pervaded by an artifactual and instrumental conception of the natural forest environment.

Maser's first error is the comparison of the human design of forests with Nature's design: "we are redesigning our forests from Nature's blueprint to humanity's blueprint."[5] Nature, of course, does not have a blueprint, nor a design, and as a zoologist, Maser knows this. His language is merely metaphorical, and it is dangerous, for it implies that we can discover the plan of natural processes and mold them to our human purposes.

Maser's second error is the comparison of nature to a mechanism. In his criticism of current forestry practices, Maser claims that when we turn forests into plantations we assume that our design for the forest mechanism is better than nature's. Maser correctly argues that "forests are not automobiles in which we can tailor artificially substituted parts for original parts."[6] But his argument against the substitution of artificial parts is empirical: "A forest cannot be 'rebuilt' and remain the same forest, but we could probably rebuild a forest similar to the original if we knew how. No one has ever done it . . . [W]e do not have a parts catalog, or a maintenance manual. . . ."[7] The implication is that if we did have a catalog and manual, if nature were as well known as an artifactual machine, then the restoration and redesign of forests would be practically and morally acceptable.

For Maser, restoration or sustainable forestry is acceptable because it more likely furthers human long-term interests. Thus, the third problem in this argument for the redesign of forests and forestry policy is that its foundation is irredeemably anthropocentric. The central problem with current practices is that they are "exclusive of all other human values except the production of fast-grown woodfiber."[8] What concerns Maser is the elimination of other human values and interests. "We need to learn to see the forest as the factory that produces raw materials . . ." to meet our "common goal[:] . . . a sustainable forest for a sustainable industry for a sustainable environment for a sustainable human population."[9] Sustainable restoration forestry is necessary because it is the best method for achieving the human goods that are extracted from nature. By using the complex knowledge of forest ecology, foresters will achieve the goal of building a better "factory-forest."

As an environmental policy, the idea of rebuilding and redesigning sustainable forests is, at the very least, extremely odd. Even a cursory examination of the concept of sustainable restoration forestry reveals the anthropocentric value system that lies at its core. The management and control of natural systems alters their natural character; management and control creates artifactual systems, which, at best, *resemble* nature. The redesign and management of natural systems is thus a paradox: once human intervention occurs, there is no longer a natural system to be preserved, there is only an artifactual system.

The example of sustainable forestry thus serves to illustrate the conceptual distinction between artifacts and natural entities. The goal of sustainable forestry is the creation of forests that best suit human purposes; these forests are thus artifacts, designed and developed for a human function, even in the limiting case where the *sole* purpose for the creation of the forest was the replication of the natural. The managed sustainable forest is (arguably) an improvement over a forest plantation; but the managed forest is still different from a natural forest, even if it appears similar, even if it develops according to the same evolutionary and ecological principles. The managed forest, as an artifact, owes its existence to intentions of human agents; the natural forest exists independently of human intention. The natural forest exists because of a historical and evolutionary process, not as the result of a human plan or design. The natural forest has no purpose, no intrinsic function; unlike an artifact, or an artifactual system, it is ontologically independent from humanity.

IV

The human intervention in and management of natural systems thus creates artifacts whose value is centered on human interests and purposes. A consideration of these artifacts, as in the policy of sustainable forestry, reveals the difference between human-centered artifacts and independent natural entities. This analysis of the difference in the ontological and axiological character of artifacts and natural entities has clear implications for normative ethics, and ultimately, for environmental policy. I argue that there is a moral obligation to preserve nonartifactual natural value, even as it exists independently from human projects, plans, and interests.

The central normative issue in this discussion is the possibility of the moral "consideration" of nonhuman and nonliving natural entities. This nontraditional and nonhuman-based moral consideration requires the determination of a plausible nonarbitrary criterion for nonhuman moral value. Since its inception, the field of environmental ethics has attempted to broaden the notion of moral considerability beyond the traditional limits of human-based criteria (such as language ability, rationality, or self-consciousness). Thus Paul Taylor has argued for a biocentric ethic which entails moral respect for all living (natural) entities.[10] The basis of this biocentric attitude of respect is the recognition that every living entity has a good-of-its-own; each living being is a "teleological centre of life."[11] Similarly, Robin Attfield has argued for "the good of trees" on essentially Aristotelian grounds: "the good life for a living organism turns on the fulfilment of its nature."[12] But the notion that nonconscious (and nonrational) living entities have an intrinsic or inherent good has been questioned. R. G. Frey, for example, suggests that a broadened notion of welfare, good, or interests cannot be limited to animals and other living entities. If we are going to talk of the good for nonhuman animals and plants, then we are also going to have to talk of the good for machines and other human artifacts: a tractor "needs" oil to run well; oil is a good that enables the tractor to fulfill its nature.[13]

The possibility of determining value for natural entities thus requires a clear distinction between artifacts—such as Frey's tractor—and living entities as teleological centers of life and activity. Gary

Varner has recently argued for the consistency of this distinction by focusing on the "biological functions" of living entities as opposed to the "artificial" functions of machines and artifacts. Unlike a machine, a living entity has needs, interests, and goods because it has biological functions, adaptive subsystems that served an evolutionary purpose in the survival of its ancestors.[14] The interests and goods of the living entity are based on the aetiology of the species; the interests and goods—if we want to call them that—of the artifact depend on the purposes ascribed to the artifact by human beings.[15] Holmes Rolston reaches the same conclusion by a consideration of organisms as "self-maintaining systems" within ecosystems and habitats: "there exist . . . systemic requirements by which the organism is tested as fit or misfit." The ecosystemic fitness of an organism is part of its nature. Artifacts have no nature of their own, merely the purposes given to them by human interests.[16] Biological and ecosystemic functions are thus the distinguishing characteristics of living entities (as opposed to artifacts); this distinction permits the possibility of the moral consideration of nonhuman living entities without the problematic inclusion of artifacts.

But the distinction between artifacts and natural *living* entities is not by itself an adequate basis for the determination of moral value in nature. First, considerations of natural teleology, biological function, and ecosystemic fitness exclude artifacts from moral consideration at the cost of excluding *nonliving* natural entities. Such an exclusion is too broad: the consideration of nonliving natural entities must be part of any comprehensive environmental ethic. There *is* a difference between artifacts and natural nonliving entities, but this difference is not describable in terms of ecosystemic or biological function, because none of these entities are alive. Nonetheless, the distinction is important for understanding the moral basis of environmental policy. A broadly conceived environmental ethic follows the holistic model of Aldo Leopold, so as to include soils, waters, mountains, the atmosphere—in sum, what Leopold termed "the land"—in the domain of moral value and moral consideration.[17] It is an ethic that is concerned with both the living and nonliving elements of the biotic system, and with the relationships between them. Thus a principle of "biological function" which eliminated the nonliving elements of the environment would exclude too much. A second problem is that the Leopoldian environmental ethic which I seek to elaborate will exclude so-called living artifacts, such as domesticated animals, biologically engineered species, and forest plantations. These human-created entities have no place in an environmental ethic since they are not natural entities. The crucial distinction then is not between living beings (with biological functions) and nonliving "things," but between artifacts and natural entities, considered as living or not.

The ethical importance of the distinction between artifacts and natural entities is thus derived from the anthropocentric nature of artifacts, their ontological reliance on human interests, plans, and projects. In contrast to natural entities, artifacts, as human instruments, are always a *means* to the furtherance of some human *end*. The normative implication of this relationship can be found in the practical moral philosophy of Kant, if we are willing to look beyond the boundaries of human rational subjects. The second formulation of the categorical imperative states that we are to treat moral subjects as ends-in-themselves, never as a mere means. If the categorical imperative is applied to a treatment of artifacts and natural entities we find a crucial difference: artifacts must be treated as means, for their existence and value only exist in a dependent relationship with human aims and goals; but natural entities, existing apart from human projects, can be considered as ends-in-themselves. Kant teaches us that the possibility of moral consideration lies in an entity's independence from rational control and design, its existence as an end-in-itself.

This consideration of Kantian moral concepts *suggests* that two crucial notions in the development of an ethical environmental policy are the Kantian ideal of "autonomy," and its moral opposite, domination. In analyzing the value of natural organisms, Rolston writes: "the values that attach to organisms result from their nonderivative, genuine autonomy . . . as spontaneous natural systems."[18] This is not true merely for organisms. Complex holistic natural systems and communities also exhibit autonomy, in that they are independent from external design, purpose, and control. Even nonliving natural entities, which do not, in themselves, develop, grow, or achieve self-realization, are essential components of autonomous natural systems. When humans intervene in nature, when we create artifacts or attempt to manage environmental systems (such as forests), we destroy that natural autonomy by imposing a system of domination. As Eugene Hargrove notes: "Historically, manipulation of nature, even to improve it, has been considered subjugation or domination.[19]

But why is the domination of nature a moral evil? Why are the products of the domination of nature less valuable than the products of a free and autonomous nature? It is clear that in the realm of human social and political thought, domination is an evil that restricts or denies individual (and social) freedom. Can the metaphor of domination be translated into the realm of nonhuman natural processes? Yes: within environmental policy, domination is the anthropocentric alteration of natural processes. The entities and systems that comprise nature are not permitted to be free, to pursue their independent and unplanned courses of development, growth, and change. Thus, the existence of domination results in the denial of free and unhindered growth and development. Wherever the process of domination exists, either in nature or in human culture, it attacks the preeminent value of self-realization.

I am not claiming that all self-realization is a moral good; even some forms of human self-realization can be morally evil. Thus a much larger question, for both environmental policy and normative human ethics generally, concerns the exploration of criteria for justifiable intervention in the free and autonomous development of human beings, natural organisms, and natural systems. I do not claim to establish a "criterion for intervention" in this essay. My point here is more simple: the denial of the self-realization of natural processes is a crucial part of the human domination of nature.

The creation of artifacts is thus central to the human project of the domination and subjugation of the natural world. Artifacts enable humanity to control the forces of nature for the betterment of human life. Generally, this artifactual control of natural forces is not a moral evil: the processes of agriculture, engineering, and medicine are necessary for the fullest possible development of human life—*human* self-realization. But the management, alteration, and redesign of nature results in the imposition of our anthropocentric purposes on areas and entities that exist outside human society. Intervention in nature creates environments based on models of human desire. This is the human project of the domination of nature: the reconstruction of the natural world in our own image, to suit our human goals and purposes.

The ontological and axiological distinctions between artifacts and natural entities are drawn most clearly when we consider the artifactual reconstruction and control of natural entities and ecosystems—when we turn wild and natural forests into tree plantations or "sustainable" woodland. Artifacts are fundamentally connected to human concerns and interests, in both their existence and their value. Natural entities and systems have a value in their own right, a value that transcends the instrumentality of human projects and interests. Nature is not merely the physical matter which is the *object* of human artifactual practice; nature is a *subject*, with its own history of development independent of human cultural intervention. As with any autonomous subject, nature thus has a value that can be subverted and destroyed by the process of human domination. The normative implication for environmental policy is that this value ought to be preserved.

Notes

1. See for example I. C. Jarvie, who writes: "Technology . . . is coterminus with our attempts to come to terms with our world . . ." in "Technology and the Structure of Knowledge," in *Philosophy and Technology: Readings in the Philosophical Problems of Technology*, ed. Carl Mitcham and Robert Mackey (New York: Free Press, 1983), p. 61.

2. Andrew Brennan, "The Moral Standing of Natural Objects," *Environmental Ethics* 6 (1984): 41–44.

3. The argument concerning "sustainable forestry" is developed more fully in Eric Katz, "The Big Lie: Human Restoration of Nature," *Research in Philosophy and Technology* 12 (1992): 231–41.

4. Chris Maser, *The Redesigned Forest* (San Pedro, Calif.: R. & E. Miles, 1988).

5. Ibid., p. xvii.

6. Ibid., pp. 176–77.

7. Ibid., pp. 88–89.

8. Ibid., p. 94.

9. Ibid., pp. 148–49.

10. Paul W. Taylor, *Respect for Nature: A Theory of Environmental Ethics* (Princeton: Princeton University Press, 1986).

11. Ibid., pp. 60–71, 100, 119–29.

12. Robin Attfield, "The Good of Trees," *Journal of Value Inquiry* 15 (1981): 35–54; reprinted in *People, Penguins, and Plastic Trees: Basic Issues in Environmental Ethics*, ed. Donald VanDeVeer and Christine Pierce (Belmont, Calif.: Wadsworth, 1986), p. 99. For a further discussion, see Robin Attfield, *The Ethics of Environmental Concern* (New York: Columbia University Press, 1983), pp. 140–65.

13. R. G. Frey, "Rights, Interests, Desires, and Beliefs," *American Philosophical Quarterly* 16 (1979): 233–39; reprinted in VanDeVeer and Pierce, pp. 41–42.

14. The living entity does have biological functions—its parts serve the wellbeing of the whole—but it itself is intrinsically functionless, not having been designed for a specific role in the environment.

15. Gary E. Varner, "Biological Functions and Biological Interests," *Southern Journal of Philosophy* 28 (1990): 258–62. Varner bases his argument on Larry Wright's analysis of function in *Teleological Explanations* (Berkeley: University of California Press, 1976).

16. Holmes Rolston, III, *Environmental Ethics: Duties to and Values in the Natural World* (Philadelphia: Temple University Press, 1988), pp. 97–105.

17. The classic statement of this position is in Aldo Leopold, "The Land Ethic," *A Sand County Almanac* (New York: Oxford University Press, 1949).

18. Rolston, p. 105.

19. Eugene C. Hargrove, *The Foundations of Environmental Ethics* (Englewood Cliffs, N.J.: Prentice-Hall, 1989), p. 195.

10

Imperialism and Environmentalism

In "Imperialism and Environmentalism" I take seriously the notion of domination as I have used it in the three previous essays to examine the idea of power in the relationship between humanity and Nature. This essay is, in part, an examination of the moral implications of the rhetoric of environmental philosophy. The concept of "ecological imperialism" has been popularized by environmental historians and philosophers to describe the process of colonization and the exploitation of natural resources of one nation-state over another. But once we view Nature as a subject worthy of moral consideration, as an autonomous system that follows its own course of development, then we can also view its exercise of power in ways analogous to human institutions. Just as humans act as imperialists in the subjugation of other peoples, Nature acts as an imperialist when it exerts its power over humanity. Using the term imperialism implies the evils of domination, but when we view Nature and humanity acting upon one another, we realize that intervention and interference are unavoidable. The interesting ethical question is thus, when is intervention permissible, when is intervention justifiable? As I suggest at the conclusion of this essay, the criterion for a justifiable intervention in the life or history of any autonomous subject is the crucial issue in all of moral philosophy.

On the evening of December 10, 1992, the Northeast coast of the United States began to experience a violent winter storm, a Nor'easter, that was described by many officials and long-time residents as the worst storm in forty years, perhaps the worst in a century. The storm had already dumped up to five feet of snow across the states of Pennsylvania and Maryland, and it hit the New York metropolitan area with driving rain and wind gusts up to ninety miles an hour. This storm was not a hurricane, for it did not originate in the tropics, but its effects were much more acute than the most vicious hurricanes of this century. One reason for the severity of the effects of the storm was that it lasted for four days, through eight high tide cycles. The shoreline communities of New Jersey, New York, Long Island, and Connecticut were devastated: seawalls collapsed, streets were flooded, bridges, tunnels, and railroads were closed, and beaches and dunes were washed out to sea. Within a mile of my summer home on Fire Island, over twenty houses were destroyed by the ocean tidal surges. In the twenty-five years that I had visited or lived on that barrier beach, I had never seen one house wash away.

I begin with this description of the so-called storm of December 1992 because it is, for me personally, the most direct representation of the power of the natural world. Whatever else nature may be, it is a complex combination of forces that exerts its various powers throughout the entire physical world. In this essay I explore an idea— imperialism—as a way for understanding the relationship of power between nature and humanity. My working assumption is that the expressions, metaphors, and representations of the power of nature that we choose determine our normative stance to the natural world. When we adopt an antagonistic attitude, as I believe we do, we interpret the natural world as an evil force that must be conquered. We view nature in terms of force and domination, as an objectified "other" that must be controlled.

The use of the concept of imperialism in conjunction with both the policy of environmentalism and the forces of nature requires an explanation. In brief, I am consciously trying to expand the normal use of the concept of imperialism—indeed, one might say, to use an appropriately violent turn of phrase, that I am attempting to explode our normal concepts, especially those concerning the relationship between humanity and the natural environment. In this essay, I consider the idea of imperialism—and all that it represents concerning power, force, and domination—as a model or metaphor for understanding the human relationship with nature. Now a metaphor of imperialism and power is rather different from the benign and optimistic metaphor of "the balance of nature" so often used by environmental philosophers, scientists, activists, and policy makers. So one purpose of this philosophical examination into the power of nature is to open a dialogue about the forms of rhetoric that help to determine environmental policy. Which metaphors or models of the human/nature relationship are more appropriate? Should we view nature as a complex of aggressive forces, or as a balanced system of cooperation and harmony? Why should we choose one metaphor over another? Should we even make one exclusive choice? Why not use both metaphors—the benign and the violent—or others that may cross our minds? The metaphor we choose in a particular situation will have a fundamental impact on our ideas concerning the appropriate role of human action in the natural world.

In this essay, the terms "nature," the "natural world," the "natural environment," and "natural processes" are used as roughly equivalent to that part of the world that lies outside human activity or human culture. Although "nature" can be used in a very broad sense to mean the natural or physical laws of the universe, I am not using that definition in this argument. The broad definition of nature as physical law does not exclude any physical phenomenon from being labeled as natural—such a characterization is virtually useless in moral philosophy or political theory, where distinctions must be made between various kinds of human and natural activity. My meaning of "nature" is more restrictive, for it only concerns the ecosystems, bioregions, and undeveloped habitats of the earth—and the entities and processes that constitute these physical spaces and systems. In brief, I use the term "nature" to mean the ecosystemic processes of the earth.

It is essential for my argument that imperialism represent more than the traditional idea of national and cultural conquest. It is more than one nation or community expanding its influence onto a less dominant nation-state, culture, or community. Imperialism is a form of domination—almost any instance of domination—in which one entity uses or takes advantage of another entity for its self-aggrandizement, to increase its power, its life, its comfort. Imperialism is thus an exercise of power. An entity uses its power to alter the world, to influence other entities, so that its own interests may be satisfied. Imperialism is, as it were, the policy that seeks to satisfy interests. It is in this sense that Bertrand Russell said that all living beings are imperialists;[1] similarly, William Leiss speaks of the "imperialism of human needs."[2] In philosophical terminology, imperialism results from any successful attempt to exert power over the "other."

This sense of imperialism is connected to environmental policies because the relationship of power need not be located in the exclusive domain of human beings, human institutions, human nation-states. Imperialism expresses a relationship of power and domination, but the entities on either end of the power relationship can be either human or non-human. Nature—natural entities and systems—can be the "other" that is dominated by humanity, or it can be the dominating and imperialistic force that subdues some aspect of humanity. Logically, there are four basic possibilities:

(1) Imperialistic humans exercise power over other humans; for example, the colonization of the Americas.
(2) Imperialistic humans exercise power over nature; for example, the practice of agriculture.
(3) Imperialistic nature exercises power over humans; for example, the destruction of beach houses in the December 1992 storm.
(4) Imperialistic nature exercises power over other nature; for example, the process of forest succession.

One immediate objection to this logical categorization is that it is based on an abnormal use of the idea of nature. Nature may be the "object" of a power-relation, in which case humans are the imperialists dominating a non-human "other," but nature cannot be the subject of an imperialistic power-relation. To regard nature as the subject exercising power, as in the third and fourth categories, is the error of anthropomorphism, seeing nature as a being with human qualities.

Although there is some truth to this objection, it is not fatal to my overall project or argument in this essay. As I noted above, I am attempting to revise the traditional ways in which we think about nature. I want to consider nature as the subject of an ongoing history, a subject that acts and develops in ways that are comparable—in some moral or axiological sense—to human action. As Colin Duncan has claimed, "While Nature is certainly not a person . . . it does have some of the attributes of a Hegelian subject. It can be both victim-like and agent-like."[3] This metaphor may be a form of anthropomorphism, but it is different from the fully developed anthropomorphizing of nature found, for example, in Greek mythology. I am not attributing to nature the emotions, intentions, and reasoning powers of human subjects; I am only suggesting that it is incorrect to think of nature as a mere object, a passive recipient of human activity.

Here we can also see how important it is to use the restricted meaning of nature introduced above—nature as the ecosystemic processes of the biological world. If we are to have a sense of nature as a subject or agent, acting upon humanity and human institutions, then it is imperative that we not view nature as simply the totality of physical laws of the universe. The laws of the universe do not *act on* anything—they are merely the *descriptions* of the ways in which the entities and systems of the universe operate. The idea that natural systems—or some parts of the natural world—act like imperialists, dominating other entities or systems, requires a sense of nature as a distinct system, able to stand in a relation with an "other." It is thus useful to use the terminology of Lynton Keith Caldwell, who distinguishes the "Earth of nature" from the "world of man." The difference, he claims, is obvious: "the Earth is a creation of the cosmos and is independent of man. The world is a human artifact; it is a conceptual creation of human experience and information." It so happens that in the present epoch, the human world is "geographically congruent" with the Earth of nature,[4] but this does not diminish their ontological distinctiveness. Nature is the sum total of non-human, biological, and evolutionary ecosystemic processes of the Earth's physical system.

But this raises a second objection: the idea that "nature" and "humanity" are opposite points in a power relationship tends to reinforce the very separation of humanity and nature that an enlightened environmental policy seeks to overcome. It is surely one goal of the environmental movement to end the common belief that humans are separate from natural processes—to instill the ecological idea that humans are an interdependent part of the natural system, requiring a well-functioning natural environment to survive. But the notion of interdependence itself requires, at least conceptually, the idea that there are separate entities that are, in fact, interrelated. To say that humans are connected to natural processes requires an idea of a distinct human presence, a distinct human ontology, that is, nevertheless, dependent on the "otherness" of the non-human natural world. It is not a mistake to claim that humans can dominate nature, or that nature can dominate humanity, even though they are inseparably related. As Don E. Marietta, Jr., once stated to me in conversation, the "sugar can dominate the pudding"—even in the case where the blending of distinct elements forms a harmonious unity, one element can dominate the whole.

This essay will not examine all four categories of imperialism, because they are not all of equal interest. The fourth type, nature's domination of nature, simply does not concern us, since we humans are not parties to the dispute, except indirectly. But what is intriguing about this schema is that almost all discussions of imperialism, even discussions of environmental imperialism, involve the first type, the domination of one human group by another. Environmental imperialism is generally seen as the alteration of natural systems by one human group as it colonizes and subsequently dominates or subdues another human group. Thus the European colonizers of the Americas used agriculture and a new conception of private property to modify the

ecology and environmental context of the indigenous American peoples. In this first type of environmental imperialism, the effects of
human activity on the natural world, although important, are indirect,
secondary, or derivative. The basic form of imperialism is understood
to be an expression of power between two human societies.

Although an analysis and understanding of this type of imperialism
is clearly important—as the work of Cronon, Crosby, and Merchant
demonstrates[5]—I believe that we should also consider the second and
third types of imperialism, the direct relationship of power between
humans and nature. At the end of this essay I will comment briefly on
the third form of imperialism, nature's power over human civilization,
but I want to consider primarily the second form of imperialism, the
human domination of nature, because this is the form over which we
have some control, and hence, for which we have some responsibility.

The human domination of nature is, of course, an old topic, even
within the field of environmental philosophy: twenty-five years ago
William Leiss's analysis of the influence of Francis Bacon was entitled
The Domination of Nature.[6] Clearly, the idea that humanity has exerted
a fundamental influence on natural processes has become a standard
and non-controversial datum of the environmentalist world-view. One
need only read the introductory chapters of Al Gore's *Earth in the Balance* to see how the idea of human domination has permeated the
mainstream consciousness of the environmental movement.[7] But to
what extent is this domination a form of *imperialism?* What is the relationship of power between humanity and nature? What is the philosophical meaning—ontological and axiological—of this relationship?

Humanity has done more than influence natural processes. It has
done more than "tame" wild nature for the increased comfort, wealth,
and power of human beings. My central thesis is that humanity has
attempted to modify and to mold natural processes for the satisfaction
of human interests, to create an artificial or artifactual world that produces the most benefit for human beings. This artificial world at best
resembles nature, where it is convenient. It is the basic policy of human
civilization—even where that policy is unarticulated—to modify or to
conquer the natural world, to subdue Nature for the furtherance of
human good. This policy has been the central project of Western civilization since the Enlightenment, and although it has proven in many
respects to be a failure, its fundamental meaning and motivation are
clear: the primary goal of Western civilization, especially Western science and technology, has been the control and domination of nature
for the promotion of human benefit—the human imperialism over
nature.

The central meaning of Western civilization regarding human activity in the natural world is that human interests, the maintenance and improvement of human life, lie at the center of all value determinations. Human progress is the purpose of all human activity. Nature and natural resources are worthless, mere objects for exploitation by the dominant human species, until they are transformed, through human labor, into cultural instruments for human betterment. The analogy with traditional notions of imperialism is obvious. Humanity conquers and colonizes the natural world, with the moral justification that human good is the only determination of value, just as one nation-state might conquer another, judging its own interests to be supreme.

One chilling example of the goal of the human imperialistic domination of nature can be found in a classic essay in the field of environmental ethics, Martin Krieger's "What's Wrong with Plastic Trees?"[8] Krieger argues that if the goal of social policy is the maximization of human satisfaction and the promotion of social justice, then there is no overriding reason to preserve nature. An adequate technology, combined with a proper education through mass culture, could create an artificial plasticized world that would produce more happiness for the human population, at a lower cost, than the preservation of the natural world. Krieger writes: "There is no lack of merit in natural environments, but this merit is not canonical,"[9] and he concludes that "Artificial prairies and wildernesses have been created, and there is no reason to believe that these artificial environments need be unsatisfactory for those who experience them."[10] Thus he proposes an environmental policy of "responsible interventions" to mold both natural processes and the popular human responses to them. The goal of this new interventionist environmental policy should be the maximization of human satisfaction and social justice.

Krieger's vision of a plastic artificial world designed for the maximization of human happiness is perhaps the most extreme case of human imperialism over the natural world. The terminology of "responsible interventions" even echoes the justification for the use of military force in U.S. foreign policy. Under Krieger's model, the natural world is not only subjugated to meet the demands of the dominating force (that is, humanity), it is virtually destroyed, replaced by a more docile, cooperative system of entities. The natural world becomes a mere pacified colony of the invading forces of humanity; aspects of the natural world that further human interests are preserved, or even augmented, while the aspects that interfere with human interests are destroyed, replaced, or exiled.

Is Krieger's theory of environmental policy merely an extreme case? If it were, then we could probably ignore it, for as an extreme it would not have much influence on mainstream environmental policy or philosophy. But Krieger's imperialistic vision has surprisingly strong echoes in other theorists of environmental policy. Chris Maser, for example, is a former research scientist for the U.S. Department of Interior Bureau of Land Management, who argues in favor of a policy of "sustainable forestry" in *The Redesigned Forest*.[11] Maser is a critic of the short-term expediency of present-day forestry practices. He attacks the plantation mentality of forest management, and argues for a forestry policy that "restores" the forest as it is harvested.

I have analyzed and criticized Maser's arguments for restoration elsewhere and will not repeat the full discussion here.[12] In brief, Maser's model of the relationship between humanity and the natural world reinforces a notion of human imperialism over nature. Maser sees the natural world as a mechanism with a design that can be discovered and manipulated by human science and technology. At one point, he compares the mechanism of a forest with an automobile as he argues empirically against the substitution of an artificial forest for a natural one: "A forest cannot be 'rebuilt' and remain the same forest, but we could probably rebuild a forest similar to the original if we knew how. No one has ever done it . . . [W]e do not have a parts catalog, or a maintenance manual. . . ."[13] The implication is that if we did have a catalog and manual, then the restoration and redesign of forests would be practically and morally acceptable.

For Maser, the ultimate motivation for forest redesign is the furtherance of long-term human interests. Maser argues that the central problem with current practices is that they are "exclusive of all other values except the production of fast-grown woodfiber."[14] What concerns Maser is the elimination of other human values and interests. "We need to learn to see the forest as the factory that produces raw materials . . ." to meet our "common goal[:] . . . a sustainable forest for a sustainable industry for a sustainable environment for a sustainable human population."[15] By using the complex knowledge of forest ecology, restorationist foresters will redesign forests to better achieve human purposes.

Maser is an interesting case because, unlike Krieger, he is a committed environmentalist, indeed a hero to enlightened foresters and government officials dealing with practical environmental policy. But a philosophical analysis of his views clearly reveals the perspective of the human imperialism over nature. The fundamental goal for Maser is the proper use of the natural world to meet human needs—this is the basic motivation for any imperialism. His only quarrel with current forestry practices is in the methodology or the style of the domination.

What then is wrong with the human imperialism over nature? Is the consideration of this type of imperialism a normative issue? Is not the human domination of nature necessary for human survival and human progress? Or is this imperialism a kind of moral evil, perhaps analogous to the human domination of other humans?

Consider two problems or reasons why the human imperialism over nature is morally suspect. First, imperialism subverts or destroys the value of the subjugated entity. The value of the subjugated entity may be either good or bad relative to human interests—for example, a good rain forest or a bad disease organism. But regardless of whether the value is good or bad, the action of human imperialism or domination changes the pre-existing status. When we replace the natural world with an artificial human substitution, we also replace a particular complex of values. The act of replacement itself imparts a new reality and a new set of values. The new system may appear to be similar to the original natural system, but it will be, in actuality, a human artifact. It will be valuable, and indeed useful, for the human goods it furthers or promotes. If the new system were not at least thought to be valuable and useful for human interests then we would not bother to create it in the first place—one is not an imperialist over a worthless entity. But at the same time that we acquire the benefits of the new subjugated system or entity, we will lose access to the values of the original system or entity—we will lose the value of the undisturbed natural world.

But is there an undisturbed natural world? Is there a nature that is independent of human power and human activity? The idea that human imperialism causes a loss to the value of the natural world raises important questions regarding the very meaning of nature itself. Thus, we can see that my original definition and discussion of the meaning of nature—as those ecosystemic processes independent from human culture and civilization—was clearly provisional; any detailed analysis of the meaning and value of human interaction with the natural world is forced to address the problem of the meaning of nature. One question results from the realization that the human impact on the natural world is so pervasive that nature as a separate system no longer exists. Is there a pure natural value that should be protected? A popular treatment of this theme can be found in Bill McKibben's *The End of Nature*,[16] where McKibben focuses on the fact that humanity has changed the chemical composition of the atmosphere. Since the atmosphere literally touches all of nature, once it has been changed, then the physical interactions that make up the natural system have also been changed. It can be argued, then, that no independent nature exists, and a concern for the value of a pristine, untouched nature is a product of a misplaced or overly sentimental nostalgia.

McKibben also suggests another question, when he writes: "When I say 'nature', I mean a certain set of human ideas about the world and our place in it."[17] Nature is not only a system of physical entities that has been subjected to pervasive human influence, it is also a set of human ideas for describing and categorizing the world. Nature is a human idea. The models by which we describe the world of nature are human constructs; our theories of nature are themselves artifacts serving human ends. This, then, is another answer to the question of what nature is—it is a human construct. We human thinkers choose the model, metaphor, or idea of nature that will best serve our purpose—just as I have chosen, in this essay, to view nature as the total set of ecosystemic processes. Thus nature is the victim of another form of human imperialism, what we can term an epistemological imperialism, for nature's very meaning is determined by human thought. The *concept* of nature, as well as its physical processes, is dominated by human thought and practice. An analysis of this domination is clearly a normative issue.

The second normative problem with the human imperialism over nature concerns the third form of imperialism, the power that nature exerts over humanity. The plain fact is that humanity has not been entirely successful in exerting its influence over nature and natural systems for the furtherance of human good. This lack of success is apparent no matter which view of nature we take to be most relevant, for humanity has not succeeded in changing the physical laws of the universe, nor has it been successful in re-creating functioning natural ecosystems. True, we have been quite effective in destroying natural systems, but our efforts at replacing them with useful human-friendly systems have been nearly catastrophic. One interpretation of the current environmental crisis is that it represents nature's backlash—its counter-insurgency—against the forces of human colonization. It is here that we recognize the awesome power of nature to reassert its independence from human attempts to control it. The ecosystemic processes that constitute nature react against human acitivity, in part by reducing our domain and dominion.[18]

The idea of nature's reaction, its counter-insurgency, gives a context and meaning to the fact of the beach houses being swept away by ocean tides and a hundred-year storm. Nature's power over humanity reveals the depth of the human arrogance that builds homes on sand. But the same point of view applies to our use of pesticides, fertilizers, nuclear energy—the list of nature's backlash is endless. So the second reason that the human imperialism over nature is a moral problem is that it cannot answer the response of nature's domination of humanity. Our attempts to dominate nature reveal a disturbing lack of prudence, to say the least. Despite our technology and science, nature is more powerful than human civilization.

Several conceptual issues invite further discussion. First is the importance of *intentionality* in the analysis of domination. It appears that using the notion of imperialism to describe the acts of nature is problematic, whether these acts are directed towards humanity (the third type) or towards other natural entities (the fourth type). Nature's actions do not have intentionality. When the December storm washed away beach houses on the northeastern coast of the United States it was not the intention of nature to exert its power over humanity. So my notion of imperialism clearly broadens the traditional use of the concept, not only in the ideas of the proper subjects and objects of imperialism and domination, but in the basic structure of the imperialistic act. The moral analysis of domination may not require the existence of intention.

It should be noted, however, that not all intra-human acts of domination require intentionality either. If racism and sexism are considered as forms of imperialistic domination (as I would so judge them), then there do exist instances of so-called institutional racism or sexism that are unconnected to specific or direct intentional actions. A person who is not a racist can act in a manner that promotes racism, for example, by following the procedures of an institution that unknowingly is structured to discriminate; thus some hiring and promotion requirements at a university may be racist (or sexist) in an institutional sense. The point is that domination can be unintentional.

The focus on intentionality becomes relevant when we consider our moral evaluation of actions and their consequences. Since humans have, in general, control over the activities that they instigate in their interactions with the natural world, it is easy to place blame or praise on the activities chosen. But it is senseless to blame nature for the destruction of beach houses or for a forest succession. Without the possibility of intention, the moral evaluation of the acting subject becomes impossible.

A related issue would be the entire complex of problems involving the teleological structure of natural systems. Do natural entities and systems lack intentionality while at the same time displaying purposive activity? Can purpose exist without intentionality? Is purposive activity all that is necessary for the concepts of imperialism and domination? Unfortunately, I do not have answers to these questions, which involve fundamental issues in the philosophy of biology and perhaps in the foundations of metaphysics. I raise the issues here only because I want to demonstrate the significance of the discussion over imperialism and environmentalism; I seek to provoke a far-ranging debate.

The final conceptual issue is, perhaps, the most important question raised by the preceding discussion. All four types of imperialism—but especially the second and third—reveal the necessity of the exercise of power over other entities. Humans must try to control some aspects of the natural world for their very survival; nature must respond as it asserts its independence from human design. The essential issue is then one of determining the proper scope of intervention and interaction. When are humans permitted to intervene in natural processes, and when should they refrain? When does an intervention become an attempt at domination? After all, humans must eat and grow food, must build houses, roads, cities, must cure disease. Are these all acts of imperialistic domination that are morally suspect?

The answer to this problem lies in determining the proper metaphor, the appropriate rhetoric, for understanding the human relationship to nature. When one nation-state interacts with another nation-state in a spirit and a structure of mutual benefit and partnership, then it cannot be considered an act of imperialism or domination. Not all interactions are instances of unequal power relationships; to use a biological concept, some actions are symbioses. Thus, to understand whether or not a human intervention into natural processes constitutes an act of imperialism, we must consider the model or metaphor under which the act is structured. Do we humans seek a balance with nature, a type of partnership, or a power relationship of control and domination? Are our agricultural processes, for example, organic, working with natural processes, or are they highly technological, seeking control through artificial fertilizers and pesticides?

To discover a criterion for the proper intervention in the natural world is the fundamental task in determining the real meaning of environmental policy. Only with a morally justifiable criterion will human activity within nature—whether this be political action, government environmental policy, resource management, ecological restoration, or wilderness and habitat preservation—avoid the stigma of domination.

By placing this problem in the framework of imperialism and domination, I am suggesting that it is the broadest possible issue regarding human action. To be morally justified, all human activity, even that between humans, requires a standard of appropriate intervention. The determination of that standard is the central question of moral philosophy.[19]

Notes

1. Bertrand Russell, *An Outline of Philosophy* (New York: New American Library, 1974), p. 30. Cited in Holmes Rolston, III, *Environmental Ethics: Duties to and Values in the Natural World* (Philadelphia: Temple University Press, 1988), p. 326.

2. William Leiss, "The Imperialism of Human Needs," *North American Review* 259, 4 (1974): 27–34.

3. Colin A. M. Duncan, "On Identifying a Sound Environmental Ethic in History: Prolegomena to Any Future Environmental History," *Environmental History Review* 15 (1991): 8. See also Eric Katz, "The Call of the Wild: The Struggle Against Domination and the 'Technological Fix' of Nature," *Environmental Ethics* 14 (1992): 265–73, and Rolston, *Environmental Ethics*.

4. Lynton Keith Caldwell, *Between Two Worlds: Science, the Environmental Movement and Policy Choice* (Cambridge: Cambridge University Press, 1990), p. 39.

5. See William Cronon, *Changes in the Land: Indians, Colonists, and the Ecology of New England* (New York: Hill & Wang, 1983), Alfred W. Crosby, *Ecological Imperialism: The Biological Expansion of Europe, 900–1900* (Cambridge: Cambridge University Press, 1986), and Carolyn Merchant, *Ecological Revolutions: Nature, Gender, and Science in New England* (Chapel Hill: University of North Carolina Press, 1989).

6. William Leiss, *The Domination of Nature* (Boston: Beacon, 1974).

7. Al Gore, *Earth in the Balance: Ecology and the Human Spirit* (Boston: Houghton Mifflin, 1992). Gore writes of the "assault of humanity on nature," of human domination of nature and the power of humanity as being equivalent to natural forces.

8. Martin Krieger, "What's Wrong with Plastic Trees?" *Science* 179 (1973): 446–55.

9. Ibid., p. 451.

10. Ibid., p. 453.

11. Chris Maser, *The Redesigned Forest* (San Pedro, Calif.: R. & E. Miles, 1988).

12. See Eric Katz, "The Big Lie: Human Restoration of Nature," *Research in Philosophy and Technology* 12 (1992): 231–41; "Artefacts and Functions: A Note on the Value of Nature," *Environmental Values* 2 (1993): 223–32, and "The Call of the Wild."

13. Maser, pp. 88–89.

14. Ibid., p. 94.

15. Ibid., pp. 148–49.

16. Bill McKibben, *The End of Nature* (New York: Random House, 1989).

17. Ibid., p. 8.

18. Duncan, p. 9, for the notion of reducing our domain.

19. An earlier and much shorter version of this paper was read at the Eighth Annual Technological Literacy Conference of the National Association for Science, Technology, and Society, Washington, D.C., January 16, 1993. I am grateful to Paul Durbin, David Rothenberg, and Chris Sellars for their comments on that earlier draft. Another version of this paper was presented at a Working Session of the Society for Philosophy and Technology Biennial Conference on the theme Technology, Nature, and Cultural Diversity, in Peñíscola, Spain, May 21, 1993. I am grateful for the comments received at that time, especially from Phil Shepard, Eduardo Sabrovsky, Andrew Light, and Laura Westra. This work is supported, in part, by the New Jersey Institute of Technology under Separately Budgeted Research Grants for the academic years 1992–1994.

Part III

Justice, Genocide, and the Environment

11

Moving Beyond Anthropocentrism: Environmental Ethics, Development, and the Amazon

Eric Katz and Lauren Oechsli

I wrote the first draft of "Moving Beyond Anthropocentrism" in the spring of 1990 in an attempt to demonstrate the differences in practical environmental policy that might arise from a nonanthropocentric environmental ethic. If the adoption of ecological holism did not lead to concrete policy results different from traditional human-based environmentalism, then the entire debate within environmental philosophy over the various foundations of an environmental ethic was merely an academic and theoretical disputation, unworthy of public concern. The next year, in fact, Bryan Norton argued in Toward Unity Among Environmentalists *(New York: Oxford University Press, 1991) that the various positions in environmental philosophy did not lead to different policies, for all environmentalists share a large common ground, a consensus in policy choices. Nevertheless, I believe that the development or preservation of the Amazon rain forest is an issue where differing environmental philosophies have a profound effect on policy decisions, particularly as they relate to questions of international and intergenerational justice. During the spring of 1990, Lauren Oechsli, an undergraduate biology major at Columbia University, wrote a term paper for my course "Ethics and the Environment" on the ethical issues in developmental policies of the rain forests. Over the summer of 1990 we modified my earlier paper on the sub-ject—which was highly theoretical—to include many of Ms. Oechsli's argu-ments on the practical effects of rain forest development. The essay was even-*

149

tually published with joint authorship in Environmental Ethics *15 (1993): 49–59.*

I. Introduction

In this paper, we consider the role of human interests in the formation of environmental policy. Are environmentalist policies justified solely because they benefit human individuals and human society? Or are there valid moral principles that transcend human concerns and justify a direct moral consideration of the natural environment?

These questions have dominated the field of environmental ethics since its inception. In general, the field has provided a critique of *instrumental* human-based arguments for environmental policies, and has attempted the development of a *nonanthropocentric* ethic or value theory which will account for a direct moral consideration of nature.[1]

We defend this rejection of anthropocentric instrumental reasoning as a basis for environmental policy. Although we do not formulate a value theory or a system of ethics that validates a nonanthropocentric regard for nature, we argue that this direction in environmental ethics is necessary for the solution of persistently difficult questions of public policy. As an example, we consider arguments about the development of the environment in the Third World, especially the destruction of the Amazon rain forests. Anthropocentric justifications concerning development—both for and against—lead to inescapable problems concerning both utility and justice. These problems can be avoided from a nonanthropocentric and non-instrumental perspective. We thus provide an *indirect* argument for the moral consideration of nature in the formation of environmental policy.

Our argument is based on a narrow, but, we believe, pervasive interpretation of the term *anthropocentric* to mean those values, goods, and interests that promote human welfare to the near exclusion of competing nonhuman values, goods, and interests. This version of anthropocentrism is closely aligned with the term *instrumentalism*, according to which the world is viewed as a resource valuable only as it promotes human good. Our purpose is to criticize *anthropocentric instrumentalism* as it is applied to developmental policies. Although we leave open the possible justification of environmental policies by *noninstrumental* forms of *anthropocentrism* (such as beauty or other intrinsic human ideals), we suggest primarily that a *nonanthropocentric instrumentalism* (based on the promotion of the goods of nonhuman nature) is a valid and necessary response to environmental problems.

II. Human Interests and Environmental Preservation

It is not surprising that anthropocentric arguments dominate discussions of policy: arguments for environmental preservation based directly on human interests are often compelling. Dumping toxic wastes into a community's reservoir of drinking water is clearly an irrational act; in such a case, a discussion of ethics or value theory is not necessary. The direct harm to humans engendered by this action is enough to disqualify it from serious ethical consideration. Nevertheless, other actions in the field of environmental policy are not so clear: there may be, for example, cases in which there are competing harms and goods to various segments of the human population that have to be balanced. The method for balancing these competing interests gives rise to issues of equity and justice. In addition, and more pertinent to our argument, are cases in which human actions threaten the existence of natural entities not usable as resources for human life. What reason do we humans have for expending vast sums of money (in positive expenditures and lost opportunities) to preserve endangered species of plants and animals that are literally nonresources?[2] In these cases, policies of environmental preservation seem to work against human interests and human good.

Anthropocentric and instrumental arguments in favor of preservationist policies can be developed in a series and arranged in order of increasing plausibility. First, it is argued that any particular species of plant or animal might prove useful in the future. Alastair Gunn calls this position the "rare herb" theory. According to this theory, the elimination of any natural entity is morally wrong because it closes down the options for any possible positive use.[3] A point frequently raised in discussions of this problem is that the endangered species we are about to eliminate might be the cure for cancer. Of course, it is also possible that it will cause cancer; the specific effects of any plant or animal species might be harmful as well as beneficial. Because we are arguing from a position of ignorance, it is ludicrous to assert either possibility as certain, or to use either alternative as a basis for policy.

A better argument is used by Paul and Anne Ehrlich: the metaphor of the airplane rivets.[4] The Ehrlichs tell a parable of an airplane passenger watching as a mechanic removes some of the rivets from the wing assembly of the plane he is boarding. When asked what he is doing, the mechanic replies that for reasons of economy, the airline is cutting down on the number of rivets used on each plane; some of the rivets are being removed and used on other planes. The procedure is not dangerous, continues the mechanic, since up to this point, no planes have been lost. The point of the parable is that although the elimination of individual species might not be directly harmful to human welfare, the aggregate elimination of many species probably will be. It is thus in the interests of humanity to remove as few "rivets" as possible, to preserve natural species even when they are "nonresources."

Without the use of a parable, Bryan Norton makes a similar point. In his discussion of the diversity-stability hypothesis in ecological theory, Norton argues that dynamically stable and mature ecosystems are important elements of that total diversity which stabilizes all ecosystems.[5] There is a danger in continually disrupting these diverse and stable ecosystems:

> Since the biological diversity of the planet has already entered an accelerating downward spiral, losses of species represent further accelerations toward local and global ecosystem breakdowns. The risks of breakdowns are so great and the contribution of species losses to them are so little understood that any rational society would exercise extreme caution in contributing to that acceleration.[6]

Diverse species populations thus contribute to stable ecosystems, which have positive impacts on human life.

Finally, this argument is broadened into a general concern for ecological function. The preservation of the natural environment insures a biosphere that supports human civilization. Degradation of the natural environment threatens human survival. Nevertheless, knowledge of ecological processes can help humans avoid damage to essential biological and physical links in the natural world. As Norton indicates, the loss of species and ecosystems is a sign that these natural connections are being "cut," lost, or damaged. The mere preservation of the natural environment halts this process of degradation. Nature thus has to be preserved because it has a value for human beings and human society: it insures the physical basis of human life.

In sum, these preservationist arguments based on "human interests" move from a narrow concern for the specific direct use of a natural entity or species, to the indirect importance of species as stabilizers of ecosystems, and finally to a general concern for the maintenance of ecosystems as the basis of human existence.

These anthropocentric instrumental arguments for environmental preservation are easily transferred to issues of environmental policy. Recent concern about the destruction of the ozone layer and the increased probability of the "greenhouse effect" reflect the fear that current environmental and economic policies are damaging the environment and threatening human life. Indeed, it is a mark of the success of the environmental movement that the public is now aware of the connections between environmental health and human survival.

A clear example of the connection between instrumental human interest arguments and concern for the preservation of an ecosystem is the current awareness of the plight of the Amazon rain forests. Although continued development of the forests and the conversion of rain forests to farmland and pasture contribute to a rapid loss of species,[7] the major problem is a threat to the overall ecosystems of the rain forests themselves. Deforestation has a significant impact on climate because of the increase of atmospheric carbon.[8] The recent increase in atmospheric carbon is a primary cause of the "greenhouse effect," which leads to global warming. Thus, the preservation of the rain forests is an important element in the maintenance of a biosphere habitable for humanity. This line of reasoning has been a clear argument and powerful motivation for environmental policies designed to preserve the Amazon rain forests. Environmentalists and ordinary citizens alike now seek a halt to the destruction of the Amazon; they now recognize that the welfare of all human life depends on the maintenance of this unique ecological region.

It thus appears that anthropocentric arguments for environmental preservation are useful in the justification and determination of environmental policy. Natural entities, species, and ecosystems are crucial, both for human survival and for the continuation of an advanced level of civilization. The important instrumental functions of the natural environment thus can be employed in debates over environmental policy throughout the Third World, and in particular, the Amazon rain forest. Should Third World nations be prevented from developing natural ecological areas in ways that would destroy the ecosystems of the region? Should policies of sustainable development, the economic use of the forest without clearcutting or other forms of destruction, be mandatory? Should such countries as Brazil be persuaded to preserve the Amazon rain forest so that the harmful consequences of the "greenhouse effect" can be avoided? A consistent environmentalist, it seems, would be forced to condemn the Third World development of the natural environment on the grounds that the Amazon rain forests must be saved.

We believe that this anthropocentric and instrumental argument for the preservation of the Amazon rain forests (or any other Third World natural area) is seriously flawed. Even though the natural environment should be preserved, arguments based on human interest fail to provide an adequate justification for the preservation of ecosystems in the Third World. We discuss the problems with the anthropocentric perspective in the following two sections.

III. Problems of Utility

The first problem is empirical: there is uncertainty about the calculation of benefits and harms to be derived from alternative policies of development or preservation. In part, the problem is a traditional one encountered with any consequentialist analysis of normative action; however, in this particular case, Amazon rain forest development, we believe that the problem is acute. Although the benefits and harms to be determined are solely those of the affected human populations, the relevant populations are clearly distinct from one another, and the level and kinds of benefits and harms appear to be incommensurable.

If a policy of preservation is adopted, the benefits to be derived are those associated with the continued maintenance of the biosphere as the basis of human life: production of oxygen, consumption of atmospheric carbon, preservation of potentially useful species, etc. If a policy of development is adopted, the benefits to be derived are primarily local and economic: increased agricultural and livestock production, industry, and exports. The costs and harms within each policy are determined by the failure to achieve the alternative benefits. A policy of preservation limits economic gain; a policy of development limits the goods of a functioning natural ecosystem.

Although the choices appear clear, we lack the kind of data that would make the utility calculations possible. Is there a quantifiable good in the preservation of x amount of rain forest acreage that can be expressed in terms of biospherical maintenance and then compared to the loss of economic gains by indigenous local populations? Can we determine a quantifiable good in various methods of rain forest development, which then can be compared to losses in ecological function? It seems unlikely that these kinds of comparisons could ever be made; they are not being made now. In a recent survey of land use and management by indigenous peoples, Jason W. Clay warns: "Until now, few researchers have examined the ways indigenous inhabitants of tropical rain forests use and sustain their region's resources.'"[9] Clay is saying that we do not know what the economic benefits and costs are in alternative policies of preservation and development. If viewed in this way, utility calculations become impossible as a basis of policy.

Our complaint is not merely with the traditional difficulties of performing real-life utility calculations. The deeper issue is the anthropocentric framework that limits ethical and policy discussions. The primary concern for human interests or benefits—anthropocentrism—creates an irreconcilable conflict between two goods that are supposedly advocated by anthropocentric policies, i.e., the ecosystem which preserves the atmosphere, thus, preserving human life, and the economic use of the land by the indigenous population. We are faced with a classic case of a conflict between a long-term support system and short-term usable goods. This conflict cannot be resolved unless we expand the framework of discussion beyond the limits of anthropocentric instrumental reasoning.

IV. The Problem of Justice

The conflict between differing kinds of goods leads directly to the problem or dilemma of justice. This problem is a classic, long-standing difficulty in normative ethics. It arises in the context of environmental and economic policy decisions because of the exclusive use of narrowly defined anthropocentric and instrumental goods. Theoretical human goods and harms (the type discussed in the previous section) are not adequate as a basis for the determination of environmental policy, because global environmental policy cannot be determined in isolation from geopolitical concerns. The history and politics of power relations cannot be ignored. Third World nations, recently freed from political colonization, see the development of indigenous natural resources as a means of attaining economic freedom. The newly formed policies of nondevelopment and preservation appear to be a subtle form of the old imperialism. The wealthy industrialized nations of the world, having developed their own natural resources, and having "stolen" the natural resources of the Third World, now are planning to prevent any further development, so that the ecological basis of humanity can be preserved—a policy which clearly limits the economic and social development of the poorer, nonindustrialized nations.[10]

These complaints of "preservationist imperialism" are difficult to answer, and open-minded environmentalists must feel uneasy about the dilemma. Nevertheless, it is our contention (in this and the next section) that if the policies of nondevelopment and preservation continue to be justified by *instrumental* arguments regarding the ecological value of nature for human survival, then the charges of imperialism and domination remain unassailable. Only by *rejecting anthropocentrism* and developing a framework of direct value for natural entities and systems, can one avoid the charges of imperialism in Third World preservation policy.

Why is anthropocentrism a critical part of the problem of justice? The simple answer is that anthropocentric arguments emphasize merely human goods, which simultaneously ignore a direct concern for environmental preservation and create insurmountable problems of balance and equity. Anthropocentric and instrumental arguments result in a merely contingent connection between human satisfaction and the maintenance of the natural environment.[11] If the final goal of our policy is the maximization of human satisfaction, then the preservation of nature only occurs when there is a congruence of interests between humanity and nature. In practical terms, thus, any discusson of policy alternatives—development, preservation, resource conservation—involves a comparison and trade-off of human goods, and only human goods. Viewed in this way, the preservation of a natural ecosystem or an endangered species becomes merely one benefit in an entire array of possible human satisfactions. For an environmentalist policy to be adopted, the results of preservation have to outweigh the results of development. Broadly speaking, the cost-benefit ratio has to favor the nondevelopment of the natural environment.

It is here that the problems of the utility calculation noted above in section three lead to the dilemma of environmental justice. Third World nations can claim that the benefits of preserving, e.g., the Amazon rain forest, are spread out thinly across the entire human race, while the costs (in this case, the cost of lost economic opportunity) are borne primarily by Brazilians and other local human populations. Development of the rain forest, however, provides benefits for the local population while spreading the costs across the rest of humanity. Demanding that Brazil and other Third World countries limit development, therefore, violates basic and intuitive notions of equity and justice. The Third World is being asked to pay for the industrialized world's profligate use of natural resources. Having been denied the benefits of past development, they are now being asked to pay for the preservation of the biosphere.

This issue of justice arises because the policy discussion has been limited to a consideration of human interests. If the criterion for policy decisions is the maximization of human satisfactions or benefits, then it becomes appropriate—even mandatory—to ask questions about the distribution of these benefits. In this way, issues of justice, in general, serve to limit and complement teleological criteria for the determination of policy. In the context of Third World environmental development, however, considerations of justice override any plausible account of benefits resulting from the preservation of the natural environment. The need for economic development seems so great that the hypothetical long-term effects on global warming appear trivial. If we restrict our analysis of policy to the maximization of human welfare and to the creation of just social institutions, then we cannot escape the problem created by the Third World's need for economic development. Conceived as a problem in maximizing and balancing human goods, the scales incline toward policies of development. The demand for anthropocentric justice dooms the preservation of the natural environment.

V. Moving Beyond Anthropocentrism

Can an environmentalist defend a policy of preservation in the Amazon rain forest without violating a basic sense of justice? We believe that the mistake is not the policy of preservation itself, but the anthropocentric instrumental framework in which it is justified. Environmental policy decisions should not merely concern the trade-off and comparison of various human benefits. If environmentalists claim that the Third World must preserve its environment because of the overall benefits for humanity, then decision makers in the Third World can demand justice in the determination of preservation policy: preservationist policies unfairly damage the human interests of the local populations. If preservationist policies are to be justified without a loss of equity, there are only two possible alternatives: either we in the industrialized world must pay for the benefits we will gain from preservation or we must reject the anthropocentric and instrumental framework for policy decisions. The first alternative is an empirical political issue, and one about which we are not overly optimistic. The second alternative represents a shift in philosophical world view.

We are not providing a direct argument for a nonanthropocentric value system as the basis of environmental policy. Rather, our strategy is indirect. Let us assume that a theory of normative ethics which includes nonhuman natural value has been justified. In such a situation, the human community, in addition to its traditional human-centered obligations, would also have moral obligations to nature or to the natural environment in itself. One of these obligations would involve the urgent necessity for environmental preservation. We would be obligated, for example, to the Amazon rain forest directly. We would preserve the rain forest, not for the human benefits resulting from this preservation, but because we have an obligation of preservation to nature and its ecosystems. Our duties would be directed to nature and its inhabitants and environments, not merely to humans and human institutions.

From *this* perspective, questions of the trade-off and comparison of human benefits, and questions of justice for specific human populations, do not dominate the discussion. This change of emphasis can be illustrated by an exclusively human example. Consider two businessmen, Smith and Jones, who are arguing over the proper distribution of the benefits and costs resulting from a prior business agreement between them. If we just focus on Smith and Jones and the issues concerning them, we will want to look at the contract, the relevant legal precedents, and the actual results of the deal, before rendering a decision. But suppose we learn that the agreement involved the planned murder of a third party, Green, and the resulting distribution of his property. At that point the issues between Smith and Jones cease to be relevant; we no longer consider who has claims to Green's wallet, overcoat, or BMW to be important. The competing claims become insignificant in light of the obligations owed to Green. This case is analogous to our view of the moral obligations owed to the rain forest. As soon as we realize that the rain forest itself is relevant to the conflict of competing goods, we see that there is not a simple dilemma between Third World development, on the one hand, and preservation of rain forests, on the other; there is now, in addition, the moral obligation to nature and its ecosystems.

When the nonanthropocentric framework is introduced, it creates a more complex situation for deliberation and resolution. It complicates the already detailed discussions of human trade-offs, high-tech transfers, aid programs, debt-for-nature swaps, sustainable development, etc., with a consideration of the moral obligations to nonhuman nature. This complication may appear counterproductive, but as in the case of Smith, Jones, and Green, it actually serves to simplify the decision. Just as a concern for Green made the contract dispute between Smith and Jones irrelevant, the obligation *to the rain forest* makes many of the issues about trade-offs of human goods irrelevant.[12] It is, of course, unfortunate that this direct obligation to the rain forest can only be met with a cost in human satisfaction—some human interests will not be fulfilled. Nevertheless, the same can be said of all ethical decisions, or so Kant teaches us: we are only assuredly moral when we act against our inclinations.

To summarize, the historical forces of economic imperialism have created a harsh dilemma for environmentalists who consider nature preservation in the Third World to be necessary. Nevertheless, environmentalists can escape the dilemma, as exemplified in the debate over the development of the Amazon rain forest, if they reject the axiological and normative framework of anthropocentric instrumental rationality. A set of obligations directed to nature in its own right makes many questions of human benefits and satisfactions irrelevant. The Amazon rain forest ought to be preserved regardless of the benefits or costs to human beings. Once we move beyond the confines of human-based instrumental goods, the environmentalist position is thereby justified, and no policy dilemma is created. This conclusion serves as an indirect justification of a nonanthropocentric system of normative ethics, avoiding problems in environmental policy that a human-based ethic cannot.[13]

VI. Concluding Remarks

Policy makers and philosophers in the Third World may not be pleased with our conclusions here. Indeed, Ramachandra Guha has recently criticized the focus on biocentrism (i.e., nonanthropocentrism) and wilderness preservation that pervades Western environmentalism. These Western concerns are at best, irrelevant to, and at worst, destructive of Third World societies. According to Guha, any justifiable environmental movement must include solutions to problems of equity, "economic and political redistribution."[14] We agree. Thus, as a final note, let us return from the abstract atmospheres of axiological theory and normative frameworks to the harsh realities of life in the non-industrialized world. If our argument is sound, then any destructive development of the natural environment in the Third World is a moral wrong, and a policy of environmental preservation is a moral requirement. Recognition of this moral obligation to preserve the natural environment should be the *starting point* for any serious discussion of developmental policy. But it is only a starting point. Once the preservationist obligation is accepted, the difficult trade-offs of goods between competing groups of humans can be debated, and questions of global equity can be addressed. Indeed, it is clear that they must be addressed, for the moral obligation to preserve the environment from destructive development creates additional human-based geopolitical obligations on the industrialized Western world. We must do more than lecture Third World nations; we must give them the economic aid that will make the development of their natural environments unnecessary. As Guha notes, we have to end the "expansionist character" of the West by developing an ethic of self-limitation. Only in this way can we begin to meet our obligation to preserve the natural environment.[15] In short, we must begin to pay the price for our centuries of environmental and developmental exploitation. We have outstanding debts, both to the nations of the Third World and to nature itself.

Notes

1. The critique of anthropocentric instrumental reasoning in environmental policy begins with Aldo Leopold's attempt to develop an ethic of ecological community. See Aldo Leopold, "The Land Ethic," in *A Sand County Almanac* (New York: Ballantine, 1970), pp. 237–64. Other important works that focus on the direct moral consideration of nature include: Holmes Rolston, III, *Environmental Ethics: Duties to and Values in the Natural World* (Philadelphia: Temple University Press, 1988); J. Baird Callicott, *In Defense of the Land Ethic: Essays in Environmental Philosophy* (Albany: SUNY Press, 1989); Peter S. Wenz, *Environmental Justice* (Albany: SUNY Press, 1988); and Paul W. Taylor, *Respect for Nature: A Theory of Environmental Ethics* (Princeton: Princeton University Press, 1986). For enlightened versions of anthropocentrism see Eugene C. Hargrove, *Foundations of Environmental Ethics* (Englewood Cliffs, N.J.: Prentice-Hall, 1989); Bryan G. Norton, *Why Preserve Natural Variety?* (Princeton: Princeton University Press, 1987); and Mark Sagoff, *The Economy of the Earth* (Cambridge: Cambridge University Press, 1988).

2. For a discussion of "nonresources," see David Ehrenfeld, *The Arrogance of Humanism* (New York: Oxford University Press, 1978), pp. 176–211.

3. Alastair Gunn, "Why Should We Care About Rare Species?" *Environmental Ethics* 2 (1980): 17–37.

4. Paul and Anne Ehrlich, *Extinction* (New York: Ballantine, 1981), pp. xi–xiv.

5. Norton, *Natural Variety*, pp. 80–84.

6. Ibid., p. 121.

7. Most sources, both popular and scientific, claim that the tropical rain forests are the source of almost half of the Earth's species. A comment by

Eugene P. Odum is typical: "Species diversity of both plants and animals tends to be high in tropical rain forests; there may be more species of plants and insects in a few acres of tropical rain forests than in the entire flora and fauna of Europe." Eugene P. Odum, *Ecology and Our Endangered Life-Support Systems* (Sunderland, Mass.: Sinauer, 1989), p. 244. See also Ehrlich and Ehrlich, *Extinction*, pp. 191–98; Thomas E. Lovejoy, "Species Leave the Ark One by One," in *The Preservation of Species*, ed. Bryan G. Norton (Princeton: Princeton University Press, 1986), pp. 13–27; Norman Myers, *The Sinking Ark* (New York: Pergamon Press, 1979) and *The Primary Source: Tropical Forests and Our Future* (New York: W. W. Norton, 1984), pp. 36–67; and E. O. Wilson, "Threats to Biodiversity," *Scientific American* 261, 3 (September 1989): 108–16. A major source of articles on all aspects of species diversity is E. O. Wilson and Frances M. Peter, eds., *Biodiversity* (Washington, D.C.: National Academy Press, 1988).

8. Deforestation has two major effects on climate, one "positive" and one "negative." Burning forests releases the carbon stored in trees into the atmosphere; and with deforestation, there are fewer trees to absorb or consume the carbon dioxide in the atmosphere. For a basic discussion in an introductory ecology text, see R. F. Dasmann, *Environmental Conservation*, 5th ed. (New York: John Wiley, 1984), p. 168, or see Myers, *The Primary Source*, pp. 283–93. Recent discussions of the effects of Amazon deforestation on climate can be found in J. Shukla, C. Nobre, and P. Sellers, "Amazon Deforestation and Climate Change," *Science* 247 (March 1990): 1322–25; and Roger A. Sedjo, "Forests: A Tool to Moderate Global Warming?" *Environment* 31 (January/February 1989): 14–20. See also Richard A. Houghton and George M. Woodwell, "Global Climatic Change," *Scientific American* 260, 4 (April 1989): 36–44; and a report on the work of Charles Keeling in Fred Pearce, "Felled Trees Deal Double Blow to Global Warning," *New Scientist* 123, 1682 (September 1989): 25.

9. Jason W. Clay, *Indigenous Peoples and Tropical Forests* (Cambridge, Mass.: Cultural Survival, 1988), p. 3. We might want to modify this bleak picture; see the argument in favor of nondestructive development of the rain forest in Charles M. Peters, Alwyn H. Gentry, and Robert O. Mendelsohn, "Valuation of an Amazon Rainforest," *Nature* 339 (June 1989): 655–56.

10. Ramachandra Guha, "Radical American Environmentalism and Wilderness Preservation: A Third World Critique," *Environmental Ethics* 11 (1989): 75–76.

11. For a discussion of the contingency of human interests in environmental policy, see Martin Krieger, "What's Wrong with Plastic Trees?" *Science* 179 (1973): 446–55; Mark Sagoff, "On Preserving the Natural Environment," *Yale Law Journal* 84 (1974): 205–67; and Eric Katz, "Utilitarianism and Preservation," *Environmental Ethics* 1 (1979): 357–64.

12. It makes many of the human interests irrelevant, but not all. See our concluding remarks below.

13. Again, we are not denying the possibility of an anthropocentric and noninstrumental ethic, a version of a so-called enlightened anthropocentrism. The

best treatments of this view are expressed by Hargrove, Norton, and Sagoff, in the works cited in note 1 above. Hargrove uses a concept of beauty, Norton a concept of "transformative " human values, and Sagoff a concept of the ideals of the community or nation. It is our contention, however, that a *direct* appeal to the goods of the nonhuman natural world is a clearer and less problematic route to the goal of environmental preservation.

14. Guha. "Radical American Environmentalism and Wilderness Preservation," p. 81.

15. Ibid., p. 80.

12

Biodiversity and Ecological Justice

In October 1990 the Center for BioDiversity Research and the Environmental Resources Research Institute at Pennsylvania State University sponsored a multidisciplinary international conference on the theme "Biodiversity and Landscapes: Human Challenges for Conservation in the Changing World." As one of the invited speakers I decided to use this opportunity—an address to scientists, policymakers, and environmental activists—to advocate the policy implications of a holistic community-based environmental ethic. The argument in this essay is a generalization of the case of the development and preservation of the Amazon rain forest, as set forth in "Moving Beyond Anthropocentrism." Here I explain in more detail the theoretical standpoint on which I base my policy decisions, using the general issue of biodiversity as the central example. Since the essay was originally written for an audience of nonphilosophers, I felt the need to justify, in some way, the entire discipline of environmental philosophy. I thus argue that the environmental crisis is primarily a crisis of moral value, a debate over fundamental beliefs about the human relationship to Nature. To solve this crisis we need to analyze and clarify the meaning and implications of our basic ideals concerning the natural world.

Introduction

The title of this essay requires explanation. The idea of "biodiversity" is rarely conjoined with the idea of "justice." This is because "biodiversity" is a scientific concept, whereas "justice" is, in part, normative. So I will have to explain why I believe the conjunction makes sense. The use of the adjective "ecological" to modify the concept of justice also

163

requires explanation. Once again I have combined a scientific idea—
that of ecology—with the normative idea of justice. Does *this* combination make sense? Is it possible to think of a system of justice that is
ecological as well as being normative, political, social? Or is this a
hopeless jumble of incompatible and contradictory ideas?

I will show that this seemingly contradictory combination of scientific and normative concepts is necessary for a full understanding of
the moral dimensions of biodiversity. I will argue that only by developing a system of justice that can properly be called "ecological justice"
can we morally justify policies that preserve the biodiversity of the
planet. If we remain trapped in the traditional categories of normative
thought we will be unable to justify acceptable and necessary environmental policies.

Two preliminary warnings: First, it must be emphasized that this
essay is an exercise and argument in applied moral philosophy. It is
an examination and criticism of a set of normative beliefs underlying
various kinds of environmental policy. Philosophical arguments have
their own standards of proof, which differ in important ways from the
standards of scientific proof. It is probably impossible to "prove" in an
"objective" way that a position in moral philosophy is "true"—
instead, philosophical rigor involves an examination of the coherence,
consistency, and implications of a given position. It is from that starting point that this exercise in applied moral philosophy proceeds.

Second, it also must be emphasized that this argument involves a
sharp criticism of conventional value judgments—concerning both
their meaning in moral philosophy in general and their specific application to environmental issues. I argue for views that lie outside the
major traditions of Western thought, precisely because the major traditions have failed to deal with the contemporary environmental crisis.
But in what is a pleasant paradox, the views I represent actually constitute the mainstream of that branch of applied moral philosophy called
"environmental ethics." Little more than twenty years old, the field of
environmental philosophy offers a continuous reexamination of conventional opinions about the meaning and basis of ethical judgments
regarding both humans and the natural environment.

A Crisis in Moral Value

The threat to planetary biodiversity caused by the technological, economic, and environmental policies of the last half century is only partly

a scientific problem. For a practitioner of moral philosophy, the threat to biodiversity is primarily a crisis in moral values. Traditional assumptions about value and the normative principles that shape moral life need to be rethought and modified. In light of increasingly complex environmental and social problems, these traditional views are, at best, inadequate; at worst, they are contributing causes of the environmental crisis.

The traditional "enlightened" interpretation of the environmental crisis is that humanity must now acknowledge the mutual interdependence of human society and the biological and ecological processes of the natural environment. The survival of individual human beings, and human civilization itself, requires the preservation of diverse biological systems and environments. Failure to recognize this interdependence could lead to a state of neobarbarism, the collapse of organized modes of local and international cooperation and stability, as a violent competition for the scarce resources necessary for human survival dominates social policy. This message—the warning that human civilization will collapse as a consequence of environmental destruction—originated, in recent years, in the work of social critics such as Paul and Anne Ehrlich, Barry Commoner, Garrett Hardin, Murray Bookchin, Norman Myers, and Rachel Carson, among others. The message is no longer the work of "extremist" critics; it is accepted, at least on the surface, as a truism. The consciousness of the environmental crisis and the need for preservation, conservation, and recycling as a requirement of human survival have spread throughout the population at large.

Why is this a problem? Why should we not rejoice that this once "extreme" position regarding the preservation of the natural environment has become the "mainstream" traditional view? What could be wrong with saving humanity?

The problem involves the determination of moral value. Any response to the environmental crisis requires the implementation of new social policies and new obligations on the part of human agents, institutions, and governments, As such, this response (or set of responses) makes explicit normative and ethical assumptions regarding human action and value. Whether they realize it or not, environmental policymakers, governmental officials, and ecological scientists are making moral decisions; these decisions reflect a (generally) unarticulated and uncritical vision of life and value. It is one task of the moral philosopher to articulate and to examine the values that are expressed through the implementation of these new policies. What values, in short, serve as the basis of the policies of conservation of the natural environment and the preservation of planetary biodiversity?

The current response to the environmental crisis expresses values that are blatantly anthropocentric: the main source of value lies in the continued existence of human life and civilization. The natural world—with its ecosystems, species, individual entities—is valued for its service to humanity, its instrumental use for the preservation of human goods. The possibility that the natural world could be valued for its own sake, that it would have a good of its own worth preserving, is hardly considered at all, and rarely plays any important part in the determination of policy.

An anthropocentric value system that only regards natural processes as important for human survival cannot serve as the basis of a comprehensive environmental policy. Anthropocentrism, in its narrow formulations of egoism, economic expediency, and utilitarianism, has been the primary force in the creation of the environmental crisis. Broadening the concept, to include the instrumental importance of the natural world for the prevention of human extinction, is hardly adequate as a solution. It merely restates the problem of the environmental crisis: why is all value based on human goods and interests?[1]

The real solution to problems in environmental policy lies in a specific transformation of values—the transcendence of human-based systems of ethics and the development of an "ecological ethic." Humanity must acknowledge that moral value extends beyond the human community to the communities within natural systems.[2] It is for this reason that the concept of "biodiversity" must be linked with "ecological justice." And it is for this reason that the problem of a diminishing planetary biodiversity is a crisis in moral value. Policies that ensure the preservation of planetary biodiversity must express values derived from a nonanthropocentric moral system, a normative theory of justice that is "ecological," i.e., a theory not based merely on human goods and interests.

The Problem of Anthropocentrism

Why is an anthropocentric value system an inadequate basis for environmental policy? This essay considers two major arguments, one theoretical, one practical. The theoretical argument involves the *contingent* relationship between the promotion of human interests and the continued preservation of the natural environmental.[3] Many human interests or goods are thought to be connected to the preservation of the natural world, connected in the sense that the satisfaction of the human interest or the production of the good derives from the continued existence of the natural processes. The environmentalist claims that the human interest or good requires the existence of the natural environment. But this connection is not necessary: human interests can probably be satisfied without nature, and certainly without a pristine nature.

A simple example is the human interest in *beauty*. It is claimed that natural environments and the biodiversity of the planet ought to be preserved because of the human need for beauty. A planet of diverse natural habitats and diverse individuals and species provides more opportunities for a necessary component of human life: appreciation of the beautiful. But the human interest in beauty can be satisfied in other ways. Urbanites, for example, New Yorkers such as myself, can satisfy their need for aesthetic stimulation and beauty by visits to the Metropolitan Museum or the Museum of Modern Art; they can view the impressive architectural designs of the city; with a heightened imagination, they can even find beauty in the dirt and debris of the urban landscape. The satisfaction of the need for beauty is thus only contingently connected to the preservation of the natural environment.

I am not claiming that humans have no interest in natural—as opposed to artifactual or cultural—beauty; I am arguing that the existence of natural beauty is not a necessary requirement for a complete human life. Thus, the environmentalist *argument* that natural diversity be maintained *because it satisfies a necessary human need for beauty* is a flawed argument: it does not provide an adequate justification for the preservation of the natural world.

This example concerning the human interest in beauty can be generalized to include all arguments for environmental preservation that are based on the satisfaction of human interests. Any such "human interest" argument is an *instrumental* argument: natural processes, environments, species, etc., are preserved for their instrumental use to humanity. The problem with instrumental arguments for preservation is that they deemphasize the intrinsic value of the object being preserved. Since the only value that matters is the use value, an adequate substitute that provides the same use will be valued just as highly as the original object. The original need not be preserved, for the instrumental use and the satisfactions derived thereby are provided by other means.[4]

It is clear that I am using a very broad notion of instrumental value. On my view, any entity or process that provides a benefit for human beings has an instrumental anthropocentric use value. Money, power, and pleasure are clearly instrumental goods—but so are beauty, friendship, and spiritual wonder. The point is that if humans preserve natural entities because of the benefits derived from the entities, their motivation and justification is instrumental, regardless of the kind of benefit being sought; this is different in fundamental ways from a justification based on moral obligation, which is not based on the maximization of benefits.[5]

In sum, anthropocentric arguments for the preservation of natural systems fail to achieve their aim. Justifications of environmental policies that are based on the satisfaction of human interest overlook the possibility of adequate substitutes for the promotion of these goods. Since the intrinsic qualities and value of natural objects and systems are ignored, these cannot be used to justify preservation. The contingent use for humanity is all that matters.

It might be objected that certain interests and goods for humanity are not contingent, but necessary: for example, the interest in human survival. Although my need for beauty can be fulfilled by looking at a Vermeer at the museum rather than a sunset over a wilderness lake in the Rockies, I cannot produce adequate substitutes for the food, water, and air I need to survive. Anthropocentric arguments for the preservation of natural environments gain force by focusing on the basic needs of human survival: the preservation of the biological cycles responsible for the production of clean food, air, and water.

There is some truth to this objection, but the argument does not take us very far. Given the increasing technological sophistication of the human race, it is unclear how many purely natural entities and processes we require for survival. We can create artificial foodstuffs, desalinate water, and purify air. How much of the natural world do we really require?[6] Because this is an open question, I am reluctant to base the justification of environmental policies of preservation on the necessity of natural soil, water, and air. The human race is surviving right now, despite the massive destruction we have imposed on natural systems and planetary biodiversity. So anthropocentric arguments that emphasize the connection between the preservation of nature and the survival of humanity are no less instrumental and contingent than those that emphasize other nonbasic human needs and interests (such as beauty). Survival arguments for environmental preservation are contingent on a given technological capability. If we have a technology that replaces nature we will no longer need to preserve it; but we do not want to base the policy on the existence or nonexistence of a specific technology.

This theoretical argument involving contingency may not be convincing to ecological scientists and policymakers who daily investigate the connection between planetary diversity and the preservation of necessary biological cycles. Scientists are often skeptical of philosophical thought experiments. Consider, then, a second, more practical argument for the inadequacy of anthropocentric justifications of environmental policy. This argument involves the problem of ecological imperialism and the development of the Third World.[7]

Consider the Amazon rainforest. The preservation of the rainforest is important, not only to preserve biodiversity but also to prevent environmental problems such as the "greenhouse" effect. The rainforest is home to millions of species with many possible instrumental uses for the betterment of human life. Destruction of the rainforest will eliminate the habitats for these species and cause their extinction. In addition, the burning of the wood from the forests increases the amount of carbon dioxide in the atmosphere, and removes carbon dioxide consuming vegetation from the planet's surface. Both processes increase the likelihood of global warming.

Policymakers and scientists therefore urge the preservation of the rainforests; these areas should not be open to development for farming and industry. This is obviously the correct environmental position. But many environmentalists, including myself, are uncomfortable with this position: it is too similar to ecological imperialism. We in the industrialized North are urging the poorer nations of the nonindustrialized South to refrain from the economic development of their own resource base. After having destroyed our own areas of diverse natural resources in the pursuit of national and individual wealth, we suddenly realize the importance of these areas for the survival of humanity, and so we prevent the rest of the world from achieving our own levels of national and individual affluence. We reap the benefits from past ecological destruction and development. The poorer undeveloped nations now pay the price: being forced to preserve their natural environments for the sake of the world and the rest of humanity.

The correct environmental policy of rainforest preservation thus raises questions of political and moral justice. Is it fair to inflict the costs of preservation on the poorer nations of the world when the benefits of this preservation (biodiversity and the slowing down of global warming) are distributed throughout the world as a whole? Is it doubly unfair that the cause of the problem has been the unchecked industrial growth of the richer nations? These are rhetorical questions: the injustice of the present situation is too obvious to argue. Environmentalists who care about broader issues of justice are faced with a painful dilemma—development or preservation; neither option produces desirable results.

There is a way out of this dilemma, and the resolution of the problem provides a *practical* argument against anthropocentric value systems. The problem of justice arises here because the issue is framed exclusively in terms of human goods and benefits; it is a dilemma involving competing claims of human values. On one side are the benefits to be derived from the preservation of the rainforest: biodiversity, less carbon dioxide in the atmosphere, etc. On the other side are the benefits to be gained from economic development: increased wealth for individuals in the poorer nations of South America. We cannot have both benefits. The dilemma arises because we do not know how to balance these competing human claims.

In thus framing the problem, we ignore the intrinsic value of the *rainforest itself*. The preservation or development of the natural environment is here conceived, as usual, as instrumentally useful for humanity, nothing more. The problem involves determining which instrumental-use value is greater and/or fairer. But the problem disappears once we focus our attention past the narrow anthropocentric interests of use and consider the rainforest, the natural environmental system, itself. Consider an analogy with two businessmen, Smith and Jones, who are arguing over the proper distribution of the benefits and costs resulting from a prior business agreement between them. If we just focus on Smith and Jones and the issues concerning them, we would want to look at the contract, the relevant legal precedents, and the actual results of the deal, before rendering a decision. But suppose we learn that the agreement involved the planned murder of a third party, Green, and the resulting distribution of his property. At that point the issues between Smith and Jones cease to be relevant; we no longer consider it important who has claims to Green's wallet, overcoat, or Mercedes. The competing claims become insignificant in light of the intrinsic value and respect due to Green.

This kind of case is analogous to the conflict over the development of the rainforest, and indeed most other environmental problems. The difference is that instead of an exclusively human case, the third party here is the rainforest. As soon as we realize that the intrinsic interests of the rainforests are relevant to the conflict of competing goods, then the claims of both the developers and the preservationists lose force. What matters is the rainforest, not the economy of Brazil or the survival of humanity.

The dilemma over the third-world development of natural environments is thus a *practical* example of the crisis in value. If we remain within the framework of anthropocentrism, we view this problem as an impossible balancing of competing human claims; but if we transcend anthropocentrism, and view the natural environment as valuable in itself, then the problem dissolves. This provides a powerful argument for abandoning our traditionally exclusive reliance on human values, goods, and interests in the determination of environmental policy.

It might be objected that I have misstated the problem: the dilemma between development and preservation of the Amazon rainforest may be more apparent than real. Development, it can be argued, will only produce short-term economic benefits that will not help the nonindustrialized nations and indigenous peoples of the region. The real goal of policy is neither preservation nor development per se, but sustainable development, the creation of an economy that uses and replenishes the natural environment of the region. There is merit in this objection, and so I remain open to possible empirical solutions to the dilemma of justice in third-world environmental policy. Nevertheless, a shift in values will be required for the successful implementation of any environmental policy. Even a policy of sustainable development will have to be based on the intrinsic respect for that which is being sustained, the natural environment.

The Need for an Ecological Ethic

My criticisms of anthropocentric value theory are based in part on a vision of moral value that extends beyond the human community to embrace the entire natural world. The failure of anthropocentric justifications of environmental policy shows that it is necessary to develop such a transhuman or nonanthropocentric ethic. But how do we develop a nonhuman ethic? On what concepts or models can it be based? Is there any possibility of demonstrating the validity of such a radical value system?

For me, the focus of moral concern and the determination of moral value must lie in the idea and the concrete existence of community. It is within communities that we perceive and acknowledge moral obligations and relationships. It is within and for communities that we act beyond the narrow confines of self-interest. Altruism and self-sacrifice only make sense within the context of communal relationships.

The origin of this view of community within the history of human-based ethical systems can be traced back to Plato and Aristotle. For Aristotle, human beings could only live an excellent life, a life of virtue, if they lived in the *polis*, the political and social community. The various social relationships that existed in the polis were the source of moral obligation: all moral value had its foundation in the functions of the social community.[8] For Plato, at least in *The Republic*, the role of community was even more important. In establishing the ideal state the good for the community was the supreme good: the well-being of the whole society had precedence over individual interests and needs.[9] The community as such was thus the primary focus of moral value and obligation.

Is it now possible to use this traditional notion of community in the establishment of a nonanthropocentric ethic? All that is required is to acknowledge that biological systems, ecosystems, natural environments, bioregions, etc., are communities in some relevant sense. Do natural systems establish mutually interdependent relationships among the members of the systems? Do various entities in the systems work towards common goals in a kind of natural cooperation? Is there greater value in the whole system than in the individual members?

These are crucial questions for the development of an environmental ethic, and many ecological theorists and environmental philosophers have debated them.[10] Although there are many differences between biological and cultural communities, the idea of an ecosystem as analogous to a moral and social community of human beings is a powerful analytical tool for the development of ethical ideals. The idea of community as a metaphor for the illumination of ethical concepts, values, and obligations was useful to Plato 2,500 years ago. Now the notion of community can be extended to include natural ecosystems, as the naturalist Aldo Leopold did 45 years ago.

Leopold used the notion of community as the heart of his seminal essay "The Land Ethic." Because community was the source of all ethical obligations, Leopold argued for the existence of a broader sense of community. "The land ethic simply enlarges the boundaries of the community to include soils, waters, plants, and animals, or collectively: the land."[11] This natural community includes human beings in their interactions with the nonhuman natural world. "A land ethic changes the role of *Homo sapiens* from conqueror of the land-community to plain member and citizen of it. It implies respect for his fellow-members, and also respect for the community as such" (p. 240). This respect for the natural community and its members is the source and justification of moral obligations. The land ethic provides a nonanthropocentric foundation for policies of environmental preservation and conservation. Actions will be evaluated from the perspective of the natural community and its interests, not from the perspective of human interests and satisfactions. Leopold concludes: "A thing is right when it tends to preserve the integrity, stability, and beauty of the biotic community. It is wrong when it tends otherwise" (p. 262). This moral imperative inspires what can be called an "ecological ethic," an ethic that derives its values from the nonhuman natural systems of the environment. The need for the establishment of an ecological ethic is apparent in the environmental crisis that engulfs us, and in the failure of traditional anthropocentric ethics to explain and to solve the crisis.

Biodiversity and the Ecological Ethic

An ecological ethic based on natural community can now be applied to the problem of biodiversity and the ethical justification of policies of preservation. The key analysis is the analogy between human and natural communities. Obligations and values inherent in strictly human communities should be found, on an analogical basis, in the natural ecosystemic community.

Consider the concept of *diversity* in human communities such as cities, universities, or classrooms. Although it is not an absolute good, we generally consider diversity in the human population to be a good worth preserving or developing. Different kinds of people, different ages, different cultural and racial heritages, all contribute to the well-being of the community and to the individuals contained therein. The community is stronger or more interesting since it has a wide variation of backgrounds to draw upon; and individuals benefit from the interaction of differing types. The kind of diversity that is beneficial is relevant to the kind of community: diverse age groups are important in a city or university, for example, but not in an elementary school classroom.

We can assume, therefore, that diversity in the natural community (biodiversity) is a similar good worth preserving and promoting. Diversity within natural ecological systems strengthens and makes more interesting the life of the member entities. It preserves the good of the community as a whole, since a diverse system provides more resources, more alternatives, for solving problems and responding to threats.

Biodiversity is thus an *instrumental* good for natural communities; it is useful for the preservation and promotion of the *intrinsic* values and goods found in natural systems. But this instrumental good should not be confused with the anthropocentric benefits previously offered as justifications for environmental policy, for here the primary goal is the continuation of the system itself, not the promotion of human goods.[12]

Pushing the analogy between human and natural communities, we can see the importance of global biodiversity, the diversity of systems spread throughout the planet. Human diversity is important and useful, not only within communities, but also *of* communities. Different kinds of communities strengthen an entire class. This is the justification for the varied mix of colleges and universities throughout the United States. The education one receives at a major university is different than the education received at a small college with limited enrollment; but both experiences are intrinsically valuable, and so a justifiable educational policy must preserve the diverse alternatives of college education. The same is true of a justifiable environmental policy: it must preserve the alternatives of biodiversity by preserving natural habitats and bioregions in their nonaltered states. This result will be beneficial for the natural systems themselves and for the planet (perhaps conceived as one large community).

This is not an argument for *absolute* diversity, either in the realm of human communities or in nature. We do not seek to multiply diverse kinds just for the sake of diversity; we do not seek to maximize diverse pathogens or other disease organisms. What we do seek to promote is a diversity of good or valuable entities. The value of these entities is determined by the relevant situational context.

In conclusion, it must be emphasized that this argument is not based on the scientific benefits to be derived from a biologically diverse habitat or community or planetary system. The point of this argument is that the benefits to be derived from biodiversity should not be conceived in exclusively human categories. An ecological ethic requires that planetary biodiversity be preserved, not as a pragmatic response to threats to human survival, nor as an instrumental betterment of human life, but as a basic moral obligation to the nonhuman members of our moral community. Our value system must be transformed, modifying the dominant concern of human interests. This transformation of value solves the moral crisis that has led to the environmental crisis. The imperative of preserving biodiversity derives from the moral structure of the natural communities of the planetary biosphere, communities in which humanity is both a "member and citizen."

Biodiversity and Ecological Justice

One problem remains: the just implementation of a nonanthropocentric ecological ethic. An ecological ethic creates disturbing results for policy. I am still bothered by the Amazon rainforest. A policy of preserving biodiversity based on an ecological ethic will require that the indigenous peoples of the poorer nonindustrialized countries refrain from the development of their national resources. The policy of preservation preserves not only the natural environment but also the economic and geopolitical status quo. Of course, the basis of the policy is now conceived differently. Preservation is required not as a means for maintaining human life and benefits, but as an ethical obligation to the natural community itself. But the policy of nondevelopment remains the same, with all the unjust implications for a fair world economic order. Must an ecological ethic be unjust?[13]

We thus return to the concept of "ecological justice" as an indispensable component of an ecological ethic. Any implementation of environmental policy must include not only the moral consideration of all members of the natural community, but also a fair distribution of the benefits and burdens resulting from the policy. Justice extends to all members of the moral community, however we have broadened the notion of community. Within this broadened human and natural community are the indigenous peoples of the third world who need to gain access to the realm of economic development. It is clearly unfair to deny them this access.

Thus, the implementation of a nonanthropocentric system of ecological justice will require a close examination and revision of environmental and developmental policies throughout the world. This examination will not proceed along the lines of a narrow comparison and trade-off of human benefits. An anthropocentrically based policy with an enlightened view of the threat to planetary biodiversity still leaves the poorer nations of the world in the position of shouldering the major burdens of environmental preservation. A truly global ecological ethic will view the problem in terms of the entire planetary system, both human and natural. From this all-encompassing perspective, it becomes incumbent upon the richer nations of the world, who have previously gained the benefits of environmental destruction and economic development, to pay their fair share in the preservation of a diverse planetary environment. In one sense, the richer developed nations owe "reparations" to both the nonindustrialized nations and to the natural community as such.[14] Only by paying for the preservation of a diverse biosphere can a *just ecological order* be maintained on the earth.

Biodiversity and ecological justice are thus necessarily connected; my title is not, I think, a jumble of incompatible ideas. The preservation of planetary biodiversity will only be achieved by the transformation of human values. Our system of ethics has to include the notion of an ecological community; our system of justice has to include a global and nonhuman perspective. I believe that we are partway to that transformation; my hope is that the transformation will be completed before the diversity of the planetary system is destroyed.

Notes

1. The critique of anthropocentrism is a major theme of the field of environmental philosophy; it would be impossible to cite all the works that develop this theme. One influential early work, accessible to the nonspecialist, is David Ehrenfeld, *The Arrogance of Humanism* (New York: Oxford University Press, 1978). Also see the major texts on "environmental ethics" cited in note 2 below.

2. The need to transform human-based ethical systems is the chief concern of what I consider "mainstream" environmental ethics. This discipline of applied moral philosophy follows the work of Aldo Leopold in the attempt to develop an ethic of ecological community. See Also Leopold, *A Sand County Almanac* (New York: Ballantine, 1970, rpt. of 1949 edition), pp. 237–64. Other important works include Holmes Rolston, III, *Environmental Ethics: Duties to and Values in the Natural World* (Philadelphia: Temple University Press, 1988); J. Baird Callicott, *In Defense of the Land Ethic: Essays in Environmental Philosophy* (Albany: SUNY Press, 1989); Peter Wenz, *Environmental Justice* (Albany: SUNY Press, 1988); and Paul W. Taylor, *Respect for Nature: A Theory of Environmental Ethics* (Princeton: Princeton University Press, 1986).

3. I first raised the problem of contingency in Eric Katz, "Utilitarianism and Preservation," *Environmental Ethics* 1 (1979): 357–65. For further discussion see Martin Krieger, "What's Wrong with Plastic Trees?" *Science* 179 (1973): 446–55; and Mark Sagoff, "On Preserving the Natural Environment," *Yale Law Journal* 84 (1974): 205–67.

4. The inadequacy of an instrumental value for the environment is also discussed in Eric Katz, "Organism, Community, and the 'Substitution Problem,'" *Environmental Ethics* 7 (1985): 241–56.

5. For a simple taxonomy of instrumental values in nature, which includes scientific knowledge and religious experience as instrumental, see William Godfrey-Smith, "The Value of Wilderness," *Environmental Ethics* 1 (1979): 309–19. For a different view, see Rolston, pp. 1–44.

6. As Martin Krieger writes, "Artificial prairies and wildernesses have been

created, and there is no reason to believe that these artificial environments need be unsatisfactory for those who experience them." See Krieger, p. 453.

7. The argument of this section is based on Eric Katz and Lauren Oechsli, "Moving Beyond Anthropocentrism: Environmental Ethics, Development, and the Amazon," *Environmental Ethics* 15 (1993): 49–59.

8. Surely this is one reason why the concept of friendship plays such a major part in Aristotle's ethics. All of Books VIII and IX concern the analysis of friendship. Different kinds of friendships determine moral obligations: "what is just is not the same for a friend towards a friend as towards a stranger, or the same towards a companion as towards a classmate" (*Nicomachean Ethics*, 1162a 32).

9. In *The Republic* Plato has Socrates answer the objection that the guardians will not be happy without private property by reemphasizing the idea that the welfare of the state as a whole is what matters: "in establishing our city, we are not aiming to make any one group outstandingly happy, but to make the whole city so . . ." (420b); and again, "We should examine . . . whether our aim in establishing our guardians should be to give them the greatest happiness, or whether we should in this matter look to the whole city and see how its greatest happiness can be secured" (421b). That this point is stressed twice in one page shows its crucial importance to Plato's ethic of community.

10. See for example, Andrew Brennan, "The Moral Standing of Natural Objects," *Environmental Ethics* 6 (1984): 35–56, and *Thinking About Nature: An Investigation of Nature, Value, and Ecology* (Athens: University of Georgia Press, 1988); Bryan G. Norton, *Why Preserve Natural Variety?* (Princeton: Princeton University Press, 1987); and Harley Cahen, "Against the Moral Considerability of Ecosystems," *Environmental Ethics* 10 (1988): 195–216.

11. Leopold, p. 239.

12. For a different argument concerning these instrumental goods, see Norton.

13. Even more than unjust, an ecological ethic seems at times to be misanthropic. As J. Baird Callicott writes, "The extent of misanthropy in modern environmentalism thus may be taken as a measure of the degree to which it is biocentric," i.e., focused on nonhuman natural values. See Callicott, "Animal Liberation: A Triangular Affair," *Environmental Ethics* 2 (1980) 326; reprinted in *In Defense of the Land Ethic*, p. 27.

14. For more on "reparations" in environmental ethics, see Eric Katz, "Buffalo-Killing and the Valuation of Species," *Values and Moral Standing*, ed. L. W. Sumner (Bowling Green, Ohio: Bowling Green State University, 1986), pp. 114–23. Taylor, *Respect for Nature*, pp. 186–92, 304–6, and generally chap. 4 and 6, and Wenz, *Environmental Justice*, pp. 287–91, also discuss the idea of "restitution."

13

The Death of Nature: First Thoughts on Ecocide and Genocide

As the title indicates, this essay was my first attempt to consider the comparison between the destruction of the natural world and the practice of genocide. Written for a joint session of the Society for the Philosophic Study of Genocide and the Holocaust, the Radical Philosophy Association, and the International Society for Environmental Ethics held in conjunction with the American Philosophical Association in December 1991, it represents an almost completely new direction in my thought about major social issues. I had never studied the Holocaust of European Jewry nor any other instance of genocide from the perspective of moral philosophy—and even more important, I had never considered these issues from the perspective of my community-based holistic environmental ethic. The catalyst for the essay lies in the fact that some environmental activists label the environmental crisis an "ecocide"—a planned killing of the natural world. As a persuasive political slogan, this terminology is intended to associate the destruction of the natural environment with the murder of thousands of human beings. Here I discuss the validity of this rhetorical and political device. From the perspective of a nonanthropocentric value system—such as my holistic environmental ethic—there appear to be basic similarities between the destruction of the natural world and genocide. But in this essay I am reluctant to endorse the comparison, for I believe that this politically motivated rhetoric cheapens or trivializes the Holocaust of Nazi Germany. I end the essay with a dilemma, for I believe in both the superiority of a nonanthropocentric value system and the singular importance of the Holocaust as an event in human history. "The Death of Nature" has not been previously published, but it established a set of problems for further research, developed in the next essay in this collection.

I

I begin this essay with a question, and I will end it with a dilemma: should the current destruction of the natural environment be called "ecocide"? This is not a descriptive problem, for my working assumption is that the facts of the contemporary environmental crisis are not in dispute. The massive destruction of habitats, the increasing rate of species extinction, the rapid elimination of the ozone layer, and the high probability of global warming due to the greenhouse effect clearly constitute a serious and immediate multidimensional threat to the continued survival of the natural environment as it presently exists. As an empirical proposition, then, we face the likely demise of the natural world.

But is this death of nature an "ecocide"? What appears as a question about terminology is actually a problem about ethics, metaphysics, and meaning: what are the essential characteristics of the environmental crisis? what are the prescriptive and normative implications of the descriptive term "ecocide"? what, in short, does "ecocide," the death of nature, *mean?*

The use of "ecocide" to describe the environmental crisis has one clear and obvious aspect: it presents the idea that the destruction of the natural environment is an activity—a killing—and not the mere coincidence of a series of interrelated but causally unconnected events. It implies that some type of decision, or complex set of decisions, has been made. It implies the formation of a policy, or, at least, the *effects* of a policy—a series of actions designed to meet a specific goal or set of goals, articulated or unarticulated—in this case, a policy to destroy or kill the natural world.

I believe that the use of the term "ecocide" is an error, that it wrongly describes the environmental crisis and the destruction of the natural environment. To call the environmental crisis an "ecocide" is an attempt to create a resonance of meaning in a comparison—and a possible equivalence—with "genocide." Although there are many instructive similarities between the destruction of the natural world and the mass slaughter of human beings, equating these activities through the use of similar terms is a dangerous mistake. Genocide, to be brief, is a *policy*, with all that implies about conscious human decision making, while the environmental crisis is not. To imply that the destruction of nature is similar to the policy of human extermination, is to distort and cheapen the meaning of the Holocaust and all other incidents of genocide in human history.

So why do I face a dilemma? My dilemma arises because my reasons for rejecting this term are at odds with my basic beliefs about the development of an environmental ethic. As an advocate of a philosophy that considers Nature and natural processes as the direct objects of moral consideration, I encounter problems in explaining the morally relevant difference between genocide and the destruction of the natural environment.

II

The comparison of ecocide with genocide must begin with a working definition of "genocide." I will use the term to mean the systematic planned elimination of a people and a culture. For a series of actions or a policy to constitute genocide, in my sense, there must be a massive killing of a national, religious, ethnic, or regional group of people—the elimination of a distinct and identifiable community that embodies a distinct and identifiable culture. Large-scale killing is not in itself a "genocide." It is not the magnitude of the action, but the intention that is the determining factor. For example, the bombings of Hiroshima and Nagasaki, as horrible as they were, were not, strictly speaking, acts of genocide—these acts were not attempts to eliminate Japanese culture. It would also be improper to call the mere elimination of a culture, without the killing of the people who embody that culture, a genocide. The attempt by the Soviet government, throughout most of this century, to prohibit the practice of organized religion, or similarly, the attempt by a nation-state to suppress the use of a regional language within its borders—even if successful—would not constitute a genocide, for the elimination of a religious culture or a particular language does not cause the massive death of human beings. The proper use of the descriptive term genocide requires a massive destruction of a certain kind—the killing or elimination of a people *and* a culture.

III

This definition is useful for making several comparisons between genocide and the destruction of the natural world. The comparisons *appear* to support the idea that the current environmental crisis is a kind of "ecocide," for there are at least three similarities between the two processes.

First: Both genocide and the destruction of Nature involve killing or destruction on two levels. As I noted above, the killing in genocide requires the elimination of a people and a culture. Similarly, the environmental crisis involves the destruction of both individual natural entities and natural ecological systems or habitats. The mere elimination of massive amounts of natural entities would not by itself constitute an ecocide or destruction of nature; what is required is the elimination of the communities or systems of which the natural entities are a part.

Both genocide and ecocide then imply a massive killing that is more than the sum of the individuals involved. Both processes exemplify what environmental philosophers call "holism," a totalizing vision—a focus on whole systems rather than on the individuals which comprise the systems. For a policy of action to be appropriately described as either a genocide or an ecocide, it must be possible to analyze the policy from a total-view or holistic perspective; that is, it must be possible to see the situation as a destruction of something that transcends the destruction of individuals. The all-too-common ethical and political perspective of individual rights, for example, would seriously misstate the evil of genocide. Although the rights of the individual human victims of a policy of genocide are clearly being violated, one cannot get at a true understanding of, let us say, the Holocaust, by analyzing individual human rights violations. The Holocaust was more than the violation of the "right to life" of six million people—it was primarily the destruction of a community, a system, a culture. It requires a holistic or systemic understanding. Similarly, the attempt to understand the meaning of the environmental crisis by focusing on the "moral rights" of individual natural entities misstates the problem. Arguments in environmental philosophy that focus on the moral consideration of individual animals or the "inherent worth" of all living entities are based on a narrow interpretation or view of the crisis. There may be good reasons for developing normative ethical theories that incorporate the moral consideration of nonhuman individuals, but the most fully developed meaning of the death of Nature requires an understanding of the destruction of ecological systems, habitats, environments—an understanding only possible from a holistic or total-view perspective.[1]

Second: Both genocide and the destruction of Nature develop from clearly focused, narrowly drawn, self-interested motivations. Genocidal policies are not created by accident; they are neither whims nor capricious lunacies, but rather deliberate social and political actions. My guess is that genocide is often the result of a complex combination of racial or ethnic hatred and an incorrectly perceived political and economic class struggle. Such, at least, is my gloss on the motivations for the Third Reich's final solution—and here I am not, I think, saying anything profound. The common dislike of Jews, stemming from their different religion and culture, was combined with the erroneous idea that the Jews were primarily responsible for the economic crisis of Germany. The Jews of the lands controlled by the Third Reich were deliberately exterminated as part of the solution to a problem perceived by the leadership of the country as real. That the problem was not real—or perhaps, that the extermination of the Jews was not a real solution—is irrelevant to the fact that the policy of deliberately killing a people and its culture was consciously chosen. So genocide always has a specific goal: to solve a political, economic, or social problem by eliminating the community, class, or ethnic-religious group that is perceived to be the source of the problem. The goal is narrowly self-interested: the purpose of genocide is to promote the political, economic, and social well-being of the dominant group or class. It is the inevitable outcome of an ethnocentric, nationalistic, or racist worldview.

The destruction of Nature has a similar motivation, a similar goal: the promotion of a narrow range of interests. The interests here are the human goods or benefits that derive from the development, use, and destruction of Nature. I consider the interests "narrow" because they are derived solely from what is considered to benefit human beings— what benefits natural entities and systems is taken into account only insofar as it works to the betterment of humanity. This motivational perspective can be called "anthropocentrism"—humans are the center, the focal point, of all value, all policy goals—and it can be compared to the similar perspective of ethnocentrism which lies at the heart of genocide. An anthropocentric worldview leads logically to the destruction of the nonhuman natural world. Because the natural world is valued merely for the maximization of human satisfactions or goods, it will be preserved only contingently, as long as it satisfies human needs. If natural entities, processes, or habitats are no longer necessary for the promotion of human goods—if, for example, humans lose their desire for natural places, or if natural entities are reproducible by technological means—then the argument for the preservation of Nature collapses.[2] Thus a narrow worldview of ethnic or human superiority leads to analogous destructions of all that is not part of the dominant class or group.

Third: But the destruction of all that is alien to the dominant class is, in both cases, merely part of the primary goal. Both genocide and the destruction of Nature are activities that remake the world according to the vision of the dominant group. The ultimate goal is the control and domination of the "other." One method for achieving this domination is by purging the alien entities—those perceived to be inferior, humans from another class or ethnic background, natural nonhuman entities. A successful purge leaves the world solely as the place of the dominant group. Another method would be to remake the subordinate group into an image acceptable by the dominant class. Thus Primo Levi describes the symbolic meaning of the three baths that marked his passage from one controlling group to another, the "black-mass bath . . . that marked [the] descent into the concentration-camp universe," the "functional, antiseptic" bath of the Americans, and the Russian bath "to human measure, extemporaneous and crude." Of the three baths, Levi writes:

> at each of those three memorable christenings, it was easy to perceive behind the concrete and literal aspect a great symbolic shadow, the unconscious desire of the new authorities, who absorbed us in turn within their own sphere, to strip us of the vestiges of our former life, to make of us new men consistent with their own models, to impose their brand upon us.[3]

Although Levi ascribes this unconscious motivation to both his liberators and his oppressors, it is clear that it is an outgrowth of control and domination—the attempt to remake those subject to the control in the image desired by those who dominate. Whether from benign or malicious motives, the "authorities" always wish to exercise their control by creating models of life consistent with their worldviews.

The same is true of the domination of Nature. The destruction of natural habitats, their development as places of human civilization and control, is an expression of humanity's desire to create an anthropocentric universe, a world built entirely subject to human interests and needs. This form of domination is best seen, I think, in the environmental policy of ecological restoration, where so-called natural ecosystems are re-created as functioning models of natural habitats. Areas once strip-mined are replanted to replace the natural scenery; a tall-grass savanna is replanted to bring back the prairies of the Great Plains; forests are managed and replanted according to ecological models of scientific forestry; wetlands are created so as to preserve the government's policy of "no net-loss." Although these ecological restorations are undertaken for a variety of reasons—aesthetics, scientific research, education, long-term productivity, nostalgia—they all share a common ontological character: they are all artifacts created by human technology. None of these ecological restorations are actually the result of natural ecosystemic or evolutionary processes; they are all artificial, built by humans for human purposes, to satisfy a human desire, a human image of the world. Humanity does not desire a world devoid of nonhuman nature; it simply wants a world in which nonhuman nature is controlled and modeled after human interests. A world filled with these ecological restorations will appear to be a world in which we have repaired the damage we have inflicted on the natural environment. But this appearance will be an illusion, obscuring the truth that we have destroyed the natural world by recasting it in the image of human desires.[4]

IV

There are, then, at least three similarities between the process of genocide and the destruction of the natural environment: (1) a proper understanding of each requires some kind of holistic or totalizing perspective, for both processes are more than the mere destruction of individuals; (2) both genocide and the destruction of Nature stem from a limited conception of value—genocide derives from a form of ethnocentrism and the destruction of Nature from anthropocentrism—so that the "other" is not considered to be a direct recipient of value; and (3) both genocide and the destruction of Nature involve a particular kind of domination and control—the remaking of the world in the image of the dominant class.

Are these similarities enough to term the destruction of Nature in the contemporary environmental crisis an "ecocide"? Are these similarities enough so that the destruction of Nature can share in the moral condemnation of the Holocaust? Or is the "ecocide" of Nature an exaggeration that distorts and trivializes the meaning of the practice of genocide?

There is one clear difference between the two activities, a difference that is probably decisive for most of those who consider the comparison. Genocide concerns the premeditated killing of humans and human cultures; the destruction of Nature is not the direct killing of humans. Since most people consider humanity superior to the nonhuman natural world, since most people consider humans to have a kind of inherent value missing from nonhumans, that one difference is crucial. For them, terming the environmental crisis a form of "ecocide" is a bad and disrespectful joke which denigrates the meaning of human life and culture.

I would prefer to argue that the human/nonhuman distinction between genocide and ecocide is not crucial. As an environmental philosopher, I have consistently argued for the adoption of a nonanthropocentric evaluation of the natural world as the basis of a coherent, consistent, and ethical environmental policy. (The essays in this volume attest to that commitment.) Although there are many problems with the notion of nonanthropocentric value, the discussion and development of such a perspective have been the principal focus of the discipline of environmental ethics for at least the past fifteen years. So the reason for drawing a distinction between genocide and the destruction of Nature must be found somewhere else than the difference between humans and nonhumans.

Thus, as I indicated at the beginning of this essay, the crucial difference between genocide and the destruction of Nature—the putative ecocide—is that genocide is a deliberate *policy* of action, while the destruction of Nature is not (usually) a conscious choice. Acts of genocide—and here I am thinking primarily of the Holocaust—are deliberately chosen to achieve clear and specific social, political, or economic ends.

But the destruction of Nature occurring throughout the contemporary environmental crisis does not appear to be the result or the intention of a conscious policy of extermination. Instead, the destruction of Nature seems to be the result of a multidimensional complex of interrelated events, some consciously chosen, some not, that have coalesced into a serious threat to the continuation of natural entities, species, processes, habitats, and systems—indeed, to the existence of the biosphere itself. The seriousness of this threat should not be minimized; the effect on human life of the destruction of the biosphere would dwarf the death and killing of any previous act of genocide in human history. So the magnitude of the negative results is not the determining factor. The destruction of the natural world is not an ecocide, not analogous to genocide, because it is not a deliberate policy chosen by human decision makers. Although it is clear that individual incidents of the destruction of Nature—such as the real estate development of coastal wetlands for housing, industry, or commercial properties, the logging of national forests for timber, and the conversion of rain forests to farmland—are consciously chosen policies, the overall destruction of Nature is not the goal of any rational human decision maker. There is nothing comparable to the "final solution" of the Holocaust in the realm of human decisions regarding the natural environment.

But what if there were? I am uncomfortable with my conclusion here because it seems contingent—the case rests solely on the empirical claim that it is not *yet* the policy of the human race to eliminate, destroy, or dominate the natural world in its entirety. But we can easily imagine that it might be—with the appropriate technology, it might be possible to eliminate Nature, to make it into a human-controlled artifactual system, without doing harm to the human race. Indeed, with the proper technology, it might be possible to improve human life by the total domination and destruction of natural processes. Such has been the goal of Western science and technology since the time of Francis Bacon. This goal is given a clear and chilling expression in one of the classic essays in the field of environmental ethics, Martin Krieger's "What's Wrong with Plastic Trees?"[5] Krieger argues quite simply that if the goal of social policy is the maximization of human satisfaction and the promotion of social justice, then there is no overriding reason to preserve Nature. With an adequate technology and the proper education, a plastic artificial world would create more human happiness at a lower cost than the preservation of the natural environment. Thus there might be nothing wrong with the planned extermination of the nonhuman natural world; the "final solution" for the natural world would help to maximize human good.

Should Krieger's plan to replace Nature with an artificial world be termed an "ecocide"? Should it be compared to the Holocaust and other acts of genocide? Even though this consciously chosen deliberate plan meets my crucial criterion, I am still reluctant to answer in the affirmative. I find myself in a quandary that defies rational explanation. My deepest emotional feeling about this comparison leads me to reject the convergence of the two concepts; the term ecocide tends to trivialize the unique meaning of the Holocaust and other acts of genocide throughout human history. But the only distinction I can see is that the destruction of Nature does not affect human beings directly, while genocide precisely *is* the direct destruction of human beings and human cultures. This is an anthropocentric analysis and distinction— perhaps, even, an individualistic one—that runs counter to all that I believe about the philosophical foundations of environmental policy. Thus my dilemma: *accept a comparison between genocide and the destruction of Nature that I find repugnant, or reject the arguments for a nonanthro-*

pocentric value theory in environmental ethics. At the present time, I simply cannot choose.

Those who do not share my belief in the truth of a nonanthropocentric basis for an ethical environmental policy will not, of course, feel the power of this dilemma. For them, the distinction between genocide and the destruction of Nature, the rejection of the concept of "ecocide," can be made easily along the line that separates humanity from the nonhuman natural world. But those who share my belief in the possibility of nonanthropocentrism should be troubled that this analysis of genocide threatens the basis of an environmental ethic. At the very least, it provides an agenda and direction for deeper analysis.

Notes

1. The most comprehensive "individualistic" position of environmental ethics is that of Paul Taylor, *Respect for Nature: A Theory of Environmental Ethics* (Princeton: Princeton University Press, 1986). Holistic accounts can be found in Holmes Rolston, III, *Environmental Ethics: Duties to and Values in the Natural World* (Philadelphia: Temple University Press, 1988); J. Baird Callicott, *In Defense of the Land Ethic: Essays in Environmental Philosophy* (Albany: SUNY Press, 1989); and Andrew Brennan, *Thinking About Nature: An Investigation of Nature, Value, and Ecology* (Athens: University of Georgia Press, 1988).

2. See my "Utilitarianism and Preservation," *Environmental Ethics* 1 (1979): 357–64.

3. Primo Levi, *The Reawakening*, trans. Stuart Woolf (New York: Collier Books, 1987), p. 8.

4. The domination and manipulation of nature has been a major theme of my work in environmental philosophy. See my essays, "The Big Lie: Human Restoration of Nature," *Research in Philosophy and Technology* 12 (1992): 231–41; "The Call of the Wild: The Struggle Against Domination and the 'Technological Fix' of Nature," *Environmental Ethics* 14 (1992): 265–73; "Artefacts and Functions: A Note on the Value of Nature," *Environmental Values* 2 (1993): 223–32; and "Imperialism and Environmentalism," *Social Theory and Practice* 21, 2 (Summer 1995): 271–85.

5. Martin Krieger, "What's Wrong with Plastic Trees?" *Science* 179 (1973): 446–55.

14

Nature's Presence: Reflections on Healing and Domination

"Nature's Presence" continues my investigation into the meaning of the Holocaust from the perspective of environmental philosophy. Although skeptical of the comparison between genocide and the destruction of the natural world, I believe that the concept of domination is critical to any analysis of these two human activities. Humans exert power over Nature, attempting to mold its processes to serve human interests; similarly some humans exert power over other humans, oppressing and killing them to meet self-interested goals. How far can the logic of domination be extended? In "Imperialism and Environmentalism" I had argued that the expression of power and domination can also be attributed to the idea of Nature itself. Since I claim that Nature can be considered as an analogue to a human subject, then we should view Nature as an imperialist, an entity or system attempting to dominate, oppress, and manipulate an alien "other"—human beings and human institutions. Do these ideas shed any light on an analysis of the Holocaust? On leave during the academic year 1995–96, I traveled to Holocaust sites in Poland and the Czech Republic to experience directly the landscapes of human destruction. I found that Nature had asserted itself in very disturbing ways, beautifying sites of unspeakable human evil. Does this mean that Nature can heal the wounds of human destruction? Or is healing another form of domination and control? This essay was first published in Space, Place, and Environmental Ethics: Philosophy and Geography I, *ed. Andrew Light and Jonathan M. Smith (Lanham, Md.: Rowman & Littlefield, 1996).*

I

The trees are like a forest. Although I can hear the sounds of traffic on Okopowa Street on the other side of the wall, inside the Jewish Ceme-

189

tery of Warsaw all is quiet. There is a light rain and fog. In the grayness of the day, the mist and the shadows prevent my eyes from seeing deep into the cemetery. All I can see are the trees and the underbrush, lush and green, growing up and over the scattered and crooked grave stones. One main walkway and a few paths have been cleared, so that tourists can view several hundred of the tombstones. Another path leads to a clearing. It is a clearing of tombstones, not of trees, the mass grave of the Jews who died in the Warsaw Ghetto before the deportations to Treblinka began in July 1942. The mass grave appears as a meadow under a canopy of tree branches. The area is ringed by grave stones, but the center of the clearing is covered with grass. Dozens of memorial candles flicker, remaining lit despite the dampness and the light rain. The beauty of this mass grave surprises and shocks me. Here is the reification of irony. This cemetery, a monument to the destructive hatred of the Nazi Holocaust, is extraordinarily beautiful. Filled with a vibrant, unchecked growth of trees and other vegetation, the cemetery demonstrates the power of Nature to re-assert itself in the midst of human destruction and human evil.

The next day I travel to Lublin, near the Ukrainian border—a two-hour drive from Warsaw, through endless flat farmland where Polish farmers still use horses to plow the fields. It is harvest season, and the car slows occasionally to pass a truck filled with sugar beets. Our destination is Majdanek, the death camp lying three kilometers from the center of Lublin. Majdanek fills a treeless meadow stretching as far as the eye can see. Standing at the entrance gate one can see in the distance, a mile off, the chimney of the crematorium.

Unlike Treblinka or Auschwitz-Birkenau, the camp at Majdanek was built near the major urban center that would supply its victims. It was not hidden in the countryside. It is easy to imagine the smoke from the crematorium drifting into the heart of downtown Lublin. Likewise, it is hard to believe that the people of Lublin did not know what was happening at the camp. Majdanek was first established as a slave labor camp in 1940, but its gas chambers began operating in November 1942. Approximately 200,000 people were killed at Majdanek, either in the gas chamber, by shootings, or because of overwork, disease, and malnutrition. In one day alone, 3 November, 1943, 18,000 prisoners were shot and killed, the bodies piled high in open ditches near the crematorium. Over 800,000 shoes were found at Majdanek when it was liberated in July 1944 by the advancing Russian army. This was the first of the camps to be liberated, the first to be seen by the Allied forces and the Western media. Unlike the camps further west that were liberated later, Majdanek was not destroyed by the retreating German forces. Although many of the wooden barracks have deteriorated through natural decay, the camp as a whole remains today as it did in 1944, relatively intact.[1]

I stand in the small open courtyard a few dozen yards beyond the entrance gate. On this spot the selections of arriving prisoners were made—who would live and work in the camp, who would be killed immediately. To my right is the gas chamber. On my left is a row of barracks, used as storerooms and work areas when the camp was in operation. These unheated and dimly lit barracks now house museum exhibits. Beyond the first row of barracks is the main camp, divided into several sections. Each section consists of two rows of barracks facing a wide open parade ground. I enter the gate and walk through the parade ground and on to the road leading to the crematorium and the site of the November 1943 mass shooting. The camp is virtually empty of visitors. As in Warsaw the day before, there is a light rain and mist, and the autumn air is cold, a harbinger of winter.

The Majdanek camp is too beautiful—the green grass of the parade ground suggests a college campus, not a site of slave labor and mass executions. Can we stand here in this lush grassy meadow and imagine the mud, the dirt, the smell—the unrelenting gray horror of the thousands of prisoners in their ill-fitting striped suits standing at roll calls? Can we imagine the perpetually gray sky, filled with smoke from the crematorium just down the road? Perhaps it would be better to see the camp in the middle of winter when one is not overwhelmed by the color of the green grass. As in the Warsaw cemetery, Nature again prevents me from seeing, understanding, and feeling the true dimensions of the remnants of the evil that confronts me.

The experience of these two places raises questions for me about the healing power of Nature—complex questions involving the ontological and normative status of Nature in its relationship to human activity, and further questions about the nature of Nature's activity. Can the study of Nature and natural processes teach us anything about the evil of human genocide? Can the study of genocide teach us anything about the human-induced destruction of the natural world, what is sometimes called the process of "ecocide"? This is not a subject that will permit facile comparisons and analogies. We study the Holocaust and the environmental crisis that currently surrounds us from different perspectives—with different attitudes and purposes. Yet the comparison may be helpful. The idea of domination can be used to link together an analysis of these two evils, and can point us in the direction of developing a harmonious relationship with both the natural world and our fellow human beings.

II

Let me begin by emphasizing the importance of my visit to the actual sites described above. This essay contains more than a philosophical argument—the ideas set forth in these pages could not have been developed by me through the typically philosophical method of argument, analysis, example, and rebuttal. The lived experience of these places not only colors my ideas but to some extent completely informs them. Indeed, the essay may be merely a written expression of my attempt to come to terms with the physical experience of these places, and to place these experiences of Holocaust sites into the context of my philosophical thoughts about the meaning of the environmental crisis and the practice of human domination.

Why connect these two areas of inquiry? Why think about the environmental crisis and the Holocaust in terms of one another? Is there a meaningful relationship between human ideas of the natural world and the concepts of domination and genocide? The Nazis thought so. As Robert-Jan Van Pelt recounts in his historical investigation of the development of Auschwitz, the reconstruction and development of Polish farmland under scientific principles of management was one of the major goals of German settlement in the conquered lands east of Germany. Quoting from a contemporary record, Van Pelt describes a trip through Poland in 1940 undertaken by Heinrich Himmler, the Reichskommissar for the resettlement of the German people. Himmler and his personal friend Henns Johst stand in a Polish field, holding the soil in their hands, and dream of the great agricultural and architectural projects to come: the re-creation of German farms and villages, the replanting of trees, shrubs, and hedgerows to protect the crops, and even the alteration of the climate by increasing dew and the formation of clouds.[2] As part of this plan, of course, there would have to be an "ethnic cleansing" of the region—the Poles, both Gentile and Jewish, would have to be moved elsewhere or otherwise eliminated so that a German agricultural utopia could be developed. Thus we see that the control of Nature—the management of agriculture so as to affect even the climate—was part of the Nazi plan. The domination of Nature and humanity are clearly linked.

The goal of the domination of Nature remains with us, in the Western world, even today. As I have argued elsewhere, the primary goal of the Enlightenment project of the scientific understanding of the natural world is to control, manipulate, and modify natural processes for the increased satisfaction of human interests.[3] Humans want to live in a world that is comfortable—or at least, a world that is not hostile to human happiness and survival. Thus the purpose of science and technology is to comprehend, predict, control, and modify the physical world in which we are embedded. This purpose is easy to understand when we view technological and industrial projects that use Nature as a resource for economic development—but the irony is that the same purpose, human control, motivates much of environmentalist policy and practice.

Consider briefly, as an example, the arguments of two writers on the theory of environmental policy: Martin Krieger's call for artificial wildernesses that will be pleasing to human visitors, and Chris Maser's plans for re-designing forests on the model of sustainable agriculture.[4] Maser is an environmentalist and Krieger is not; yet their views on environmental policy are strikingly similar. Maser is considered a spokesperson and leader of enlightened environmental forestry practices, but his goal is to manage forests in such a way as to maximize the wide variety of human interests in forest development: sustainable supplies of timber, human recreation, and spiritual and aesthetic satisfaction. Krieger is a public policy analyst interested in the promotion of social justice. His goal is to develop an environmental policy consistent with the maximization of human economic, social, and political benefits. Thus he argues that education and advertising can re-order public priorities, so that the environments that people want and use will be those available at the lowest cost. Natural environments need not be preserved if artificial ones can produce more human happiness at a lower cost.

What ties together views such as Krieger's and Maser's is their thoroughgoing anthropocentrism—human interests, satisfaction, goods, and happiness are the central goals of public policy and human action. This anthropocentrism is, of course, not surprising. Since the Enlightenment, at least, human concerns—rather than the interests of God—have been the central focus of almost all human activities, projects, and social movements. The institutions of human civilization believe that it is their mission to improve the lives of human beings. Although methods may differ, and the class of people that is the primary object of this concern may differ, the central anthropocentric focus is consistent regardless of ideology or social position or political power—humanity is in the business of creating and maximizing human good.

Anthropocentrism as a worldview quite easily leads to the practices of domination, even when the domination is not articulated. In the formation of environmental policy, Nature is seen as a nonhuman "other" to be controlled, manipulated, modified, or destroyed in the pursuit of human good. As a nonhuman other, Nature can be understood as merely a resource for the development of human interests; as a nonhuman other, Nature has no valid interests or good of its own. Even the practice of ecological restoration, in which degraded ecosystems are restored to a semblance of their original states, is permeated with this anthropocentric ideology. Natural ecosystems that have been harmed by human activity are restored to a state that is more pleasing to the current human population. A marsh that had been landfilled is re-flooded to restore wetland acreage; strip-mined hills are replanted to create flowering meadows; acres of farmland are subjected to a controlled burn and replanting with wildflowers and shrubs to recreate the oak savanna of pre-European America. We humans thus achieve two simultaneous goals: we relieve our guilt for the earlier destruction of natural systems, and we demonstrate our power—the power of science and technology—over the natural world.[5]

But the domination of nonhuman Nature is not the only result of an anthropocentric worldview—the ideology of anthropocentric domination may also extend to the oppression of other human beings, conceived as a philosophical "other," as nonhuman or as subhuman. Or as C. S. Lewis wrote fifty years ago, "what we call man's power over Nature turns out to be a power exercised by some men over other men with Nature as its instrument." The reason that this exercise of power is justifiable is that the subordinate people are not considered human beings: "they are not men at all; they are artefacts."[6] Anthropcentrism does not convert automatically into a thoroughgoing humanism, wherein all humans are treated as equally worthwhile. As we have seen historically, the idea of human slavery has been justified from the time of the ancient Greeks onward by designating the slave class as less than human. In this century, the evaluation of other people as subhuman finds its clearest expression in the Nazi propaganda concerning the Jews, but we find its echoes in the ethnic civil war in the former Yugoslavia and in the continuing hatred of extreme right-wing Israelis for the Palestinians. From the starting point of anthropocentrism, domination and oppression are easily justified. The oppressed class—be it a specific race or religious group, or even animals or natural entities—is simply denied admittance to the elite center of value-laden beings.[7] From within anthropocentrism, only humans have value and only human interests and goods need to be pursued. But who or what counts as a human is a question that cannot be answered from within anthropocentrism—and the answer to this question will determine the extent of the practice of domination.

Thus the ideas of anthropocentrism and domination tie together a study of the Holocaust and the current environmental crisis. Genocide and ecocide are only possible when we conceive of our victims as less than human, as outside the primary circle of value.

III

The resurgence of trees in the Warsaw cemetery and the lush green grass of the meadow at Majdanek serve as a catalyst for rethinking the relationships among Nature, humanity, and the practice of domination. In these places, one can only describe the processes of Nature as a kind of healing, a soothing of the wounds wrought by the evil of the Holocaust. Does Nature make everything better? Can we say that dominated and oppressed entities are saved—redeemed—by the ordinary processes of the natural world? Does Nature have this power? And if it does, what are the implications for the way in which humanity acts in relationship to the natural world?

First, we should note a possible objection to this entire line of analysis. One might argue that in thinking of Nature as having a redeeming power over human evils, we are, in part, treating Nature as if it possessed a kind of intentional activity. But Nature is not a rational subject. Nature makes no decisions, rational or otherwise. If the lush vegetation hides the horrors of Majdanek this is not the result of any natural plan, merely the effects of natural processes in their normal operations. According to this objection, we should be wary of anthropomorphizing natural processes, of being misled by metaphor and analogy.

This objection serves as an important warning to the analysis that follows. Nature has no intentions—and no other thoughts, desires, wants, or needs. Nevertheless, we can consider Nature to be analogous to a human subject. Human activities can benefit or harm natural processes in ways similar to the benefits and harms inflicted on other humans, on human institutions, and on nonhuman living beings. More-over, Nature does act in predictable ways similar to a thinking being. As Colin Duncan has claimed, "While Nature is certainly not a person . . . it does have some of the attributes of a Hegelian subject. It can be both victim-like and agent-like."[8] Most important, we can consider Nature as the subject of an ongoing history that can be interfered with or destroyed by human action. From the perspective of normative value theory, Nature develops in ways similar to human subjects—the continuous processes of Nature produce good and bad consequences for itself and for other entities. Morally and axiologically, then, Nature can be considered to be equivalent to a subject. Without anthropomor-phizing Nature—without attributing to it the emotions, feelings, and rational will of human subjects—we can understand that it is not merely a passive object to be manipulated and used by humanity.[9]

Nature, in fact, acts upon human beings, human institutions, and the products of human culture in powerful ways. So-called natural disas-ters, such as earthquakes and floods, are the prime examples of events in which natural forces impact on humanity. But ordinary weather, small changes in climate, and even the rotation of the earth are also activities of Nature—natural processes—that affect human life. Else-where I have categorized this type of activity as Nature's imperialism over humanity, for it has a parallel structure to the basic kind of human imperialism over other humans, as well as to the human imperialism over Nature. Imperialism is a form of domination, in which one entity uses, takes advantage of, controls, or otherwise exerts force over an-other. If we consider Nature as both a possible subject and object of imperialism, then we can think of Nature as exerting its power—attempting to dominate—humanity, just as we can think of humanity attempting to dominate Nature.[10]

But my experiences in the Warsaw cemetery and at Majdanek sug-gest that Nature's domination in these places is benign. It appears to heal the scars of human atrocities. Nature here does not exert the op-pression of an imperialist. Nature provides the balm to restore the health and goodness of a world wounded by human evil. Nature's domination—its resurgence in these areas of human atrocities—serves as the corrective to the effects of human domination, in this case to the oppression and genocide of Eastern European Jewry. Is this an appro-priate way to interpret the experiences of these places?

Perhaps not. One objection to viewing Nature as a benign healer of human-induced wounds is that such a view of Nature is yet another expression of an anthropocentric worldview. Rather than use Nature as a physical resource for economic purposes, we are here using Nature as an emotional resource, to make us feel better about the horrors of human destruction.[11] We are blinded to the fact that natural processes develop independent from human projects; Nature follows its own logic. The desire to see Nature as a healer demonstrates how pervasive is the anthropocentric perspective. We humans seem incapable of viewing the natural world on its own terms, free of the categories and purposes of human life and human institutions.

Even more important, the question arises whether or not Nature can heal these wounds of human oppression. Consider the reverse process, the human attempt to heal the wounds of Nature. We often tend to clean up natural areas polluted or damaged by human activity, such as the Alaskan coast harmed by the *Exxon Valdez* oil spill. But we also attempt to improve natural areas dramatically altered by natural events, such as a forest damaged by a massive brush fire, or a beach suffering severe natural erosion. In most of these kinds of cases, human science and technology are capable of making a significant change in the appearance and processes of the natural area. Forests can be replanted, oil is removed from the surface of bays and estuaries, sand and dune vegetation replenish a beach. But are these activities the healing of Nature? Has human activity—science and technology—restored Nature to a healthy state?

No. When humans modify a natural area they create an artifact, a product of human labor and human design.[12] This restored natural area may resemble a wild and unmodified natural system, but it is, in actuality, a product of human thought, the result of human desires and interests. All humanly created artifacts are manifestations of human interests—from computer screens to rice pudding. An ecosystem restored by human activity may appear to be in a different category—it may appear to be an autonomous living system uncontrolled by human thought—but it nonetheless exhibits characteristics of human design and intentionality: it is created to meet human interests, to satisfy human desires, and to maximize human good.

Consider again my examples of human attempts to heal damaged natural areas. A forest is replanted to correct the damage of a fire because humans want the benefits of the forest—whether these be timber, a habitat for wildlife, or protection of a watershed. The replanting of the forest by humans is different from a natural re-growth of the forest vegetation, which would take much longer. The forest is replanted because humans want the beneficial results of the mature forest in a shorter time. Similarly, the eroded beach is replenished—with sand pumped from the ocean floor several miles offshore—because the human community does not want to maintain the natural status of the beach. The eroded beach threatens oceanfront homes and recreational beaches. Humanity prefers to restore the human benefits of a fully protected beach. The restored beach will resemble the original, but it will be the product of human technology, a humanly designed artifact for the promotion of human interests.

After these actions of human restoration and modification, what emerges is a Nature with a different character than the original. This is an ontological difference, a difference in the essential qualities of the restored area. A beach that is replenished by human technology possesses a different essence than a beach created by natural forces such as wind and tides. A savanna replanted from wildflower seeds and weeds collected by human hands has a different essence than grassland that develops on its own. The source of these new areas is different—man-made, technological, artificial. The restored Nature is not really Nature at all.

A Nature healed by human action is thus not Nature. As an artifact, it is designed to meet human purposes and needs—perhaps even the need for areas that look like a pristine, untouched Nature. In using our scientific and technological knowledge to restore natural areas, we actually practice another form of domination. We use our power to mold the natural world into a shape that is more amenable to our desires. We oppress the natural processes that function independent of human power; we prevent the autonomous development of the natural world. To believe that we heal or restore the natural world by the exercise of our technological power is, at best, a self-deception and, at worst, a rationalization for the continued degradation of Nature— for if we can heal the damage we inflict we will face no limits to our activities.

This conclusion has serious implications for the idea that Nature can repair human destruction, that Nature can somehow heal the evil that humans perpetuate on the earth. Just as a restored human landscape has a different causal history than the original natural system, the re-emergence of Nature in a place of human genocide and destruction is based on a series of human events that cannot be erased. The natural vegetation that covers the mass grave in the Warsaw cemetery is not the same as the vegetation that would have grown there if the mass grave had never been dug. The grass and trees in the cemetery have a different cause, a different history, that is inextricably linked to the history of the Holocaust. The grassy field in the Majdanek parade ground does not cover and heal the mud and desolation of the death camp—it rather grows from the dirt and ashes of the site's victims. For anyone who has an understanding of the Holocaust, of the innumerable evils heaped upon an oppressed people by the Nazi regime, the richness of Nature cannot obliterate nor heal the horror.

IV

What we see in the Warsaw cemetery and the Majdanek death camp is another example of Nature's imperialism over humanity—the mirror image of the human destruction of the natural environment. Nature here acts—without an intention or design—to erase the remnants of human evil. To speak in metaphor, Nature imposes its vision of the world on its human interpreters. But Nature's vision is not our vision, and in this case it does not express the essence of the places we experience. Nature's restoration of a site of human destruction alters the character of the site, just as the human restoration of a degraded ecosystem turns a natural area into an artifact. Although the beauty of the trees in the cemetery cannot be denied, the meaning and value of the cemetery lies not in the trees but in the historical significance of the Nazi plan to kill the Jews of Eastern Europe.

Nature's reemergence at these Holocaust sites is a form of domination: the domination of meaning. Nature slowly exerts its power over the free development of human ideas, human history, and human memory. Now it may seem strange to think of the healing power of Nature—the healing power of anything—as a form of domination. But Primo Levi describes his liberation from Auschwitz in terms that suggest this relationship.[13] He recounts the series of baths that he and the other prisoners were given by the Allies: "it was easy to perceive behind the concrete and literal aspect a great symbolic shadow, the unconscious desire of the new authorities, who absorbed us in turn within their own sphere, to strip us of the vestiges of our former life, to make of us new men consistent with their own models, to impose their brand upon us."

But Levi also compares these baths of liberation with the "devilish-sacral" or "black-mass" bath given by the Nazis as he entered the universe of the concentration camps. All of these baths served as symbols of domination—the molding of human beings into artifacts appropriate for their current situations. The cleansing of liberation is thus comparable to the oppression of imprisonment, for both actions deny the autonomy of the free human subject. Healing thus can be an expression of domination, if it modifies or destroys the meaning and the freedom of the original entity.[14]

To understand the multiplicity of the forms of domination, however, is the first step toward developing a comprehensive ethic for evaluating human activity in relationship to both the natural environment and the human community. We must resist the practice of human domination in all of its forms. We must act so as to preserve the free and autonomous development of human individuals, communities, and natural systems. We must understand the moral limits of our power to control Nature and our fellow human beings.

And so I am reminded of the last verse of the kaddish, the prayer that closes all Jewish services, and also serves as the prayer of mourning for the dead. This verse is a call for the healing power of peace. *Osay shalom bimromov hoo ya-ahsay shalom, olaynoo v'al kol yisroayl.* "May He who establishes peace in the heavens, grant peace unto us and unto all Israel." In viewing the Warsaw cemetery and the Majdanek death camp, I was moved by the hope that Nature could be the agent who establishes peace. But Nature alone cannot accomplish this. If there is a God, He works through human decisions. Only humans can understand the meaning and history of evil. Only humans who understand the need to control our power can halt the practice of domination, can halt the destruction of people and the natural environment. It is only through human actions that peace can be restored to our planet and our civilization.

Notes

1. For a general discussion of Majdanek and the overall history of the Holocaust, see Leni Yahil, *The Holocaust: The Fate of European Jewry*, trans. by Ina Friedman and Haya Galai (New York: Oxford University Press, 1990), especially 362–63; Ronnie S. Landau, *The Nazi Holocaust* (Chicago: Ivan R. Dee, 1994); and Martin Gilbert, *The Holocaust: A History of the Jews of Europe during the Second World War* (New York: Henry Holt, 1985). The death statistics cited in these recent works differ by an order of magnitude from Dawidowicz's classic work, which claims that 1.3 million Jews died at Majdanek (Lucy S. Dawidowicz, *The War against the Jews, 1933–1945* [New York, Holt, Rinehart, and Winston, 1975], 149). Gilbert reports that Hitler was enraged that the German SS forces did not destroy the camp before the Russian advance (711).

2. Robert-Jan Van Pelt, "A Site in Search of a Mission," in *Anatomy of the*

Auschwitz Death Camp, ed. Yisrael Gutman and Michael Berenbaum (Bloomington: Indiana University Press, 1994), 101–103.

3. See Eric Katz, "The Call of the Wild: The Struggle against Domination and the 'Technological Fix' of Nature," *Environmental Ethics* 14 (1992): 265–73; "Artefacts and Functions," *Environmental Values* 2 (1993): 223–32; and "Imperialism and Environmentalism," *Social Theory and Practice* 21:2 (summer 1995): 271–85.

4. See Martin Krieger, "What's Wrong with Plastic Trees?" *Science* 179 (1973): 446–55; and Chris Maser, *The Redesigned Forest* (San Pedro: R&E Miles, 1988).

5. See Eric Katz, "The Big Lie: Human Restoration of Nature," *Research in Philosophy and Technology* 12 (1992): 231–41, and "Restoration and Redesign: The Ethical Significance of Human Intervention in Nature," *Restoration and Management Notes* 9:2 (1991): 90–96.

6. C. S. Lewis, "The Abolition of Man," reprinted in *Philosophy and Technology: Readings in the Philosophical Problems of Technology*, ed. Carl Mitcham and Robert Mackey (New York: Free Press, 1983), 143–50, esp. 143 and 146. Lewis's *The Abolition of Man* was originally published in 1947.

7. Thus the power of Peter Singer's argument that animal liberation is necessary to correct speciesism, a prejudice akin to racism or sexism (Peter Singer, *Animal Liberation: A New Ethics for Our Treatment of Animals* [New York: Avon, 1975], 1–23).

8. Colin A. M. Duncan, "On Identifying a Sound Environmental Ethic in History: Prolegomena to Any Future Environmental History," *Environmental History Review* 15:2 (1991): 8. See also Katz, "The Call of the Wild," and "Imperialism and Environmentalism."

9. See Katz, "Imperialism and Environmentalism," 274. Holmes Rolston, III presents a sustained account of the idea of Nature as the subject of an ongoing history (Rolston, *Environmental Ethics: Duties to and Values in the Natural World* [Philadelphia: Temple University Press, 1988], esp. 342–54).

10. See Katz, "Imperialism and Environmentalism," esp. 273–74.

11. I am indebted to Avner de-Shalit for bringing this argument to my attention.

12. The argument in this section is based on Katz, "The Big Lie," "Call of the Wild," and "Artefacts and Functions."

13. Primo Levi, *The Reawakening*, trans. Stuart Woolf (New York: Collier Books, 1987), 8.

14. Although it may appear paradoxical to think of the act of healing as a form of domination, consider the long-standing issue of paternalism in the field of medical ethics. The use of medical procedures against the wishes of a fully rational patient is a violation of individual autonomy, even when these medical procedures are clearly in the best interests (i.e., the health) of the patient.

Part IV

History and Tradition

15

Judaism and the Ecological Crisis

Although I was raised in the Jewish religion, my philosophical work has been entirely secular. I rarely consider religious issues or the nature of the divine in my philosophical analysis or arguments. Yet in the spring of 1990 I started working on the subject of the Jewish response to the environmental crisis with Rabbi Steven Shaw, the director of community education at the Jewish Theological Seminary of America in New York. Rabbi Shaw and I together taught a five-week mini-course in the Lehrhaus *program of the seminary on the subject of environmental ethics from both a Jewish and a secular philosophical perspective. I began to discover that there were elements of Jewish religious and moral law that were compatible with my basic position in environmental philosophy—particularly, the Jewish ideal of* bal tashchit, *do not destroy.*

In the summer of 1992 I was asked to contribute to Worldviews and Ecology, *a special issue of the* Bucknell Review, *edited by Mary Evelyn Tucker and John A. Grim.* Worldviews and Ecology *presents a survey of the world's major religions and philosophies as they relate to environmental issues. Since I am not trained in Jewish thought, I relied on a host of secondary sources to produce a comprehensive review of basic ideas in Judaism that deal with the environment and the natural world. My goal, as always, was to show that nonanthropocentrism was a viable option as the basis of environmental thought and policy.*

What does Judaism say about nature and the environmental crisis? Any discussion of the Jewish view of the natural world, the ecological principles underlying natural processes, and the obligations relevant to human activity in relation to nature must begin with the concrete and specific commandments binding upon all practicing Jews. A so-

205

called worldview of Judaism would be a mere abstraction from the specific rules and principles of Jewish life, for in Judaism, perhaps more than any other religion, philosophical meaning arises out of the procedure of concrete daily activity. As Robert Gordis writes: "The true genius of Judaism has always lain in specifics." Thus, Gordis continues, an understanding of Jewish teachings on the environmental crisis is "not to be sought in high-sounding phrases which obligate [Jews] to nothing concrete; rather [it] will be found in specific areas of Jewish law and practice."[1]

This reluctance to focus on abstract philosophical principles or a generalized worldview as a replacement for concrete obligations regarding the natural environment is a recurrent theme in the expositions of contemporary commentators on the Jewish tradition. After a discussion of the Hebrew concepts of nature in the Bible, Jeanne Kay concludes, in part, that "the Bible views observance of its commandments, rather than specific attitudes toward nature or techniques of resource protection, as the prerequisite of a sound environment."[2] In an essay that predates the current environmental crisis by more than a generation, E. L. Allen claims that in the Jewish tradition nature is neither an abstraction nor an ideal, but rather one of the realms in which humans interact with God. "Nature is envisaged as one of the spheres in which God meets man personally and in which he is called upon to exercise responsibility."[3] Thus, "for the man of the Bible nature is never seen in abstraction either from God or from the tasks which He has assigned to man in the world."[4] Within Judaism, then, the human view of nature and the environment is grounded in the specific obligations and activities of Jewish life, the tasks and commandments that God presented to the Jewish people.

Subdue the Earth: Dominion and Stewardship

Given this turn away from the abstract, an examination of the Jewish perspective on nature and the environmental crisis must begin with specific texts and commands, and none is more important than Genesis 1:28 in which God commands humanity to subdue the earth:

> And God blessed them [Adam and Eve]; and God said unto them: "Be fruitful and multiply, and replenish the earth, and subdue it; and have dominion over the fish of the sea, and over the fowl of the air, and over every living thing that moves upon the earth."

This notorious passage appears in almost every discussion of the religious foundations of the environmental crisis. It is used by Lynn White, Jr., and others, to demonstrate that the Judeo-Christian tradition is fundamentally biased toward the dominion—if not the actual domination—of the earth by humanity.[5] It suggests that the earth and all nonhuman living beings in nature belong to the human race, mere means for the growth ("be fruitful and multiply") of humanity.

This is not the place for a full discussion of White's controversial thesis concerning the Christian tradition.[6] But if we are to understand the Jewish perspective on the environmental crisis, we must examine the meaning of the command to "subdue" the earth and its relationship to the process of domination. Does this passage represent God's gift of title to humanity? Does this passage mean that the earth belongs to the human race?

The Jewish tradition clearly answers in the negative. Norman Lamm points out that the very next line from Genesis, which is usually ignored in the discussions of this passage, restricts humans to a vegetarian diet, hardly the prerogative of one who has dominion, control, and ownership of all the living creatures in nature! "And God said: 'Behold, I have given you every herb yielding seed, which is upon the earth, and every tree in which is the fruit of a tree yielding seed—to you shall it be for food' " (Gen. 1:29). The Torah thus limits the human right to "subdue" and use nature; this command is not title to unbridled domination.[7]

Indeed, Jewish scholars throughout history have gone to extraordinary lengths to disavow any idea that Genesis 1:28 permits the subjugation of nature by humanity. The Talmud (*Yebemot* 65b) relates the phrase "subdue it" to the first part of the sentence, "be fruitful and multiply," and then through a tortuous piece of logic, connecting the act of "subduing" with warfare—a male activity—claims that the passage really means that the propagation of the human race is an obligation of the male. And the medieval commentators Nachmanides and Obadiah Sforno connect the phrase to the activities of humanity in the use of natural resources, not their destruction or misuse. Nachmanides sees the passage as granting permission to humanity to continue their activities of building, agriculture, and mining. Sforno's explanation is even more restrictive: *"And subdue it*—that you protect yourself with your reason and prevent the animals from entering within your boundaries and you rule over them."[8] These interpretations recognize the power of humanity to use natural resources, and indeed the necessity of them so doing, but they emphasize limitations in the human role. Dominion here does not mean unrestricted domination.

The reason for the restrictions is also clear: in the Jewish tradition, humanity is the steward of the natural world, not its owner. Stewardship is a position that acknowledges the importance of the human role in the care and maintenance of the natural world without permitting an unrestricted license. David Ehrenfeld and Philip Bentley thus consider it a middle position, but one that is definitely on the side of the spectrum that advocates the human use of the natural environment, rather than the opposite extreme of the sacred reverence and noninterference with nature suggested by Eastern religions such as Jainism.[9] To use a comparison widespread in the literature of environmental philosophy, the concept of stewardship in Judaism advocates neither the *domination-destruction* nor the *preservation* of the natural environment but its *conservation* and wise developmental use. Genesis 2:15 lends support to the idea of stewardship, as it declares: "And . . . God . . . put him into the garden of Eden to till it and to keep it." This suggests, as Ehrenfeld and Bentley point out, that the human dominion over nature should not be interpreted in a harsh or exploitative way, and the rabbinic tradition has not done so.[10] The whole idea of stewardship implies care for an entity that is in one's power; it does not imply exploitative use.

The idea of care implicit in stewardship is, however, based on a more fundamental concept: the proper ownership of the entity under care. From a mere analysis of the meaning of concepts, the difference between dominion and stewardship is that the former includes an unrestricted ownership and total power over the subordinate entity, while the latter strictly limits power because it denies ownership. Humanity does not own the natural world. *In Judaism, the world belongs to God.* Judaism is a theocentric religion, at least when it concerns the relationships between humans and nature. God himself, not human life and welfare, is the source of all religious and moral obligation. The divine ownership of nature is most clearly and directly stated in Psalm 24: "The earth is the Lord's and the fulness thereof, the world and those who dwell therein." Humanity cannot have an unrestricted dominion over the natural world because the world belongs to God; humanity is merely the divinely appointed guardian or steward of what belongs to God.

This general theocentric worldview is expressed in many ways throughout Jewish ritual and practice, so much so that Jonathan Helfand can declare that "in both content and spirit the Jewish tradition negates the arrogant proposal that the earth is man's unqualified dominion."[11] God does not forsake the ownership of the world when he instructs Adam and his descendants to master it. As Helfand notes, the existence of the laws concerning the sabbatical—and the Jubilee—year clearly indicate that God is the owner of the earth: "And the land is not to be sold in perpetuity, for all land is Mine, because you are strangers and sojourners before Me" (Lev. 25:23).[12] In Samuel Belkin's words, man possesses but a "temporary tenancy of God's creation."[13] Thus, the prohibition on farming the land in the seventh year, which is detailed in Leviticus 25:3–4, is not to be understood as a primitive attempt at enlightened agricultural methods. Belkin argues that "the sages refuse to assign purely economic, agricultural or social motives to this law," for Rabbi Abahu cites the ownership of God as the primary reason for the existence of the Sabbath and Jubilee years (*Sanhedrin* 39a).[14] Belkin himself is even more emphatic about the theocentrism of Judaism: "the entire structure of Judaism rests" on the principle "that creation belongs to the Creator." Without such a principle, humans would own the world and the entities within it; they would then be able to use those things without regard to any laws or principles other than their own will. But this is not the case: the moral code of the Torah, the ritual commands, and the laws of Judaism all strongly imply that the world belongs to God, and he has "instructed man concerning what he is permitted to do or prohibited from doing with His creation . . . [God] alone dictates the terms of man's tenancy in this world."[15]

One commonplace example of the way ritual action reinforces the notion of God's ownership is the commandment concerning the blessings over food. Helfand cites the *Tosefta: Berakhot* 4:1:

> "Man may not taste anything until he has recited a blessing, as it is written: 'The earth is the Lord's and the fulness thereof.' Anyone who derives benefit from this world without a [prior] blessing is guilty of misappropriating sacred property."[16]

The fact that God owns the world requires us to ask permission before we ingest any item of food. All the objects of the material world are as sacred as the entities of heaven, for they are all the creation of God, and belong to him.[17]

Perhaps the significance of the theocentric ownership of the world by God in Judaism is best summarized by the rituals concerning not the sabbatical year, but the ordinary *weekly* Sabbath. Ehrenfeld and Bentley articulate the meaning of the Sabbath for contemporary environmentalists: "For Jews, it is the Sabbath and the idea of the Sabbath that introduces the necessary restraint into stewardship."[18] For these authors, the Sabbath acquires this meaning because of three elements of the observance of Sabbath: "we create nothing, we destroy nothing, and we enjoy the bounty of the Earth." The fact that nothing is created serves to remind us that we are not as supreme as God; the fact that nothing is destroyed emphasizes that the world does not belong to us, but to God; and our enjoyment of the earth's bounty reminds us that God is the source of nature's goodness.[19] Thus the concept of the Sabbath itself—the absence of work and the appreciation of God—imposes a strict limit on human activity and achievement. Humanity in no way possesses dominion over the nonhuman world since it does not even possess dominion over its own activities.

Observance of the Sabbath thus returns us to the notion of stewardship, for without dominion, humanity is merely the steward of God's creation. But stewardship strongly implies a notion of responsibility, for the steward is responsible for the condition of the entities in his care. To illustrate this point, Ehrenfeld and Bentley recount a story told by the eleventh-century Spanish rabbi, Jonah ibn Janah. A man walks into a house in the midst of a deserted city; he finds a table with food and drink and begins to eat, thinking to himself, "I deserve all this, it is mine, I will act as I please." Little does he know that the owners are watching him, and that he will have to pay for all that he consumes. Thus man, as merely the appointed steward of God's creation, is responsible to God for the use of his property, the natural world.[20]

Environmentalism in Practice: Rituals and Commandments

An abstract notion of responsibility for the guardianship of the natural world is not, however, an adequate account of Judaism's perspective on the environmental crisis. For this notion of responsibility to be part of the practice of religious belief, it must be distilled into a series of specific commandments regarding human actions affecting the natural world. An examination of Jewish law and ritual does reveal these specific commandments, involving many different aspects of everyday Jewish life.

Several commandments involve the general health and well-being of the human community as it is situated in the natural environment. Deuteronomy 23:13–15, for example, requires the burial of human sewage in wartime, with the command that the soldiers must possess a spade for that very purpose among their other weapons: "and it shalt be when thou sittest down outside, thou shalt dig therewith, and shalt turn back and cover that which cometh from thee."[21] A more general principle is *yishuv ha-aretz* ("the settling of the land") which mandates both restrictions on the type of animals that can be raised and the type of trees that could be used for burning on the sacrificial altar. Goats and sheep were thought to be destructive to the land, and vine and olive trees were too valuable to be used in religious services.[22] Helfand argues that *yishuv ha-aretz* is also the basis of the mandate to establish a *migrash*, an open space one thousand cubits wide around all cities in Israel, in which agriculture and building would be prohibited. "The operative principle . . . calls upon the Jew in his homeland to balance the economic, environmental, and even religious needs of society carefully to assure the proper development and settling of the land."[23]

The existence of the *migrash* is, indeed, only one aspect of the laws regulating life in early Jewish cities, what amounts to a fully realized notion of town planning. Aryeh Carmell discusses many of these restrictions in an essay detailing the rabbinic concern for the quality of the environment in Jewish life.[24] Rambam in the *Hilchot Shechenim* ("Laws of Neighborly Relations"), explains that there are four classes of nuisance in which injury is always presumed: smoke, dust, noxious smells, and vibration. There is also a right to quietness.[25] This leads to rabbinic regulations—a kind of ancient zoning ordinance—regarding the specific placement of certain "industries" within the town: threshing floors, cemeteries, tanneries, and slaughterhouses.[26] The basis of these rabbinic regulations was a limitation of individual property rights for the sake of the entire community.[27] It seems clear that these limitations of individual property rights can also be traced to the notion that all property belongs ultimately to God, and thus that the use of the property by human individuals must be regulated by the laws of the Torah and the rabbinical interpretations of these laws.

Another category of Jewish law concerns the human relation to the divine plan. Nature is conceived, in Judaism, as the result of a divine plan or intelligence, which is not to be altered by human activity. Thus, in Leviticus 19:19 we find a prohibition against the hybridization of plants and animals, and even a restriction on wearing two types of cloth: "you shall not let your cattle mate with a different kind, you shall not sow your field with two kinds of seed, you shall not wear a garment of wool and linen." Helfand explains that this passage falls in the midst of a discussion of the proper and improper forms of human relationships, thereby reinforcing the idea that there is a fixed divine plan for both the social and the natural order of the universe.[28] The intrinsic significance of the divine plan is further revealed by Jewish traditions that aim, in modern terminology, to protect endangered species. Thus Helfand cites the commentator Nachmanides on the meaning of two biblical commands—not to slaughter a cow and her calf on the same day (Lev. 22:28) and not to take a mother bird with her young (Deut. 22:6): "Scripture will not permit a destructive act that will cause the extinction of a species."[29]

A concern for animals is further emphasized in Jewish thought by the fundamental principle of *tza'ar ba'alei chayim* ("the pain of living creatures"). Although it is not strictly a principle concerning the ethical treatment of the environment, it is the basis for the compassionate treatment of animals throughout Jewish life. Gordis considers it one of the two basic principles constituting the Jewish attitude to the nonhuman natural world—the second principle, *bal tashchit*, will be discussed below.[30] *Tza'ar ba'alei chayim* requires a concern for the well-being of all living beings—if not a full-scale sacred reverence for all life, at least an attitude of universal compassion.[31] The laws of kosher slaughtering, as well as the law forbidding the yoking together of animals of unequal strength (Deut. 22:10), are based on this compassion for animal suffering.

As Gordis emphasizes, one of the most unlikely textual affirmations for *tza'ar ba'alei chayim* is the conclusion of the book of Jonah, in which Jonah complains to God about the destruction of a gourd, a plant that had been shielding Jonah from the sun as he awaited God's decision about the destruction of the city of Nineveh. Jonah is angry for two reasons: God has spared the city, thereby making Jonah's prophecy appear foolish or pointless; and God has caused the gourd that shaded him to wither and die. God's reply is this:

> "You pity the gourd, for which you did not labor, nor did you make it grow, which came into being in a night, and perished in a night. And should I not pity Nineveh, that great city, in which there are more than a hundred and twenty thousand persons who do not know their right hand from their left, and also much cattle?" (Jon. 4:9–11)

God's rebuke compels a consideration of three different kinds of entities; the human inhabitants of Nineveh, the nonhuman domesticated animals that live in Nineveh, and the wild gourd—the plant life—outside the city. Clearly God does not consider the potential loss of the cattle to be a minor point; the loss of the cattle with the human population is an event to pity, an event requiring divine compassion. But the passage also suggests that pity for the gourd—wild, undomesticated plant life—is not an absurdity. Jonah's mistake is not that he felt compassion for the gourd, but that his level of concern was too great. It is wrong to value the wild gourd more than God values the inhabitants of Nineveh. Compassion for all living beings is a moral obligation in Judaism, but the context will determine the appropriate level of response.

Bal Tashchit: Do Not Destroy

Although the preceding section listed several principles and commandments that prescribe specific actions regarding the nonhuman environment, the most important and fundamental principle of the Jewish response to nature is *bal tashchit*—"do not destroy"—which is first outlined in Deuteronomy 20:19–20:

> When you besiege a city for a long time . . . you shall not destroy its trees by wielding an ax against them. You may eat of them, but you may not cut them down. Are the trees in the field men that they should be besieged by you? Only the trees which you know are not trees for food you may destroy and cut down, that you may build siege-works against the city.

In the context of warfare, specific moral rules apply. As Gordis notes, "this injunction ran counter to accepted procedures in ancient war," particularly the actions of the ruthless Assyrians.[32] But more importantly, the principle of *bal tashchit* forbids the wanton destruction of an enemy's resources, a so-called scorched earth policy of warfare. Lamm comments that "what the Torah proscribed is not the use of the trees to win a battle, which may often be a matter of life and death, but the wanton destruction of embattled areas, so as to render them useless to the enemy should he win."[33]

The principle here is the prohibition on wanton destruction or vandalism, the destruction of trees for no (or little) redeeming purpose. Lamm also notes that Jewish law extends the law to situations in peacetime as well as war; the Bible merely used an example of a situation in wartime to emphasize the seriousness of the restriction, for the commandment "do not destroy" is so powerful that it cannot even be overridden for the sake of victory in war.[34] Thus both Lamm and Gordis claim that *bal tashchit* is the establishment of a general principle in the expression of a concrete situation.[35]

There is much evidence from rabbinical texts to support the idea that *bal tashchit* is a general and fundamental principle regarding human actions within the nonhuman and natural environment. The idea of "wielding an ax" is extended to any means of destruction, even the diverting of a water supply.[36] Moreover, the principle is extended to any natural entity or to any human artifact. In the *Sefer Hahinuch* ("Shoftim" Commandment 529) is written this comment on *bal tashchit*: "In addition [to the cutting down of trees] we include the negative commandment that we should not destroy anything, such as burning or tearing clothes, or breaking a utensil—without purpose." Lamm also cites Maimonides, who includes the stopping of fountains, the wasting of food, or "wrecking that which is built" as violations of *bal tashchit*.[37] Thus Gordis concludes: "The principle of *bal tashchit* entered deep into Jewish consciousness, so that the aversion to vandalism became an almost psychological reflex and wanton destruction was viewed with loathing and horror by Jews for centuries."[38]

The precise meaning of *bal tashchit* and its application in the affairs of humans interacting with and using natural objects raises, however, interesting issues. First is the relationship of *bal tashchit* to economic considerations. The original passage in Deuteronomy appears to make a distinction between food-producing (fruit-bearing) trees and trees that do not produce fruit. Although wanton destruction is prohibited regarding all trees, fruit-bearing trees should be protected even from appropriate military uses. It is permitted to destroy trees that do not produce fruit for good reasons. Lamm explains that this special concern for food-producing trees may be tied to commercial considerations, either "an economy of scarcity" or the existence of property rights. And there is rabbinical evidence for the importance of economic values: a fruit-bearing tree may be destroyed if the value of its crop is less than the value of the lumber the tree would produce; moreover, the tree may be destroyed if the land is needed for the construction of a house. These exceptions to *bal tashchit* are not permitted for purely aesthetic reasons, such as landscaping.[39] Eric Freudenstein echoes this conclusion (which he derives from *Baba Kama* 91b): "the standards of bal tashchit are relative rather than absolute. The law is interpreted in the Talmud as limited to purposeless destruction and does not prohibit destruction for the sake of economic gain."[40] But Freudenstein supplements this conclusion with the point that what constitutes an appropriate economic value differs from generation to generation, and thus the correct use of *bal tashchit* at any time must be left to the authorities to decide. The keeping of goats and sheep was once banned because of the destructive impact on the environment, but it is now permitted.[41] Thus the moral evaluation for the destruction of an object or natural entity will depend on the economic and social context of the act. *Bal tashchit* prohibits *wanton* destruction, but the meaning of "wanton" will change throughout history.

An additional economic issue is the relationship of *bal tashchit* to notions of private property. Both Lamm and Gordis claim that the principle is not tied in any way to our modern notion of private property; one is not permitted to destroy one's own property any more than one is permitted to destroy another's. *Bal tashchit* is concerned with "the waste of an economic value per se" i.e., the social utility of the object being destroyed. Lamm even cites the interpretation of the principle to include the idea that it is permissible to destroy a fruit tree if it is somehow damaging the property of others—thus the basis of the principle would be social concern. *Bal tashchit* is a religious and moral law that requires a consideration of the social implications of actions that harm nonhuman entities; it is not a law of financial and personal property.[42]

But even this focus on social consequences does not reveal the true depth of *bal tashchit*. Questions of private property and social utility reintroduce the issue of the real ownership of the world. It was noted above that the fundamental basis of the idea of stewardship was the theocentric perspective of Judaism: the world belongs to God. When *bal tashchit* is combined with this theocentrism, we arrive at the ultimate argument against the destruction of natural entities: such entities are the property of God. This position easily renders insignificant the economic or utilitarian justifications for *bal tashchit*. The principle is not designed to make life better for humanity; it is not meant to insure a healthy and productive environment for human beings. In the terminology of environmental philosophy, it is not an *anthropocentric* principle at all: its purpose is not to guarantee or promote human interests. The purpose of *bal tashchit* is to maintain respect for God's creation.

Gordis thus ties *bal tashchit* to the laws of the sabbatical year and the Jubilee year—the reaffirmation of God's ownership of the land.[43] But as an explanation of the philosophical worldview that underlies *bal tashchit*, I find sections of the book of Job even more compelling. Near the end of the story, Job is finally able to question God about the reasons for the several misfortunes that have befallen him. God speaks to Job out of the whirlwind, but his answer is not a direct justification of the seemingly incomprehensible divine actions that have radically altered Job's life. Instead, God discusses aspects of the natural world—

the wild domain outside of human control—and challenges Job to acknowledge the limits of human wisdom:

> Where wast thou when I laid the foundations of the earth?
> Declare, if thou hast the understanding.
> Who determined the measures thereof, if thou knowest?
> Or who stretched the line upon it?
>
> (Job 38:4–5)

And God continues to paint a picture of a world that exists independent of human concerns and free from human notions of rationality or
cause and effect:

> Who hath cleft a channel for the waterflood,
> Or a way for the lightning of the thunder;
> To cause it to rain on a land where no man is,
> On the wilderness, wherein there is no man;
> To satisfy the desolate and waste ground,
> And to cause the bud of the tender herb to spring forth?
>
> (Job 38:25–27)

And more than the useless rain on land where humans do not live,
there are the animals, the great beasts "behemoth" and "leviathan,"
which do not exist for human purposes; they lie outside the sphere of
human life (Job 40:15ff).

God's speech to Job out of the whirlwind is a dramatic reaffirmation
of the theocentrism of the universe, God's creation. Job, as well as any
other human being, errs when he believes that the events of the world
must have a rational explanation relevant to human life. The events
of the world are ultimately explained only in reference to God. This
theocentrism is the driving force of *bal tashchit*, for it gives meaning to
the reasons behind a prohibition on wanton destruction. Destruction
is not an evil because it harms human life—we humans should not
believe that God sends the rain for us—it is an evil because it harms
the realm of God and his creation.

The remarkable philosophical conclusion from this perspective of
theocentrism is that it serves to resolve a long-standing dispute among
secular environmental philosophers: should anthropocentric (i.e.,
human-centered) or nonanthropocentric arguments be used to support
environmental practices? Should policies of environmental preservation be pursued because such policies will benefit humanity, or be-

cause such policies are *intrinsically* beneficial to the natural world? Both positions encounter ethical and policy-oriented problems. The anthropocentric perspective would permit the use (and destruction) of natural entities for a correspondingly greater human benefit; but the nonanthropocentric intrinsic value perspective implies a policy of strict nonintervention in natural processes, an absolute sanctity of nature. One position may lead to the destruction of nature, and the other may lead to worshipful noninterference: thus the dilemma for environmental philosophers.

On a practical level, the theocentrism of Judaism resolves this dilemma because it is functionally equivalent to a nonanthropocentric doctrine of the intrinsic value of nature without endorsing the sacredness of natural entities in themselves. Natural objects are valued, and cannot be destroyed, because they belong to God. They are sacred, not in themselves, but because of God's creative process. This worldview is, in part, derived from the Kabbalistic strand of Jewish thought, as is expressed quite clearly by David Shapiro: "The quality of lovingkindness is the basis of all creation. It is God's steadfast love that brought this world into being, and it is His steadfast love that maintains it."[44] Thus, "all creation is linked together in a bond of unity," which humans must act to preserve and not to destroy.[45] A further description of this view is offered by Lamm, who writes that "Judaism . . . refuses to ascribe the quality of holiness to nature and natural objects as such."[46] The Jewish view of the human relationship to nature can be represented by the opposition of two extreme views, with the mainstream Jewish tradition taking the middle position. On the one side is the form of Hasidism that follows the Kabbalistic tradition of God's immanence throughout nature, the extreme of nature-deification. On the other side is the Mitnagdic criticism of Hasidism which radically separates the divine and natural realms, the extreme of nature-as-profane. Lamm argues that the two extremes tend to converge, for the Hasidic tradition teaches respect for nature without ascribing sanctity to it, while the Mitnagdic tradition acknowledges that from God's perspective the world is suffused with his presence. For Lamm, this "theological tension is resolved . . . [in] . . . practice . . . [as] Nature is not to be considered holy, but neither is one permitted to act ruthlessly towards it, needlessly to ravage it and disturb its integrity."[47] As Gordis concludes, "every natural object is an embodiment of the creative power of God and is therefore sacred."[48] Its sacredness and its integrity—its intrinsic value, let us say—rests on its status as God's creation. Thus, it is the theocentric basis of *bal tashchit* that requires Jews to act with a practical respect for the value of nature without regard to human concerns.

The Jewish View of Nature

This survey of Jewish principles and commandments regarding nature and the environment does not lead easily into a unified worldview. Is it possible to summarize this examination of the specific regulations of Judaism concerning nature? Is there a coherent Jewish perspective? Yes: the Jewish worldview holds that nature has a value independent of human interests, as an expression of the creative power of God. This divinely inspired value thus inspires respect and requires obedience on the part of humanity, the servants and stewards of God's creation.

As stewards of God's earth, humans serve as partners in the never-ending task of perfecting the universe. Gordis concludes that "Judaism . . . insists that human beings have an obligation not only to conserve the world of nature, but to enhance it" as a "copartner with God in the work of creation."[49] The universe is God's creation, and that is the undeniable and fundamental starting point of the Jewish view of nature. Understanding the universe as an outgrowth of God's power is the most important aspect of the value of nature in the Jewish worldview. It gives the natural world a force, a presence, that cannot be ignored.

Allen ends his discussion of the value of nature with a return to the book of Job, for in God's speech out of the whirlwind we are presented with the essence of the wild: a world beyond the control and understanding of humanity. But the lack of control does not breed disrespect; on the contrary, it creates a sense of awe, wonder, and responsibility, for we are in the presence of the divine. "The untamed world beyond the frontiers of human society is fraught with the numinous, it is a constant reminder that man is not master in the world but only a privileged and therefore responsible inhabitant of it."[50]

Notes

1. Robert Gordis, "Judaism and the Environment," *Congress Monthly* 57, no. 6 (September/October 1990): 8. This article is a revised version of "Judaism and the Spoilation of Nature," which appeared in *Congress Bi-Weekly*, April 2, 1971. Another version of the essay, with substantial similarities, appeared as

"Ecology and the Jewish Tradition" in *Judaic Ethics for a Lawless World* (New York: Jewish Theological Seminary, 1986), 113–22. This 1986 essay is reprinted in *Judaism and Ecology, 1970–1986: A Sourcebook of Readings*, ed. Marc Swetlitz (Wyncote, Pa.: Shomrei Adamah, 1990), 47–52.

2. Jeanne Kay, "Concepts of Nature in the Hebrew Bible," *Environmental Ethics* 10 (1988): 326–27.

3. E. L. Allen, "The Hebrew View of Nature," *The Journal of Jewish Studies* 2, no. 2 (1951): 100.

4. Ibid.

5. Lynn White, Jr., "The Historical Roots of Our Ecologic Crisis," *Science*, 155 (1967): 1203–7.

6. For a full philosophical discussion, see John Passmore, *Man's Responsibility for Nature: Ecological Problems and Western Traditions* (New York: Scribner's, 1974), 3–40, and Robin Attfield, *The Ethics of Environmental Concern* (New York: Columbia University Press, 1983), 20–87.

7. Norman Lamm, "Ecology and Jewish Law and Theology," in *Faith and Doubt* (New York: KTAV, 1971), 164–65; reprinted in Swetlitz, *Judaism and Ecology*, 77.

8. See Gordis, "Judaism and the Environment," 7–8.

9. David Ehrenfeld and Philip J. Bentley, "Judaism and the Practice of Stewardship," *Judaism* 34 (1985): 301–2; reprinted in Swetlitz, *Judaism and Ecology*, 97–98.

10. Ibid., 305 (in Swetlitz, 99).

11. Jonathan I. Helfand, "The Earth Is the Lord's: Judaism and Environmental Ethics," in *Religion and Environmental Crisis*, ed. Eugene C. Hargrove (Athens: University of Georgia Press, 1986), 39.

12. Ibid., 40.

13. Samuel Belkin, "Man as Temporary Tenant," in *Judaism and Human Rights*, ed. Milton R. Konvitz (New York: Norton, 1972), 253; reprinted in Swetlitz, *Judaism and Ecology*, 25.

14. Ibid., 253–54 (in Swetlitz, 25–26).

15. Ibid., 255 (in Swetlitz, 26).

16. Helfand, "The Earth Is the Lord's," 40–41.

17. Belkin, "Man as Temporary Tenant," 252 (in Swetlitz, 25).

18. Ehrenfeld and Bentley, "Judaism and Stewardship," 309 (in Swetlitz, 101).

19. Ibid., 310 (in Swetlitz, 102).

20. Ibid., 306–7 (in Swetlitz, 100).

21. See discussion in Eric G. Freudenstein, "Ecology and the Jewish Tradition," *Judaism* 19 (1970): 409–10; reprinted in Swetlitz, *Judaism and Ecology*, 30–31. See also Richard H. Schwartz, *Judaism and Global Survival* (New York: Vantage Press, 1984), 49.

22. Helfand, "The Earth Is the Lord's," 46. See also Aryeh Carmell, "Judaism and the Quality of the Environment," in *Challenge: Torah Views on Science*

and Its Problems, ed. Aryeh Carmell and Cyril Domb (New York: Feldheim, 1978), 511; reprinted in Swetlitz, *Judaism and Ecology*, 39.

23. Helfand, "The Earth Is the Lord's," 46.

24. Carmell, "Judaism and the Quality of the Environment," 500–525 (in Swetlitz, 34–46).

25. Ibid., 503 (in Swetlitz, 35).

26. Ibid., 504 (in Swetlitz, 36). Carmell cites the Mishna, *Bava Bathra* 2:8–9.

27. Ibid., 505 (in Swetlitz, 36).

28. Helfand, "The Earth Is the Lord's," 42.

29. Ibid., 45.

30. Gordis, "Judaism and the Environment," 8.

31. Allen explains that Judaism is not a Schweitzerian ethic, an ethic for all life, because there is a difference between domestic and wild animals. Humans have a specific covenant with domestic animals to protect them; the concern for wild nature is more mysterious, as it is based on the recognition of the divine presence in the entire world of creation. This point will be expanded below. See Allen, "Hebrew View of Nature," 103.

32. Gordis, "Judaism and the Environment," 9.

33. Lamm, "Ecology and Jewish Law," 169 (in Swetlitz, 79).

34. Ibid.

35. Lamm, 169 (in Swetlitz, 79) and Gordis, 9.

36. Gordis, ibid., cites *Sifre Shofetim*, section 203.

37. Lamm, 169 (in Swetlitz, 79).

38. Gordis, 9.

39. Lamm, 170 (in Swetlitz, 80). Lamm cites *Turei Zahov* to *SH.A.Y.D.* 116:6, and Responsa *Havot Yair*, no. 195.

40. Freudenstein, "Ecology and Jewish Tradition," 411 (in Swetlitz, 31).

41. Ibid., 411–12 (in Swetlitz, 31–32).

42. Lamm, 171–72 (in Swetlitz, 80–81). See also Gordis, 9.

43. Gordis, 9.

44. David S. Shapiro, "God, Man and Creation," *Tradition* 15 (1975): 25; reprinted in Swetlitz, *Judaism and Ecology*, 64.

45. Ibid., 41 (in Swetlitz, 73).

46. Lamm, 173 (in Swetlitz, 81).

47. Ibid., 173–77 (in Swetlitz, 81–83).

48. Gordis, 10.

49. Ibid., citing *B. Shabbat* 10a.

50. Allen, "Hebrew View of Nature," 103. I have discussed these themes from a secular standpoint in Eric Katz, "The Call of the Wild: The Struggle against Domination and the Technological Fix of Nature," *Environmental Ethics* 14 (1992): 265–73.

16

The Traditional Ethics of Natural Resources Management

"The Traditional Ethics of Natural Resources Management" was written for an interdisciplinary textbook. My assignment was the historical background of ethical attitudes toward the environment, and in particular, toward the human use of natural resources. Although my philosophical arguments in defense of a community-based holism are not based on historical texts, I was able to use this opportunity to discuss the origins of modern anthropocentrism and the beginning of an ethic centered on respect of natural entities. In the philosophy of John Locke we can find the traditional justification of environmental policies based on the satisfaction of human interests, for Locke viewed Nature in itself as worthless until it was transformed by human labor to meet human needs. Locke's philosophical outlook finds its application in the wise-use conservation policies of Gifford Pinchot, the first head of the U.S. Forest Service. But in the writings of John Muir we find the beginning of a minority tradition that advocates the direct moral consideration of Nature. The ideological clash between Pinchot and Muir is then resolved in the scientific and ethical ideas of Aldo Leopold, who developed a "land ethic" based on the concept of ecological community. This essay is reprinted with permission from A New Century for Natural Resources Management, *ed. Richard L. Knight and Sarah F. Bates, pp. 101–16. Copyright © Island Press 1995. Published by Island Press, Washington, D.C., and Covelo, Calif.*

> God, who hath given the World to Men in common, hath also given them reason to make use of it to the best advantage of Life, and convenience. The Earth, and all that is therein, is given to Men for the Support and Comfort of their being.
>
> —John Locke,
> *The Second Treatise of Government*

221

The human use of natural resources is a practice as old as humanity itself. As the species *Homo sapiens* evolved, it necessarily made use of the material in its environment, as did every other species and living entity on Earth. The use of the natural environment by itself is not an ethical issue; it is a biological fact. Human life—indeed, all life—depends on the proper exploitation of the environment.

Ethics enters the picture when we begin to think about the meaning and value of the use of the environment, when humans examine the nature of their relationship with nature. Within ethics, judgments are made concerning the good or evil of specific actions, policies, and practices. This type of judgment, this type of self-conscious examination of the relationship with the natural environment, is also as old as humanity itself. Even the humans of prehistory reflected on their relationship with the natural world, as the famous Paleolithic cave paintings of animals and the hunt demonstrate.

Since both the use of nature and the reflective examination of this use are as old as the human species, we can very well ask what is meant by the "traditional" ethics of the use of natural resources. Within the duration of the human species there have been countless traditions, countless institutional practices and belief systems regarding the human relationship with the natural world. Most of these traditions are lost in prehistory. But even in the last 10 thousand years, the era of a recorded culture and history, there are a multitude of traditional world views. Where then do we begin to understand the ethical history of the human relationship with nature?

Older Western Traditions

In the Western cultural tradition, it is perhaps appropriate to begin with the first Greek philosophers (Thales, Anaximander, Anaximenes, Heraclitus) who, beginning in the 6th century B.C., began to ask fundamental questions about the physical relationship between humans and the natural world. The birth of the discipline of physics is really the birth of an environmental philosophy and an ethic of nature, for the essential questions the pre-Socratic Greek philosophers asked were "what is the nature of the physical universe?" and "what is the human place or role in this system?" These metaphysical questions provide the basis of the ethics of the use of natural resources. They establish a framework for any serious investigation into the meaning and value of human activity in the natural world. For unless we humans know what the universe is like, we cannot judge our actions concerning the natural system as either good or evil.

Yet the early Greek philosophers had no explicit conception of what we 20th-century humans would call an environmental policy; they made no conscious effort to develop a set of principles governing human action in the environment. Perhaps the first such set of principles appeared in the Old Testament, in the book of Genesis, where God commanded Adam and Eve to subdue the Earth:

> And God blessed them; and God said unto them: "Be fruitful and multiply, and replenish the Earth, and subdue it; and have dominion over the fish of the sea, and over the fowl of the air, and over every living thing that moves upon the Earth." (Genesis 1:28)

This passage is invoked in almost every discussion of the Biblical foundations of environmental philosophy, and it has aroused much controversy among scholars of the Judeo-Christian religious tradition. Much of the controversy originated with Lynn White, Jr.'s argument in "The Historical Roots of Our Ecologic Crisis" that this passage has served to justify the domination of all natural resources on Earth—all nonhuman entities—for the sole benefit of humanity.[1] According to White, the passage suggests that humanity rules over all nonhuman beings, that it is proper to "subdue" the Earth and all natural entities for the growth and maintenance ("be fruitful and multiply") of human life. If so, the Bible explicitly states what we will call an *anthropocentric* perspective on the value of nature and natural resources: the value of nature centers on humanity. Nature's effect on humanity and the use of nature by humanity are the major if not the sole determinants of the value of natural resources.

Obviously, this is not the proper place for a full discussion of the meaning of Genesis for the development of an ethics of environmental policy. Its importance for us, in this chapter, is to see that an anthropocentric attitude toward the use of natural resources is embedded so deeply into the Western philosophical and religious tradition that it is rarely articulated, examined, or criticized. The anthropocentric world view is the basic vision of Western civilization: nature and all its components are only evaluated—only seen—through the category of usefulness for humanity.

The Early Modern Tradition: John Locke
and Nature as Property

The basic Western tradition of anthropocentrism was fully articulated when we entered the age of modern thought, after the Renaissance, at the beginning of the ages of exploration, the Enlightenment, and the Industrial Revolution. One convenient place to begin an investigation of the modern tradition would be with the thinker Francis Bacon. Bacon expressed the basic motivations and methodologies of modern empirical science. The goal of the new empirical science was not mere contemplation, but the active manipulation and understanding of Nature, to unlock the secrets of Nature, to bend her to the will of humanity, to better the lives of human beings and human society. This view of science and the human relationship to nature is summed up in Bacon's famous aphorism, "Knowledge is power." It has been the dominant view of the meaning of science and technology in the world today, an unquestioned and noncontroversial credo of modern humanity and the contemporary scientist. But Bacon, of course, wrote with little regard for the adverse impact of human power on the natural environment—although a true visionary, he was a creature of his times, almost completely ignorant of ecological relationships and natural systems. In that way too, he exemplified the modern age.

Although Bacon explained the presuppositions, methods, and purposes of modern science, it was the 17th-century philosopher John Locke who more explicitly established the traditional modern world view of the human relationship with the natural environment. Bacon argued for the use of science to aid human life. Locke argued for the human evaluation of the natural world. Thus, Locke was the great modern theorist of anthropocentrism. For Locke, nature was valuable solely as it was used as property by human beings. Natural entities were valuable only insofar as they were actually removed from the natural system and became part of human culture.

It is important that we examine Locke's views in detail, for Locke, more than any other modern philosopher, truly formulated the foundation of the modern tradition of the use of natural resources. It is ironic however, that Locke formulated this radically anthropocentric view of nature as a minor theme in the development of his political philosophy. His chief concern in the *Second Treatise of Government* was to establish the legitimacy of a popularly elected democratic government, and thereby to oppose the prevalent view of the divine right of the monarchy. He based the argument on a theoretical model of a "state of Nature" that supposedly preceded the establishment of the first government or civil society. It was from this state of nature that humans established a social order. Thus, it became important to understand the conditions of human life prior to the development of civil society.

> To understand Political Power right . . . we must consider what State all Men are naturally in, and that is, a *State of perfect Freedom* to order their Actions, and dispose of their Possessions, and Persons as they think fit, within the bounds of the Law of Nature, without asking leave, or depending on the Will of any other Man. (II. 4)[2]

From this state of perfect individual freedom, humans agree to form a social order, by means of a social contract.

Governments, or civil societies, however, exert power over free and independent individuals and create an inherent political inequality. The existence of this unequal power can only be morally justified if it is the result of the rational consent of free individuals. The central idea of the social contract is the consent of free individuals, joining together to limit their freedom, each expecting to benefit in this contract.

> Men being . . . by Nature, all free, equal and independent, no one can be put out of his Estate, and subjected to the Political Power of another, without his own *Consent*. The only way whereby any one divests himself of his Natural Liberty, and *puts on the bonds of Civil Society* is by agreeing with other Men to joyn and unite into a Community, for their comfortable, safe, and peaceable living one amongst another. . . . (VIII. 95)

The source of legitimate political power, then, is the rational freedom of individual human subjects that exists as a condition of the state of nature. Political legitimacy lies in the consent of the governed, not in the absolute power of the king.

Within the context of this argument for a democratic political philosophy, Locke also examined and defended a specific notion of property. The right to property must be seen as an essential (or natural) right if meaningful political power is to reside in the consent of free people. Without property, political power would be empty, for individuals would have no possessions necessary for the maintenance of life. The right to property thus exists within the state of nature, prior to the establishment of the social contract.

According to Locke, property is just those parts of nature that are used and valued by human individuals. In this philosophy, it must be emphasized that Nature is deemed valuable solely because it is used by humans, solely as it becomes property, a possession of a human individual. Nature—the Earth, the natural environment, land and water—begins as a common resource that exists for the maintenance of human life. The natural world and all natural entities and resources exist to be useful for human beings. The quotation at the beginning of this chapter expresses the foundation of Locke's anthropocentric view of nature.

The usefulness of any natural resource depends on its private appropriation as property. Parts of the natural environment must be removed from the"commons" and used privately if they are to have any significant effect on the comfort and well-being of the individual humans. The"fruits" and "beasts" of the commons are given to all, "yet being given for the use of Men, there must of necessity be a means to appropriate them some way or other before they can be of any use, or at all beneficial to any particular Man" (V. 26). Locke appears to have employed a model of eating as the basic method of using a natural resource. That is why the fruits and beasts must be individually appropriated before they can be used. After a natural resource is eaten it is no longer a part of the commons, but in the most literal way imaginable a private part of the individual. Locke completed the argument: "The Fruit, or Venison, which nourishes the wild *Indian* . . . must be his, and so his, *i.e.*, a part of him, that another can no longer have any right to it, before it can do him any good for the support of his Life" (V. 26). A person may eat something that is common property, but once it is eaten it is clearly private property, a part of the individual. The consumption of natural resources therefore requires the establishment of private property. For Locke, consumption was the primary, if not the only, model of the use of natural resources.

Although the appropriation of a natural resource from the commons is physically necessary to sustain life, Locke needed to determine its moral legitimacy, if he was to justify a right to property as an element of the natural freedom that precedes the social contract in the state of nature. He began with the physical body of the individual human being, since this was clearly the property of the individual. "Though the Earth and all inferior Creatures be common to all Men, yet every Man has a *Property* in his own *Person*. This no Body has any Right to but himself" (V. 27). If the physical body is the property of the individual, so is the labor of the body; a person owns the actions or physical motions of its body. Locke continued: "The Labour of his Body, and the Work of his Hands, we may say, are properly his" (V. 27). Thus the individual is morally free to use his labor to act on the common resources of nature. In Locke's metaphor, he "mixes" his labor with the natural entity. The mixing of the private property of individual labor with the unowned commons creates that act of appropriation. Locke used the example of harvesting acorns or apples:

> He that is nourished by the Acorns he pickt up under an Oak, or the Apples he gathered from the Trees in the Wood, has certainly appropriated them to himself. No Body can deny the nourishment is his. I ask then, When did they begin to be his? When he digested? Or when he eat? Or when he boiled? Or when he brought them home? Or when he pickt them up? And 'tis plain, if the first gathering made them not his, nothing else could. That *labour* put a distinction between them and common. (V. 28)

The moral basis of the existence of private property is thus the labor used by the individual to remove natural resources from the commonly owned natural world for the purpose of physical sustenance. "Whatsoever then he removes out of the State of Nature hath provided . . . he hath mixed his *Labour* with, and joyned to it something that is his own, and thereby makes it his *Property*" (V. 27).

To complete the argument for the moral legitimacy of privately owned natural resources, Locke imposed two limitations on the extent of the act of appropriation. The limitations appeared to protect people from the acquisition of private property by others. The first limitation was that no one could take more than could be used before spoilage. "Nothing was made by God for Man to spoil or destroy," and thus:

> But how far has [God] given it [i.e., the commons] us? To enjoy. As much as any one can make use of to any advantage of life before it spoils; so much he may by his labour fix a Property in. Whatever is beyond this, is more than his share, and belongs to others. (V. 31)

This restriction even applies to the appropriation of real property (land). A person cannot enclose, and thus acquire by labor, more land than he can cultivate.

The second limitation required that one leave enough common natural resources for others to use. As with the first limitation, this requirement seems imposed to ensure that no individuals are harmed by the general acquisition of private property. An individual only makes a justifiable appropriation of a natural resource if others can appropriate a similar amount. "Nor was this *appropriation* . . . any prejudice to any other Man, since there was still enough, and as good left; and more than the yet unprovided could use" (V. 33). Locke illustrated this point with one of his finest metaphors: "No Body could think himself injur'd by the drinking of another Man, though he took a good Draught, who had a whole River of the same Water left him to quench his thirst" (V. 33). As long as there are natural resources left in the state of nature, the commons, for the use of other individuals, then the creation of private property through labor for the purpose of consumptive use is not immoral or illegitimate.

The two limitations helped reinforce the moral foundation of the acquisition of private property, since they protected against two potential abuses: the waste of natural resources and harm to other human beings. From the perspective of an ethic of the use of the natural environment, these limitations may also have helped to demonstrate the roots of an awareness of environmental responsibility. Yet the existence of the limitations was clearly a minor theme in Locke's philosophy of the use of nature. The primary significance of Locke's notion of private property was that it established the anthropocentric use-value of nature, explicitly endorsing a model of the natural world as a reservoir of resources for the use of humanity.

An anthropocentric conception of value pervaded Locke's language and argument. He was so tied to an anthropocentric perspective of the natural world that he even defined the "intrinsic" value of natural entities as their use. "The intrinsick value of things . . . depends only on their usefulness to the Life of Man" (V. 37). This is a total reversal of the current meaning of the terms, for a value based on usefulness is what philosophers call an "instrumental" value, the exact opposite of intrinsic value. An intrinsic value of an entity would be the value in itself without regard to its use by anyone or anything. For Locke however, natural entities were resources, only valuable as they were used by human beings, having little or no value in themselves.

The key to Locke's argument was an empirical claim that cultivated land was almost a hundred times more valuable than uncultivated land lying fallow, in common:

'tis *Labour* indeed that *puts the difference of value* on every thing. . . . I think it will be but a very modest Computation to say, that of the *Products* of the Earth useful to the Life of Man 9/10 are the *effects of labour*; nay, if we will rightly estimate things as they come to our use . . . what in them is purely owing to *Nature*, and what to *labour*, we shall find, that in most of them 99/100 are wholly to be put on the account of *labour*. (V. 40)

Locke illustrated the point by a comparison of the productivity of the land in England with the vast amount of common land in America. Despite the richness of American soil, it lacked the value and productivity of the land of the advanced nations, because the land lay unused, fallow, uncultivated, as *waste*.

For Locke, then, the value of natural resources, the value of the natural world, depended on the labor of human beings to bring the natural world within the realm of human culture. Humans domesticated, cultivated, and used wild nature for the furtherance of human purposes. In discussing the value of a harvested corn crop, Locke concluded that "Nature and the Earth furnished only the almost worthless Materials" (V. 43). The value of natural entities in themselves was virtually worthless, since Locke perceived value only in the productive use of natural resources for human life.

Nature, for Locke, was merely the raw material for the development of human property. It was only human property—nature converted to a human resource through productive labor—that was useful for humanity. Locke's vision of the natural world was thoroughly anthropocentric. Nature, and all the living and nonliving entities therein, was evaluated almost entirely on its contributions to human well-being. Nature and natural entities had no intrinsic value; their value was determined by their instrumental use by humanity. The maintenance of human life and comfort was the primary focus of all policies of action, all determinations of value.

Locke's philosophy of nature thus expressed the dominant tradition of the modern age. In many ways, Locke represented the entire movement of modernism, the intellectual milieu of Western civilization since the Renaissance. According to one recent commentator, modernism was that historical movement that considered "science, technology, and liberal democracy" as the agents of change, "to transform a base and worthless wilderness into industrialized, democratic civilization."[3] We find in Locke a fusion of political philosophy (the source of the moral legitimacy of the state) with a philosophy of nature and the environment—a fusion based on the value of human progress. Human interests, the maintenance and improvement of human life, lie at the center of all value determinations. Human progress is the end of all policy, the purpose of all human activity. Nature and natural resources are worthless, mere objects for exploitation by the dominant human species, until they are transformed, through human labor, into instruments for human betterment. The entire nonhuman world becomes an instrument for the fulfillment of human needs and desires, for human life and comfort.

John Locke was no ordinary philosopher, for his ideas exerted enormous influence across the entire domain of Western civilization. His theory of political society, based on the fundamental natural rights of individual human beings, established the framework for political discussion throughout the period of modern liberalism, a period in which we still reside. In addition, his ideas concerning the value and meaning of nature and property established the primacy of the anthropocentric use-values of natural resources. This view of nature and property still sets the framework for the debate in environmental policy, as we will see in the ideas of Gifford Pinchot, John Muir, and Aldo Leopold. In the analysis of natural value, we are heirs to the Lockean tradition.

Recent Traditions: Utilitarianism and Beyond

The dominant tradition of the value of natural resources has focused on the use of these resources for humanity. The concept of use enframes the philosophical discussion of environmental policy: one is either an advocate or a critic of use and development, but the concept of use is inescapable. All environmental policies that affect the protection and/or development of natural resources are analyzed, evaluated, and criticized with some regard to their usefulness for humanity. The dominant tradition in the history of the ethics of environmental policy could not be clearer. In the modern world, we accept, at least as the starting point for discussion, the Lockean paradigm for the analysis of nature's value.

But it was only after Locke's lifetime that the philosophy of use-value was given a technical name by moral philosophers: *utilitarianism*. Utilitarianism is the ethical theory that claims that the morally correct action is the one, among several alternatives, that maximizes the good, pleasure, or happiness of those human beings affected by the action. It is an ethical doctrine based on the *consequences* of actions (or policies), for it is the *result* of an action that determines the amount of good or evil that it produces. Utilitarianism is, in the field of academic philosophy, a complicated, subtle, and controversial doctrine—and it is beyond the scope of this chapter to give it a full hearing and analysis. But the basic idea of utilitarianism appeals to common sense, since it encapsulates the idea that ethical judgments should, in the long run at least, promote good consequences and happiness. Its central idea can be summarized by the familiar maxim, "the greatest happiness for the greatest number."

In the late 19th and early 20th centuries, natural resource policy was debated along utilitarian lines. Gifford Pinchot was the leading proponent of the utilitarian analysis of natural resource policy. John Muir was the leading critic of that view.[4] Aldo Leopold was the visionary who offered a compromise ethic of environmental respect.[5] In the remainder of this chapter, I will briefly survey the basic philosophical and ethical ideas of these three thinkers.

Gifford Pinchot, who ultimately rose to the position of head of the new United States Forest Service, was trained, as a young man, in the science of forest management in Europe. The philosophical and ethical foundation of forest management was clearly the use-value of forests for human beings. The entire concept of "management" implies that the forests be directed, controlled, or designed for a particular purpose. The forests, or any other natural resource, must be used in such a way as to create benefits for humanity, and at the same time preserve the resource base for the future. Pinchot, in his autobiography, described the new policy with language that was an exact replication of the utilitarian maxim: "the use of the natural resources for the greatest good of the greatest number for the longest time."[6] All the aspects of policy that fell under the purview of the Forest Service—public lands, mining, agriculture, erosion, game management—could be understood as part of a utilitarian objective: "the one great problem of the use of Earth for the good of man."[7]

As Roderick Nash's history of wilderness preservation in the United States recounts, this utilitarian outlook was central to the arguments that helped to establish the first national and state parks and wilderness preserves.[8] Land was to be set aside, protected from the normal economic development of forestry, grazing, and farming because better results for humanity could be produced by preservation. The best possible use of the land was, paradoxically, not to use it in the manner of traditional development. New empirical evidence demonstrated that the overcutting of forests in sensitive watershed areas caused drought, flood, and erosion. Alternatively, the preservation of wilderness in these areas could prevent catastrophic results. Wilderness preservation was thus seen as compatible with economic progress, development, and the use-value of natural resources.[9]

The arguments for the establishment of Yellowstone National Park and New York State's "Forest Preserve" of the Adirondacks were essentially utilitarian: the preserves would be more useful if they were not developed. Yellowstone was to be protected from the "private acquisition and exploitation of geysers, hot springs, waterfalls, and similar curiosities."[10] The key idea was that the public—not private individuals—should maintain ownership and access to these natural wonders because this would be of the greatest benefit for the greatest number. Most important, Nash recounts that the supporters of Yellowstone had to show that the area of the park was useless for development because of its altitude and temperature (its preservation would not harm material progress.)[11] In New York, the preservation of the Adirondacks was urged because of the effects on water supply, not because of recreation or other noneconomic amenities. Preservation had to be seen as a matter of economic self-interest, entirely compatible with industry and development.[12]

There were those who urged the preservation of natural wilderness on other than the utilitarian grounds of economic development—for reasons of aesthetics, recreation, and religious awe. John Muir, who founded the Sierra Club, was the leading advocate of this nonutilitarian position. But at the beginning of the movement for wilderness preservation, both kinds of "preservationists" were united in their fight against the so-called despoilers of nature—those developers who saw no reason not to use natural resources to the maximum degree, those who perceived natural resources to be limitless. To prevent the ever-increasing, rapid deterioration of nature and its resources, all kinds of environmentalists united, despite differing motivations and values, to fight a common enemy. Eventually, however, the differing bases of the environmentalist position would lead to divergent policy choices, and the division of the movement into warring factions. This historical result is not surprising, since it appears to validate the logic of the connection between ethical values and policy. The values that lie at the foundation of a policy are the ultimate justification of the policy; if one introduces a different set of values, then in the long run, policies will emerge that conflict with the original set of values.

John Muir's relationship with Gifford Pinchot is a perfect example of this clash of values.[13] Muir's ideas of the value of wilderness were not based on the utilitarian use-value of natural resources. Although there is much scholarly debate about the precise meaning of Muir's thought, it seems clear that he had a nearly mystical, almost religious sense of the value of nature. In perhaps his most famous statement in the debate over wilderness preservation, when he fought to prevent the construction of a dam at Hetch Hetchy that would supply water for San Francisco, he clearly alluded to the sacredness of the undisturbed wilderness: "Dam Hetch Hetchy! As well dam for water-tanks the people's cathedrals and churches, for no holier temple has ever been consecrated by the heart of man."[14] For Muir, the wilderness was an expression of God's harmony, of the spiritual power of the universe—it was the place in which people could come closest to God.

It is easy to characterize Muir as a critic of utilitarian thought regarding natural resources; but it is also important to understand the source of his criticism, his own view of the value of wild nature. Muir rejected anthropocentrism and adopted what is now called a "biocentric" perspective, centering value on all living entities, rather than humans alone. He viewed nature as an organism in constant flux, not a fixed and determinate mechanism. This view of nature and the value of life was based on pantheism—a view that holds all of Nature sacred—that was itself informed by the new evolutionary insights of Darwin and other scientists of the late 19th century. He was also a critic of modernism, the relentless push for materialistic progress.[15]

Muir's pantheistic view of nature was, of course, a religious view of the value of nature, but it yielded important philosophical and ethical conclusions. These conclusions helped to establish a rival tradition of the ethics of the use of natural resources. In a pantheistic perspective, God is in the world in its entirety: all the parts of the world are part of God. This view thus implies a radical equality among all the beings of nature as well as a universal harmony and kinship, a web of life in which humans do not dominate, use, or destroy. "The universe would be incomplete without man; but it would also be incomplete without the smallest transmicroscopic creature that dwells beyond our conceitful eyes and knowledge." We are, Muir wrote, "part of wild nature, kin to everything." This implies a deep and equal respect among humans and all of wild nature.[16] It is a view that is the exact opposite of the anthropocentric utilitarianism espoused by Pinchot (and explicitly formulated in the modern age by Locke). Nature is not the material for the development of human happiness. Nature is valuable in itself—intrinsically—as a manifestation of the Divine.

Originally allies in the fight for wilderness preservation, Muir and Pinchot clashed, and ended their relationship permanently, over the proposal to dam Hetch Hetchy. Pinchot argued on simple utilitarian grounds: which policy alternative created the most benefits for the affected human population? In his testimony before Congress on June

25, 1913, Pinchot claimed that the central issue was whether there was more advantage in leaving the valley natural and wild, or in using the water resources for the benefit of San Francisco. Preserving wilderness should not prevent the citizens of San Francisco from obtaining an adequate water supply. Pinchot defended his view by expressing his basic belief in conservation policy: "the fundamental principle of the whole conservation policy is that of use, to take every part of the land and its resources and put it to that use in which it will serve the most people."[17] The greatest good for the greatest number—utilitarianism pure and simple.

Muir, on the other hand, saw Hetch Hetchy as the first great test of the nation's new commitment to the preservation of wilderness. Although San Francisco clearly had a need for an adequate water supply, there was no reason to obtain this water from a beautiful, pristine wilderness park. Muir argued on aesthetic and spiritual grounds that the need for beautiful areas of wilderness was important for the human soul and the minds of human beings. Moreover, the wilderness valley was a sacred or divine place that needed to be protected from the materialistic and commercial interests of the age.[18]

Hetch Hetchy represented a classic case of the conflict between utilitarian and nonutilitarian values. These are different kinds of values, since one is based on the amount of benefit or happiness to be produced as a result of a particular policy of action, and the other is based on nonquantifiable and intangible spiritual values, such as beauty and divinity. The early American environmentalist movement was inspired by both traditions. It was inevitable that a case like Hetch Hetchy would expose the inherent contradiction within a movement governed by two distinct ethical traditions.

As Nash comments, the most surprising aspect of the battle over the proposal to dam Hetch Hetchy was that it even happened.[19] For the first time in American history, serious consideration was given to a position other than the direct material use of a natural resource. It was not surprising, however, that the dominant tradition of utilitarian use-values carried the day, but at least a minority tradition concerning natural resources and the preservation of wilderness was beginning to take hold in American consciousness.

With the thoughts of Aldo Leopold, the minority tradition would be combined with a scientific theory of ecological land-use. Leopold invoked both the use-value tradition of natural resources and the spiritual or ethical tradition of respect for nature in itself. His ideas played a central part in the history of the ethics of environmental policy. Leopold's classic essay "The Land Ethic" in *A Sand County Almanac* is probably the most widely cited source in the literature of environmental philosophy. His view of the moral consideration of the land-community is the starting point for almost all discussions of environmental ethics. Although his views are not accepted among all professionals in the field of environmental policy, Leopold's ethic of land use is clearly the dominant tradition in the philosophy of nature and the environment today—and his influence continues to grow.

Leopold was trained as a forester at the Yale School of Forestry, and so was an early follower of the wise-use tradition of natural resource policy. But his ideas matured over the years into a deep-seated respect for the harmonious dynamics of ecological processes. It was the biotic community, the interrelated system of living and nonliving natural entities, that was the source of value. He recounted his conversion in an essay, "Thinking Like a Mountain," about the overhunting of wolves. Once the wolves are killed, the deer population explodes, the vegetation on the mountainside is eaten until it too is dead, and then the deer die also. "Only the mountain has lived long enough to listen objectively to the howl of a wolf." We must think of the entire ecological system, and not try to manage one isolated part. If we try to over-manage parts of the natural system, without an appreciation of the interconnections, then we have "not learned to think like a mountain. Hence we have dustbowls, and rivers washing the future into the sea."[20]

In "The Land Ethic," Leopold presented the first ecologically based statement of an ethic based on the direct moral consideration of natural nonhuman entities. His guiding ethical maxim was simple: "A thing is right when it tends to preserve the integrity, stability, and beauty of the biotic community. It is wrong when it tends otherwise."[21] This statement is a remarkably clear alternative to the dominant tradition of anthropocentric use-value of the natural environment.

A detailed look at Leopold's land ethic reveals two major strands of thought: (1) the extension of ethical consideration to nonhumans, and (2) the recognition of an ecosystemic community. For Leopold, the extension of moral consideration to an ever increasing range of individuals and kinds of entities so as to include the natural environment was not only an "evolutionary possibility" but also "an ecological necessity." He called this extension of ethical consideration the "ethical sequence," and he saw it as an empirical and historical fact of human social development: as human society progresses, it increases the range of moral significance. Leopold begins "The Land Ethic" with a striking image from the *Odyssey* of Homer, where human female slaves are treated as property—they are considered mere things, outside of moral categories, subject only to the decisions of the owner regarding expediency and economics.[22] Nonhuman nature, "the land," is treated similarly, as mere property. But Leopold thought that ethics was continually advancing, becoming more complex as a mode of cooperation and control. It enlarges its focus from the individual to the family to the society, and ultimately to nature itself.

The extension of ethical vision rests on the idea of community, and it is here that Leopold was able to combine his ecological insights with the foundation of ethics. Community, for Leopold, was the foundation of all moral activity. "All ethics so far evolved rest upon a single premise: that the individual is a member of a community of interdependent parts."[23] It is within communities that we perceive and acknowledge moral relationships and obligations. But from the perspective of ecological science, Leopold saw that biological systems, ecosystems, natural environments—in short, the land—are communities in the sense relevant for ethical obligation. Natural systems establish mutually interdependent relationships among the members of the systems; the members of natural systems also work toward common goals in a kind of natural cooperation, which we term symbiosis. Thus Leopold argues for the existence of a broader sense of community. "The land ethic simply enlarges the boundaries of the community to include soils, waters, plants, and animals, or collectively: the land."[24] Membership in this land community is the source of moral respect and obligation. Since membership is not limited to human beings, the land ethic expresses a *nonanthropocentric* tradition of the ethics of the use of natural resources.

Leopold's vision of an ethic directed toward the land, and not merely toward the human use of the land, does contain utilitarian elements. Even Leopold could not escape the dominant tradition of the modern age. The surprise was that Leopold could be interpreted as proposing a *nonanthropocentric utilitarianism*, an ethical theory that seeks to maximize the good, not for humans, but for the natural world as a whole. Since he includes in his calculations of ethical behavior the good for the nonhuman world (its "integrity, stability, and beauty"), he can acknowledge the kinds of goods that Muir sought to maximize (the beauty, harmony, and divinity of the wilderness) with the kinds of goods that Pinchot sought (the overall maintenance of the natural system as a reserve for resources for the future). Preserving all of these goods tends to preserve the ecological system as a whole. An ethic of respect for natural processes and communities will result in benefits for both nature and humanity.

Leopold's contribution to the traditions of ethics regarding the use of natural resources can be defined by his rejection of an anthropocentric perspective and his focus on whole systems and natural communities. Although he celebrates many of the values of nature proposed by John Muir and other advocates of wilderness preservation, he does so from the perspective of a trained forester and game manager with a secure grounding in ecological science and ecosystemic relationships. Like Gifford Pinchot, he sought to use land wisely and conservatively, but this use must also imply a direct respect for the entities and processes of the natural world. His land ethic offers the best hope of developing an ethic for the use of natural resources while simultaneously respecting the integrity of the natural world.

Notes

1. Lynn White, Jr., "The Historical Roots of Our Ecologic Crisis," *Science* 155 (1967): 1203–7. For a fuller discussion of this philosophical tradition, see John Passmore, *Man's Responsibility for Nature: Ecological Problems and Western Traditions* (New York: Scribner's, 1974), pp. 3–40, and Robin Attfield, *The Ethics of Environmental Concern* (New York, Columbia University Press, 1983), pp. 20–87.

2. All references to Locke are to chapter and paragraph of the *Second Treatise of Government*.

3. Max Oelschlaeger, *The Idea of Wilderness* (New Haven, Conn.: Yale University Press, 1991), p. 68.

4. My discussion of Pinchot and Muir owes much to three secondary sources that focus on the philosophical examination of the Pinchot/Muir split: Roderick Nash, *Wilderness and the American Mind*, third edition (New Haven, Conn.: Yale University Press, 1982); Bryan G. Norton, *Toward Unity Among Environmentalists* (New York: Oxford University Press, 1991); and Oelschlaeger, *The Idea of Wilderness*.

5. Norton has a similar view of Leopold, though we may differ in the details of how Leopold effected a compromise. See Norton, *Toward Unity*, pp. 39–60.

6. Gifford Pinchot, *Breaking New Gound* (Washington, D.C.: Island Press, 1987; originally published 1947), pp. 325–26. Cited in Norton, *Toward Unity*, p. 23.

7. Pinchot, *Breaking New Ground*, p. 322. Cited in Norton, *Toward Unity*, p. 22.

8. See Nash, *Wilderness and the American Mind*, esp. pp. 108–21.

9. Ibid., p. 105. The crucial argument was presented in George Perkins Marsh, *Man and Nature: or, Physical Geography as Modified by Human Action* (1864).

10. Nash, p. 108.

11. Ibid., p. 112.

12. Ibid., pp. 117–18.

13. Note that Norton offers a revisionist interpretation of this clash, stressing the similarities between Pinchot and Muir. See Norton, *Toward Unity*, pp. 31–38.

14. John Muir, *The Yosemite* (New York, 1912). Cited in Nash, p. 168.

15. My view of Muir is based primarily on the interpretation of Oelschlaeger, *The Idea of Wilderness*, pp. 172–204. Nash sees Muir as primarily a Transcendentalist, a follower of Thoreau and the Romantic traditions of the nineteenth century. See Nash, pp. 125–29, and Oelschlaeger, pp. 173, 178–82.

16. Muir quotations cited in Nash, pp. 128–29.

17. Pinchot's testimony before the House Committee on Public Lands is summarized in Nash, pp. 170–71.

18. Nash, pp. 163–68.

19. Ibid., p. 181.

20. Aldo Leopold, *A Sand County Almanac: With Essays on Conservation from Round River* (New York: Ballantine, 1970. Originally published by Oxford University Press 1949), pp. 137–40.

21. Ibid., p. 262.

22. Ibid., pp. 238–39.

23. Ibid., p. 239.

24. Ibid.

Bibliography

The following list contains the works cited in the sixteen essays collected in this book. It is not meant to be a comprehensive bibliography of the field of environmental ethics, nor even a complete list of the books and essays that I have read over the past twenty years. Many important and influential works in the field are not listed, because I did not use these works directly in writing the essays collected here. Readers interested in a more complete bibliography of environmental ethics should consult my two annotated bibliographies in *Research in Philosophy and Technology*, volumes 9 and 12 (full bibliographic information listed below).

Adams, E. M. "Ecology and Value Theory." *Southern Journal of Philosophy* 10 (1972): 3–6.

Allen, E. L. "The Hebrew View of Nature." *Journal of Jewish Studies* 2, 2 (1951): 100–104.

Attfield, Robin. *The Ethics of Environmental Concern*. New York: Columbia University Press, 1983.

——. "The Good of Trees." *Journal of Value Inquiry* 15 (1981): 35–54.

Belkin, Samuel. "Man as Temporary Tenant," in *Judaism and Human Rights*, ed. Milton R. Konvitz. New York: Norton, 1972, pp. 251–258.

Bentham, Jeremy. *An Introduction to the Principles of Morals and Legislation*. 1989; rpt. *The Utilitarians*, Garden City, N.Y.: Anchor, 1973.

Birch, Thomas H. "The Incarceration of Wildness: Wilderness Areas as Prisons." *Environmental Ethics* 12 (1990): 3–26.

Blackstone, William T., ed. *Philosophy and Environmental Crisis*. Athens: University of Georgia Press, 1974.

Bookchin, Murray. *Our Synthetic Environment*. New York: Knopf, 1962.

Brennan, Andrew. "The Moral Standing of Natural Objects." *Environmental Ethics* 6 (1984): 35–56.

239

————. *Thinking About Nature: An Investigation of Nature, Value, and Ecology.* Athens: University of Georgia Press, 1988.

Cahen, Harley. "Against the Moral Considerability of Ecosystems. *Environmental Ethics* 10 (1988): 195–216.

Caldwell, Lynton Keith. *Between Two Worlds: Science, the Environmental Movement and Policy Choice.* Cambridge: Cambridge University Press, 1990.

Callicott, J. Baird. "Animal Liberation: A Triangular Affair." *Environmental Ethics* 2 (1980): 311–38.

————. "Animal Liberation and Environmental Ethics: Back Together Again." *Between the Species* 4 (1988): 163–69.

————. "The Case Against Moral Pluralism." *Environmental Ethics* 12 (1990): 99–124.

————. "Hume's *Is/Ought* Dichotomy and the Relation of Ecology to Leopold's Land Ethic." *Environmental Ethics* 4 (1982): 163–74.

————. *In Defense of the Land Ethic: Essays in Environmental Philosophy.* Albany: SUNY Press, 1989.

————. "Intrinsic Value, Quantum Theory, and Environmental Ethics." *Environmental Ethics* 7 (1985): 257–75.

————. "Non-anthropocentric Value Theory and Environmental Ethics." *American Philosophical Quarterly* 21 (1984): 299–309.

————. "On the Intrinsic Value of Nonhuman Species," in *The Preservation of Species,* ed. Bryan G. Norton. Princeton: Princeton University Press, 1986, pp. 138–72.

————. Review of Tom Regan, *The Case for Animal Rights. Environmental Ethics* 7 (1985): 365–72.

Carmell, Aryeh. "Judaism and the Quality of the Environment," in *Challenge: Torah Views on Science and Its Problems,* ed. Aryeh Carmell and Cyril Domb. New York: Feldheim, 1978, pp. 500–525.

Carson, Rachel. *Silent Spring.* Boston: Houghton Mifflin, 1962.

Cebik, L. B. "Forging Issues from Forged Art." *Southern Journal of Philosophy* 27 (1989): 331–46.

Cheney, Jim. "Ecofeminism and Deep Ecology." *Environmental Ethics* 9 (1987): 115–45.

Clay, Jason W. *Indigenous Peoples and Tropical Forests.* Cambridge, Mass.: Cultural Survival, 1988.

Colwell, Thomas B., Jr. "The Balance of Nature: A Ground for Human Value." *Main Currents in Modern Thought* 26 (1969): 46–52.

Commoner, Barry. *The Closing Circle: Nature, Man, and Technology.* New York: Knopf, 1971.

Cronon, William. *Changes in the Land: Indians, Colonists, and the Ecology of New England.* New York: Hill & Wang, 1983.

Crosby, Alfred W. *Ecological Imperialism: The Biological Expansion of Europe, 900–1900.* Cambridge: Cambridge University Press, 1986.

Dasmann, R. F. *Environmental Conservation,* 5th ed. New York: John Wiley, 1984.

Dawidowicz, Lucy S. *The War Against the Jews 1933–1945*. New York: Holt, Rinehart, and Winston, 1975.

Delattre, Edwin. "Rights, Responsibilities, and Future Persons." *Ethics* 82 (1972): 254–58.

Diamond, Cora. "Eating Meat and Eating People." *Philosophy* 53 (1978): 464–79.

Duncan, Colin A. M. "On Identifying a Sound Environmental Ethic in History: Prolegomena to Any Future Environmental History." *Environmental History Review* 15 (1991): 5–30.

Ehrenfeld, David. *The Arrogance of Humanism*. New York: Oxford University Press, 1978.

Ehrenfeld, David, and Philip J. Bentley. "Judaism and the Practice of Stewardship." *Judaism* 34 (1985): 301–11.

Ehrlich, Paul. *The Population Bomb*. New York: Ballantine, 1968.

Ehrlich, Paul, and Anne Ehrlich. *Extinction*. New York: Ballantine, 1981.

Elliot, Robert. "Faking Nature." *Inquiry* 25 (1982): 81–93.

Feinberg, Joel. "The Nature and Value of Rights." *Journal of Value Inquiry* 4 (1970): 243–57.

———. "The Rights of Animals and Unborn Generations," in *Philosophy and Environmental Crisis*, ed. William T. Blackstone. Athens: University of Georgia Press, 1974, pp. 43–68.

Freudenstein, Eric G. "Ecology and the Jewish Tradition." *Judaism* 19 (1970): 406–14.

Frey, R. G. "Rights, Interests, Desires, and Beliefs." *American Philosophical Quarterly* 16 (1979): 233–39.

Gilbert, Martin. *The Holocaust: A History of the Jews of Europe During the Second World War*. New York: Henry Holt, 1985.

Gilligan, Carol. *In A Different Voice: Psychological Theory and Women's Development*. Cambridge: Harvard University Press, 1982.

Godfrey-Smith, William. "The Value of Wilderness." *Environmental Ethics* 1 (1979): 309–19.

Goldblatt, David. "Do Works of Art Have Rights?" *Journal of Aesthetics and Art Criticism* 35 (1976): 69–77.

Golding, M. P. "Obligations to Future Generations." *Monist* 56 (1972): 85–99.

Goodpaster, Kenneth E. "From Egoism to Environmentalism," in *Ethics and Problems of the 21st Century*, ed. K. E. Goodpaster and K. M. Sayre. Notre Dame: University of Notre Dame Press, 1979, pp. 21–35.

———. "On Being Morally Considerable." *Journal of Philosophy* 75 (1978): 308–25.

Gordis, Robert. "Ecology and the Jewish Tradition," in *Judaic Ethics for a Lawless World*. New York: Jewish Theological Seminary, 1986, pp. 113–22.

———. "Judaism and the Environment." *Congress Monthly* 57, 6 (September/October 1990): 7–10.

Gore, Al. *Earth in the Balance: Ecology and the Human Spirit*. Boston: Houghton Mifflin, 1992.

Guha, Ramachandra. "Radical American Environmentalism and Wilderness Preservation: A Third World Critique." *Environmental Ethics* 11 (1989): 71–83.

Gunn, Alastair S. "Why Should We Care About Rare Species?" *Environmental Ethics* 2 (1980): 17–37.

Hardin, Garrett. "The Tragedy of the Commons." *Science* 162 (1968): 1243–48.

Hargrove, Eugene C. *The Foundations of Environmental Ethics.* Englewood Cliffs, N.J.: Prentice-Hall, 1989.

———., ed. *Religion and Environmental Crisis.* Athens: University of Georgia Press, 1986.

Helfand, Jonathan L. "The Earth Is the Lord's: Judaism and Environmental Ethics," in *Religion and Environmental Crisis,* ed. Eugene C. Hargrove. Athens: University of Georgia Press, 1986, pp. 38–52.

Hill, Thomas, Jr. "Ideals of Human Excellence and Preserving Natural Environments." *Environmental Ethics* 5 (1983): 211–24.

Houghton, Richard A., and George M. Woodwell. "Global Climatic Change." *Scientific American* 260, 4 (April 1989): 36–44.

Jarvie, I. C. "Technology and the Structure of Knowledge," in *Philosophy and Technology: Readings in the Philosophical Problems of Technology,* edited by Carl Mitcham and Robert Mackey. New York: Free Press, 1983, pp. 54–61.

Jones, Hardy. "Genetic Endowment and Obligations to Future Generations." *Social Theory and Practice* 4 (1976): 29–47.

Katz, Eric. "Environmental Ethics: A Select Annotated Bibliography, 1983–1987." *Research in Philosophy and Technology* 9 (1989): 251–85.

———. "Environmental Ethics: A Select Annotated Bibliography II, 1987–1990." *Research in Philosophy and Technology* 12 (1992): 287–324.

Kay, Jeanne. "Concepts of Nature in the Hebrew Bible." *Environmental Ethics* 10 (1988): 309–27.

Krieger, Martin H. "What's Wrong with Plastic Trees?" *Science* 179 (1973): 446–55.

Lamm, Norman. "Ecology and Jewish Law and Theology," in *Faith and Doubt.* New York: KTAV, 1971, pp. 162–85.

Landau, Ronnie S. *The Nazi Holocaust.* Chicago: Ivan R. Dee, 1994.

Leiss, William. *The Domination of Nature.* Boston: Beacon Press, 1974.

———. "The Imperialism of Human Needs." *North American Review,* 259, 4 (1974): 27–34.

Leopold, Aldo. *A Sand County Almanac.* New York: Oxford University Press, 1949.

———. "Some Fundamentals of Conservation in the Southwest." *Environmental Ethics* 1 (1979): 131–41.

Levi, Primo. *The Reawakening,* trans. Stuart Woolf. New York: Collier Books, 1987.

Lewis, C. S. "The Abolition of Man," in *Philosophy and Technology: Readings in the Philosophical Problems of Technology,* ed. Carl Mitcham and Robert Mackey. New York: Free Press, 1983, pp. 143–50.

Light, Andrew, and Eric Katz, eds. *Environmental Pragmatism*. London: Routledge, 1996.

Locke, John. *Second Treatise on Goverment*. London, 1690.

Lockwood, Jeffrey A. "Not to Harm a Fly: Our Ethical Obligations to Insects." *Between the Species* 4 (1988): 204–11.

Losonsky, Michael. "The Nature of Artifacts." *Philosophy* 65 (1990): 81–88.

Lovejoy, Thomas E. "Species Leave the Ark One by One," in *The Preservation of Species*, ed. Bryan G. Norton. Princeton: Princeton University Press, 1986, pp. 13–27.

Lovelock, J. E. *Gaia: A New Look at Life on Earth*. Oxford: Oxford University Press, 1979.

Marietta, Don E., Jr. "The Interrelationship of Ecological Science and Environmental Ethics." *Environmental Ethics* 1 (1979): 195–207.

Marsh, George Perkins. *Man and Nature; or Physical Geography as Modified by Human Action*. 1864; rpt. Cambridge: Harvard University Press, 1965.

Martin, John N. "The Concept of the Irreplaceable." *Environmental Ethics* 1 (1979): 31–48.

Maser, Chris. *The Redesigned Forest*. San Pedro, Calif.: R. & E. Miles, 1988.

McKibben, Bill. *The End of Nature*. New York: Random House, 1989.

Merchant, Carolyn, *Ecological Revolutions: Nature, Gender, and Science in New England*. Chapel Hill: University of North Carolina Press, 1989.

Mesthene, Emmanuel G. "Technology and Wisdom," in *Philosophy and Technology: Readings in the Philosophical Problems of Technology*, ed. Carl Mitcham and Robert Mackey. New York: Free Press, 1983, pp. 109–15.

Mill, John Stuart. "Nature," in *Three Essays on Religion*. London, 1874.

Muir, John. *The Yosemite*. New York: 1912.

Myers, Norman. *The Primary Source: Tropical Forests and Our Future*. New York: Norton, 1984.

———. *The Sinking Ark*. New York: Pergamon Press, 1979.

Naess, Arne. *Ecology, Community and Lifestyle*, trans. and ed. David Rothenberg. Cambridge: Cambridge University Press, 1989.

———. "The Shallow and the Deep, Long-Range Ecology Movement: A Summary." *Inquiry* 16 (1973): 95–100.

Narveson, Jan. "Moral Problems of Population." *Monist* 57 (1973): 62–86.

———. "Utilitarianism and New Generations." *Mind* 76 (1967): 62–72.

Nash, Roderick. *Wilderness and the American Mind*, 3rd ed. New Haven: Yale University Press, 1982.

Norton, Bryan G. "Environmental Ethics and Nonhuman Rights." *Environmental Ethics* 4 (1982): 17–36.

———. "Environmental Ethics and Weak Anthropocentrism." *Environmental Ethics* 6 (1984): 131–48.

———., ed. *The Preservation of Species*. Princeton: Princeton University Press, 1986.

———. *Toward Unity Among Environmentalists*. New York: Oxford University Press, 1991.

―――. *Why Preserve Natural Variety?* Princeton: Princeton University Press, 1987.

Odum, Eugene P. *Ecology and Our Endangered Life Support Systems*. Sunderland, Mass.: Sinauer, 1989.

Oelschlaeger, Max. *The Idea of Wilderness*. New Haven: Yale University Press, 1991.

Pacey, Arnold. *The Culture of Technology*. Cambridge: MIT Press, 1983.

Packard, Steve. "Just a Few Oddball Species: Restoration and the Rediscovery of the Tallgrass Savanna." *Restoration & Management Notes* 6,1 (Summer 1988): 13–22.

Passmore, John. *Man's Responsibility for Nature: Ecological Problems and Western Traditions*. New York: Scribner's, 1974.

Pearce, Fred. "Felled Trees Deal Double Blow to Global Warming." *New Scientist* 123, 1682 (September 1989): 25.

Peters, Charles M., Alwyn H. Gentry, and Robert O. Mendelsohn. "Valuation of an Amazon Rainforest." *Nature* 339 (June 1989): 655–56.

Pinchot, Gifford. *Breaking New Ground*. 1947. rpt. Washington, D.C.: Island Press, 1987.

Pluhar, Evelyn B. "The Justification of an Environmental Ethic." *Environmental Ethics* 5 (1983): 47–61.

―――. "Two Conceptions of an Environmental Ethic and Their Implications." *Ethics and Animals* 4 (1983): 110–27.

Regan, Tom. "Animal Rights, Human Wrongs." *Environmental Ethics* 2 (1980): 99–120.

―――. *The Case for Animal Rights*. Berkeley: University of California Press, 1983.

―――. "The Moral Basis of Vegetarianism." *Canadian Journal of Philosophy* 5 (1975): 181–214.

―――. "The Nature and Possibility of an Environmental Ethic." *Environmental Ethics* 3 (1981): 19–34.

Rodman, John. "The Liberation of Nature?" *Inquiry* 20 (1977): 83–131.

Rolston, Holmes, III. "Are Values in Nature Subjective or Objective?" *Environmental Ethics* 4 (1982): 125–51.

―――. "Can and Ought We to Follow Nature?" *Environmental Ethics* 1 (1979): 7–30.

―――. *Environmental Ethics: Duties to and Value in the Natural World*. Philadelphia: Temple University Press, 1988.

―――. "Is There an Ecological Ethic?" *Ethics* 85 (1975): 93–109.

―――. *Philosophy Gone Wild: Essays in Environmental Ethics*. Buffalo: Prometheus, 1986.

―――. "Values Gone Wild?" *Inquiry* 26 (1983): 181–207.

―――. "Valuing Wildlands." *Environmental Ethics* 7 (1985): 23–48.

Russell, Bertrand. *An Outline of Philosophy*. New York: Norton, 1927; rpt. New York: New American Library, 1974.

Russow, Lilly-Marlene. "Why Do Species Matter?" *Environmental Ethics* 3 (1981): 101–12.

Ryder, Richard. *Victims of Science*. London: Davis-Poynter, 1975.

Sagoff, Mark. "Do We Need a Land Use Ethic?" *Environmental Ethics* 3 (1981): 293–308.

———. *The Economy of the Earth: Philosophy, Law, and the Environment*. Cambridge: Cambridge University Press, 1988.

———. "On Preserving the Natural Environment. *Yale Law Journal* 84 (1974): 205–67.

Sapontzis, Steve F. "Predation." *Ethics and Animals* 5 (1984): 27–38.

Scherer, Donald, and Thomas Attig, eds. *Ethics and the Environment*. Englewood Cliffs, N.J.: Prentice-Hall, 1983.

Schwartz, Richard H. *Judaism and Global Survival*. New York: Vantage Press, 1984.

Sedjo, Roger A. "Forests: A Tool to Moderate Global Warming?" *Environment* 31 (January/February 1989): 14–20.

Shabecoff, Philip. "New Battles over Endangered Species." *New York Times Magazine*, June 4, 1978, pp. 38–44.

Shapiro, David S. "God, Man and Creation." *Tradition* 15 (1975): 25–47.

Shepard, Paul. "Ecology and Man—A Viewpoint," in *The Subversive Science*, ed. Paul Shepard and Daniel McKinley. Boston: Houghton Mifflin, 1969, pp. 1–10.

Shukla, J., C. Nobre, and P. Sellers. "Amazon Deforestation and Climate Change." *Science* 247 (March 1990): 1322–25.

Sikora, R. I. "Utilitarianism: The Classical Principle and the Average Principle." *Canadian Journal of Philosophy* 5 (1975): 409–19.

Singer, Peter. *Animal Liberation*. New York: Random House, 1975.

Stearns, J. Brenton. "Ecology and the Indefinite Unborn." *Monist* 56 (1972): 612–25.

Stone, Christopher. *Earth and Other Ethics: The Case for Moral Pluralism*. New York: Harper & Row, 1987.

———. *Should Trees Have Standing? Towards Legal Rights for Natural Objects*. Los Altos, Calif.: Kaufmann, 1974.

Swetlitz, Marc, ed. *Judaism and Ecology, 1970–1986: A Sourcebook of Readings*. Wyncote, Pa.: Shomrei Adamah, 1990.

Sylvan, Richard. "A Critique of Deep Ecology." *Radical Philosophy* 40 (Summer 1985): 2–12.

Taylor, Paul W. *Respect for Nature: A Theory of Environmental Ethics*. Princeton: Princeton University Press, 1986.

———. "The Ethics of Respect for Nature." *Environmental Ethics* 3 (1981): 197–218.

Tormey, Alan. "Aesthetic Rights." *Journal of Aesthetics and Art Criticism* 32 (1973): 163–70.

Tribe, Laurence H. "Technology Assessment and the Fourth Discontinuity: The

Limits of Instrumental Rationality." *Southern California Law Review* 46 (1973): 617–60.

———. "Ways Not to Think About Plastic Trees." *Yale Law Journal* 83 (1974): 1315–48.

Tribe, Laurence H., Corrine S. Schelling, and John Voss, eds. *When Values Conflict*. Cambridge, Mass.: Ballinger, 1976.

Van Pelt, Robert-Jan. "A Site in Search of a Mission," in *Anatomy of the Auschwitz Death Camp*, ed. Yisrael Gutman and Michael Berenbaum. Bloomington: Indiana University Press, 1994, pp. 93–156.

VanDeVeer, Donald, and Christine Pierce, eds. *People, Penguins, and Plastic Trees: Basic Issues in Environmental Ethics*. Belmont, Calif.: Wadsworth, 1986.

Varner, Gary. "Biological Functions and Biological Interests." *Southern Journal of Philosophy* 28 (1990): 251–70.

———. "No Holism Without Pluralism." *Enviromental Ethics* 13 (1991): 175–79.

Wenz, Peter. *Environmental Justice*. Albany: SUNY Press, 1988.

———. "Minimal, Moderate, and Extreme Moral Pluralism." *Environmental Ethics* 15 (1993): 61–74.

Weston, Anthony. "Beyond Intrinsic Value: Pragmatism in Environmental Ethics." *Environmental Ethics* 7 (1985): 321–39.

White, Lynn, Jr. "The Historical Roots of Our Ecologic Crisis." *Science* 155 (1967): 1203–7.

Wilson, E. O. "Threats to Biodiversity." *Scientific American* 261, 3 (September 1989): 108–16.

Wilson, E. O., and Frances M. Peter, eds. *Biodiversity*. Washington, D.C.: National Academy Press, 1988.

Wright, Larry. *Teleological Explanations*. Berkeley: University of California Press, 1976.

Yahil, Leni. *The Holocaust: The Fate of European Jewry*, trans. Ina Friedman and Haya Galai. New York: Oxford University Press, 1990.

Index

Footnote references are not indexed unless the note contains a discussion that augments or extends a discussion in the main text.

247

About the Author

Eric Katz received a B.A. in philosophy from Yale University and a Ph.D. from Boston University. He is an associate professor of philosophy and director of the Science, Technology, and Society Program at the New Jersey Institute of Technology in Newark, New Jersey. Katz is the author of two annotated bibliographies of the field of environmental ethics published in *Research in Philosophy and Technology* in addition to several dozen articles and chapters in scholarly publications. He is the coeditor, with Andrew Light, of *Environmental Pragmatism* (Routledge, 1996). Funded by a grant from the U.S. Environmental Protection Agency, he has coauthored (with colleagues at NJIT) a textbook, *Environmental Protection: Solving Environmental Problems from Social Science and Humanities Perspectives* (Kendall Hunt, 1997).

Katz was the founding vice president of the International Society for Environmental Ethics and is now a member of the editorial board and book review editor of the journal *Environmental Ethics*. He has worked as a consultant in environmental policy and philosophy for the United Nations, the State of Maryland, the New Jersey Environmental Educational Coalition, the National Coalition on the Environment in Jewish Life, and the Jewish Theological Seminary of America. Katz lives with his family on Long Island, New York, and Fire Island.